To: Doug Parr

Enjoy!

Spencer Boatright

The Unknown Journey

An Autobiography of Spessard Boatright

SPESSARD BOATRIGHT

authorHOUSE®

AuthorHouse™
1663 Liberty Drive, Suite 200
Bloomington, IN 47403
www.authorhouse.com
Phone: 1-800-839-8640

First published by AuthorHouse 12/23/2008

ISBN: 978-1-4389-3829-5 (e)
ISBN: 978-1-4389-3828-8 (sc)
ISBN: 978-1-4389-3827-1 (hc)

Library of Congress Control Number: 2008911543

Printed in the United States of America
Bloomington, Indiana

This book is printed on acid-free paper.

COME YE NOW AND KNOW my story is presented to AuthorHouse
Publishing in the 2008th year of Our Lord and Savior Jesus Christ, and the 232nd
year of our American Independence, and my 68th year as a sojourner in this present,
though temporary life. The story is mine, and the words are mine. In some cases, I
have used the names of relatives to make the story personal to my family. In other
cases, I have used the names of public figures or people who are well known to be in
the public domain. All places and products used in the telling of my story are in the
public domain. I have either asked for nor received any endorsements from or by
individuals, companies, governments, or any other entity. I alone am responsible for
the contents of this autobiography.

DEDICATION

This book is dedicated to the memory of my beloved parents, Joseph Arch (Joe) Boatright and Susan Elizabeth Starling (Lizzie) Boatright. They were the greatest set a parents any child could ever dream of having, and to my wonderful and faithful wife of over 40 years, JoAnn Newton Boatright—she has let me walk among the stars.

ACKNOWLEDGEMENTS

It is not possible to acknowledge everyone who has played an important part in my life or in the publication of this book. Suffice it to say that I am deeply indebted to more people than the pages of a book could hold.

First, my parents deserve to be recognized because they gave me life and then guidance. My brothers and sisters added their parts because I was the youngest child in our family and some of them filled almost a parent's role in my infancy and early years. My devoted wife, JoAnn, has stood by me no matter what was going on in our lives; our daughters, Rebecca and Brenda, have supported me and offered sincere understanding when I had to be at work or was away performing National Guard Duty and missing many of the important events in their lives as they grew up. To all of these, I owe a debt of gratitude that cannot be fully expressed or repaid; so I can only offer my humble appreciation.

My military career was full of soldiers that contributed to my success, many of whom I will not mention, but their contributions were significant and appreciated nonetheless. Those whom I will mention encouraged, mentored, supported, and demonstrated strong loyalty, had faith in my abilities; some entrusted me with the command of military units at varying levels. At the top of the list was Warrant Officer Four Lawrence W. Lee, followed by Major General Robert F. Ensslin, Major General Ronald O. Harrison, Major General Louie C. Wadsworth, Brigadier General George H. Dale, Brigadier General Harold McLeod, Brigadier General Thomas Sprenger, Colonel Edwin P. Stewart, Colonel D. O. Tsoulos, and Colonel Paul Oehler.

My civilian life was also touched by many who would influence what I did and where I went. Some of those who encouraged, mentored, supported, had faith in my abilities, were loyal, and entrusted me with management and supervisory positions and responsibilities were Dr. Jack Foley, Mr. Eustice Collins, Mr. Henry Mangles, Mr. Alvin Brown, Mr. Pete Collins, Dr. Clyde Bass, Mrs. Brenda (Clark) Gamble, Mrs. Dorothy Fann, Mr. Arthur Lawrence, Mrs. Madelyn Baucom, Mr. Laurie (Pop) Duval, Mr. Marvin Johns, Mr. Hugh Mills, Commissioner of Education Betty Castor, Dr. Cecil Golden, Dr. Gene Chick, Dr. James H. Schroeer, Mr. Alfred Bowen, Mr. Don Lott, Mr. Wayne V. Pierson, Mr. Bill Lindner, Mr. Ed Woodruff, Mr. John Newman, Mrs. Lynn Cobb, Mrs. Patricia Levesque, Commissioner of Education Jeanine Blomberg, and Mrs. Irene Schmutz.

Finally, I would like to thank Dr. Charles L. Wooten for his technical assistance in editing this manuscript to help me tell my story. As an author, he understands the mechanics of storytelling; as a friend, he helped me with the personal flavor of writing.

PREFACE

How vain it is to sit down to write when you have not stood up to live. Henry David Thoreau.

In my wildest imagination, I never dreamed of writing a book. I was not planning to write my autobiography even though some friends and family encouraged me to do it. Yet with their support, I really never gave serious thought to putting pen to page. That was until our family reunion in March 2008, when I was once again asked to record the stories and times about our common history for our family's sake. Oddly enough, just a few weeks earlier, JoAnn and I were having breakfast with our daughter Brenda and we begin discussing my time as Superintendent of Schools. It was then that I realized I had been in the office as Superintendent almost four years when she was born. She certainly knew what my job was, but she had no idea what it entailed. I knew then, for her and our other daughter Rebecca's benefit, and especially for Cooper and Chandler, our grandsons, that if I didn't tell the stories with a certain level of detail, they would never have the opportunity to know my history and a little bit about their roots. Also, with the large number of brothers and sisters in my family, my many nieces and nephews, and their extended families, if someone in my generation didn't reduce to writing some of our past, those precious memories would be lost forever.

This is a personal memoir; this is how I remember times, places, and events. Even though I have made every effort to accurately portray events, situations, and circumstances as completely as possible, I did it in a summary fashion. This story is not written as, or intended to be, a detailed description or history of the major events I was privileged to take part in. I wrote it principally to share my story with my immediate and extended family, and hope the book will prove useful to and inspire future generations regarding how as least one person dealt with life's events that happen day by day.

I faced the problem all authors have to contend with, that of selecting events and the level of detail I wanted to share. I had neither the time or wanted to use book space to tell everything. I was determined to produce a book that was easy reading and of reasonable length.

My story is of a rural north-Florida country kid who comes from a large family, grows up on a family farm with limited means, goes to college, returns to teach school in his hometown, and less than four years later is elected as county Superintendent of Schools at the age of 27. I joined the Florida Army National Guard while still in high school, and somehow rose through the military ranks from the lowest level Private to become a Brigadier General. At the time of my retirement, I had served 39½ years on active duty and National Guard service proudly wearing the uniform of the United States Army.

My story is one of hard work, being at the right place at the right time, and good fortune. For me, occasionally times were rough, but for the most part, they were good times. It is a dual story of civilian service and soldiering. It is a story about the people, circumstances, and situations that helped make me what I am, and who I am. It is a story of my benefiting from opportunities created by the sacrifices of my parents, and by others throughout my walk through life. It is a story of me believing in myself, and my abilities coupled with determination, hard work, honesty, integrity, and never sacrificing personal principles of values, morals, and ethics.

I told this story primarily because of my love for my family. My life has been great, and this is my story so far. I'm sure there will still be more to come.

Contents

Follow virtue and knowledge. Dante.

FAMILY LIFE
THE EARLY YEARS

Children, obey your parents in all things: for this is well pleasing unto the Lord. Colossians 3:20.

THERE WAS NOTHING UNCOMMON or unique about my birth. I was born May 20, 1940, at the time when the Great Depression was coming to an end and just as the dawn of World War II was beginning. Although this was a time that produced a generation that would reshape America into its modern mold, all of those who started life in that era laid no claim to being different or special. Like most children, I can't remember much before I was four or five years old. But there was one thing I knew with absolute certainty before I could walk, talk, or remember; I knew that I was loved and was a member of a large family where love was shown daily by my parents and by my brothers and sisters.

I was the youngest of 13 children born to my parents, nine boys and four girls, of whom 11 survived well into adulthood. The first and fourth child born to my parents died at 15 and 19 months, respectively, from flu epidemics in the early and mid 1920s. In order to understand how I got to where I am today, I need to briefly tell a little bit about my parents and their backgrounds. Both sets of grandparents, like my own parents, were born and raised on farms and became farmers just as my parents did. I was the youngest grandchild on both sides of my family; consequently, entering into a very large family, I had a whole host of cousins who were a lot older than me.

In 1940, the average car cost $800 and a gallon of gas was never more than 18 cents. A new home averaged about $6,500, though most homes weren't that expensive in our area. A loaf of bread was eight cents, and milk was about 34 cents a gallon. It cost three cents for a first-class postage stamp and you could buy a stamped postcard for a penny. When I entered the world, the average annual salary was about $1,900—and that was pretty good, because in the rural South most folks didn't reach that level even though the minimum wage was 30 cents an hour.

MY LINEAGE

Daddy, Joseph Arch (Joe) Boatright, was born March 26, 1892, in Taylor County, Florida; he moved to Suwannee County as a very young child and became a lifelong citizen of Suwannee County. Daddy's father, Alexander Monroe (Mon) Boatright, was born in 1861 and died in 1927 (age 66); his mother was born in 1869 and died in 1902 (age 32). Daddy's parents had two sets of twins, and, as was common in earlier generations that didn't have the miracles of modern medicine, his mother died during childbirth giving life to the second set of twins.

Eight children were born, five boys and three girls, to this marriage of my paternal grandparents. At the time of my grandmother's death, their children ranged from 15 years old to infant twins; Daddy was third from the oldest and 12 years old when he lost his mother. Life was very difficult for my Dad's family and it was especially hard for my grandfather because he had to struggle against nature to provide food, clothing, and shelter to raise and keep the family together, as well as mourn the loss of his beloved wife. Several years later Grandpa Boatright was blessed to marry again; he expanded his family by marrying a widow with two girls, and they had two children together, a boy and a girl. In those days it was common for widowed parents of young children to marry and have a large blended family.

Mama, Susan Elizabeth (Lizzie) Starling, was born July 6, 1897, in Dowling Park, Suwannee County, Florida. Her father, William Allan Starling, was born in 1866 and died in 1960 (age 94); her mother Susan Ann (Bell) Starling was born in 1869 and died in 1948 (age 79). Ten children were born, five boys and five girls, to the marriage of my maternal grandparents; Mama was fifth from the oldest. Grandpa Starling was a successful and prosperous farmer in the area. His father, Levi Starling, was a Confederate soldier in the American Civil War. Mama's family all grew up on the family farm and in the same house where both her parents passed away.

My parents were married December 12, 1917, at the home of Mama's parents near Dowling Park, Florida. At the time of their wedding, Daddy worked plowing a mule six days a week and was paid $10 a month along with room and board; somehow, he scraped together enough money from his meager earnings and paid $25 for an engagement ring for my mother. You can see pictures of our parents in the back of the book—both young and old; they are precious memories.

OUR HOMEPLACE

As my parents started out in married life, they faced many difficulties and severe struggles to survive those hardships that were common to farmers. My Dad was able to purchase 80 acres from one of his uncles. He and my mother cut the timber from the land and together built a small smokehouse in which they lived while they were building the house where all their children, including me, were born and raised. The house was built entirely using manual tools, handsaws, hammers, a square, ax, foot adz, jackplanes, drawing knife, and lots of hard work and sweat. Our home was all wood. It had a lapboard exterior that was painted white; inside, it had wooden walls and ceiling that were painted white, and in keeping with the available building materials, our home had a wooden shingle roof.

Daddy and Mama moved into the house about 1920. Only their bedroom and the hallway were finished; the remainder of the house had all the walls up, but the other rooms didn't have ceilings. The house was renovated completely in about 1947; the refurbishing included finishing the installation of ceilings in all rooms, putting in additional electrical wall outlets, and replacing the wood-shingle roof with a new tin roof. Once the major work was done, the old home place was totally repainted inside and out—it was like a new home. You can see pictures of our house and the smokehouse in the back of the book—my parents started their life together under rugged conditions and then built a home and family through a lifetime of love and hard work.

During the 1920s, farmers in our area had to plan and produce crops that would sell to the large markets; the main cash crops were corn and cotton. During the Great Depression of the 1930s, corn and cotton continued to be the primary cash crops, but a few farmers began to grow the crop that was increasing in demand: tobacco; and we participated in the supply side of this economic venture. During the 1940s, and after World War II, the main cash crop shifted almost completely to tobacco; cotton crops almost disappeared because of governmental control. Most farmers also grew and sold livestock periodically. All farmers, at least all those whom I knew, had the basic assortment of livestock, which included hogs, cows, horses, and chickens. And, like all farmers, we maintained a large garden that constantly changed with each season to take advantage of whatever produce would grow to provide food for the family, livestock, or serve as a bumper for some extra money.

Even though there were 13 children born to my parents, there were never more than 10 of us living at home at the same time—though 10 certainly was no small number to clothe, house, feed, and provide for their moral and spiritual guidance while trying to ensure we got a decent education. My oldest sister was married three years before I was born. By the time I came along, Dad had acquired adjoining property and owned 200 acres of farm and timber land. The house my parents built sat on top of a sandy hill and faced east. There were seven rooms: my parent's bedroom, a combination living room/bedroom for my sisters, a boy's bedroom with two double beds, a small bedroom built by closing in part of the back porch, a large kitchen with a wood stove, dining room, a hallway, and large front and back porches. I slept in a steel-framed baby bed in the corner of the living room until I was probably five years old. We had to use all available space and make the best use of it. You can see a picture of all my parents' children together at one time in the back of the book—we didn't have many pictures made where all of us were together at the same time simply because there were so many of us and we just couldn't get together all at once.

Our home didn't have hot water, a bathroom, a telephone, or a heater, and we had no automobile. We did have an outdoor toilet that was about 150 yards from the main house. We also had a bathing area about 30 feet from the back porch in a building we called the pump house. The pump house was easily accessible using the concrete walkway from the back porch and contained two small rooms; one room for the water pump and water storage tank, and the other room had a concrete floor, which served a dual purpose. Primarily, it was a washhouse, which Mama used for laundering clothes, complete with a *Maytag* washing machine and three washtubs; its secondary function was for our personal cleanliness because it was equipped with a showerhead, or we could use one of the washtubs for bathing. The smaller children bathed in a washtub, and the older ones used the shower. If we weren't really dirty, we didn't have to take a bath every night, but we always had to wash our feet before bedtime. However, we always had to wash our face and hands before every meal.

The Rural Electrification Administration (REA) began providing electricity to outlying areas in the late 1930s; Daddy signed up and we started getting electrical service in December 1939. Our house had two wall outlets and one electric light in each room; we also had a light on the front and back porches. The house had, in addition to lights, four things powered by electricity: a water pump, a washing machine, a refrigerator, and an electric AM radio. We had the radio in the living room and its usual place was to the left of the fireplace.

FUN CHILDHOOD MEMORIES

Some of my earliest memories are of Daddy coming in from the fields early for lunch and listening to the noon news; he was always anxious to get the latest update on the progress of the war in Europe. Daddy always sat near the radio and was its sole operator; we (us children) were never allowed to touch the radio dials. We would listen to whatever Daddy wanted to hear, which usually was the news every night, again for an update on the war. Some of his favorite news reporters were Edward R. Murrow, Gabriel Heatter, and Eric Severeid. Often, when the world news programs ended, we would listen to such programs as *Amos 'n' Andy*, *The Lone Ranger*, *Fibber McGee and Molly*, or some selection from the many other shows that provided wholesome family entertainment. Our family being gathered around that radio, enchanted by stories, is one of my favorite childhood memories; it was exciting and, unlike most families today, we were all interested and involved in the same thing as a family.

A BAD MEMORY OF WAR

The period of World War II, especially 1944-45, was a very difficult time for our family. My two older brothers were in the war; the oldest was drafted into active duty while serving as a member of Company E, 124th Infantry Regiment, Florida Army National Guard. The second oldest brother quit high school and joined the Navy; he served in the Pacific Theater of operations during the last two years of the war.

I guess my earliest memory goes back to late spring of 1944 when my parents received a telegram from the War Department notifying them that my oldest brother, Thomas Lee (Tom), was missing in action in Germany. Daddy was always a strong and stern individual; seeing how his heart was broken and saddened so deeply affected the entire family, and it left a lasting impression on me. Whenever I remember the image of his pain, the memory still hurts today just like a fresh wound.

The news about Tom only increased Daddy's interest in the progress of the war. Our mailbox was about a half mile from the house. The mail carrier, Mr. Russell Goff, was a very good friend of my Dad. He was also a veteran of World War I and knew a lot about the anguish families go through in troubled times. Mr. Goff delivered our mail Monday through Saturday at about 12:30 p.m. Mr. Goff lived in Pine Mount (about three miles North of O'Brian on US Highway 129), where our Post Office was located—and he had a telephone. Mama always made sure that at least one of us children was at the mailbox when the mailman came; my parents were always anxious to see if we received any letters from Tom, or from the War Department. Daddy asked Mr. Goff to open and read any letters to us from the War Department if the mail came after he returned from his route each day. Whenever there was any news, Mr. Goff would drive back to our house with any information regarding the status of Tom, or any other critical new knowledge from the War Department.

During this perilous time, the government rationed many things: sugar, gasoline, rubber products including tires, automobiles, and many other commonly used items. The entire nation was at war, not just parts of it, and everything was geared toward support of the war effort; no one during that time felt put upon or inconvenienced by the sacrifices that were required of our national effort.

I recall when my parents received word from the War Department confirming that Tom was alive and in a German concentration camp. While there was still the pain of Tom being in such a terrible place, there was a measure of joy and relief at knowing he was alive. I was too young to understand much, but I knew there was a lot of hurt in the hearts of my parents.

Tom was a prisoner of war (POW) for a year and seven days. He spent five months of that time in a concentration camp living on a slice of bread and a cup of water a day. Tom's weight went from about 180 pounds at the time of his capture, down to about 80 pounds at the time of his release from the concentration camp. During his incarceration, Tom was forced to stand in a cell about 12 inches by 18 inches, of course at some point he got so weak that he couldn't stand and his body simply relaxed and conformed to the shape of the cell.

Mercifully, for the last seven months as a POW, they sent Tom to work on a German homestead as a farm hand. This was a blessing for him since he had been raised on a farm and was good at all farm-related work. However; when he arrived at the German farm, he was so weak that he wasn't physically able to do any work. The German family where he was conscripted consisted of the mother, six girls, and one boy; the boy was the youngest—he was my age. I believe the father had been killed in the war. The mother and daughters worked in the hay fields and did all the manual work while Tom drove the horses. The entire family was very good to him; he was blessed to have been placed on this particular farm. The mother took excellent care of him and helped Tom regain his strength.

Tom remained on that farm until he was liberated on May 3, 1945; less than a week later Germany and Italy surrendered on May 8th. Tom arrived home on June 8th. He and Marie Turner, his fiancée, were married 11 days later on the front porch of our home on June 19, 1945. I guess we could have made jokes about his trading one captivity for another by getting married so soon after being released as a prisoner of war; but some things just aren't funny. That never has been.

Tom and Marie stayed in touch with the lady who owned the farm where Tom was placed as a prisoner of war. They exchanged Christmas cards and often sent gifts to each other and their families. Since there was a language barrier, they had to get their letters translated, which shows the level of concern each had for the other. In 1974, Tom went back to Germany and visited with the children of the German lady who had, in a sense, served as his warden; he stayed in the same home as a guest where he had once been a captive. I guess that shows just how much freedom is worth, and how we should treat it: paradise lost and paradise found. Nations go to war; soldiers kill, wound, and imprison each other; but caring people find a way to be at peace no matter who they are or what their circumstances may be.

THE WAY WE WERE

I have been blessed in many ways; some of the ways I consider myself set apart probably would seem strange to most. Having older parents was kind of like being raised by grandparents, and that was a special blessing. Many of my peers at school had grandparents the age of my parents. All four of my grandparents were born in the nine year period from 1861 to 1870 which is the era just before, during, and after the American Civil War. I don't have to reach very far back, generation wise, to get to the time of the Civil War. Also, being raised in the rural South gave me experiences and exposure that was about a generation behind many of my peers. But I think that was a good thing, another blessing.

My parents were brought up in a time when there was little money, frugal life styles, few clothes, no bought entertainment, minimal recreation, very few home conveniences, precious little public education, long work hours, and a lot of hard work. We were taught to be contented and make do with what we had; there was no welfare, no social security, no automobiles, no airplanes, and no travel. By necessity we had to be self sufficient, plan ahead to provide food (always having a garden and livestock for slaughter), care for neighbors, and use home remedies whenever we were sick. There was no such thing as telecommunications and even the US Mail service wasn't all that dependable. With our limited money, we could only buy the essential items required to sustain our existence. But that too was a blessing;

it taught us how to survive and how to appreciate the small things in life.

No matter how hard the times were, there was always a strong belief in God and Country. Many of the ways in which my parents were brought up, and their positive and caring attitude about life itself, was manifested in the way they managed and operated our household, and reared children. My parents and grandparents lived in the era of President Theodore Roosevelt, and they understood his adage, "Do what you can, with what you have, where you are." Self-sufficiency was their way of life, which is a polar opposite of today's entitlement-minded generation.

Sir George Savile said that we should avoid too much gaudiness in our clothes. That's how our family lived. Daddy's everyday work clothes consisted of blue-denim bibbed overalls, a light-blue chambray shirt, a pair of brogan shoes, and a brimmed felt hat. His dress up clothes were a couple of suits, white shirt with a long wide tie, and a dress pair of high top shoes. Mama's everyday work clothes were simple dresses, usually homemade and frequently made from the cloth material used to sack flour or cattle feed. She always wore a large apron with a bib top; and if working the fields, she always wore an old-fashioned bonnet. From my memories, she had long graying hair, and wore it pulled straight back and made into a small bun in the back of her head. She had several nice stylish dresses, and since this was an era when women wore hats, Mama had her fashionable headwear. Mama stood about 5 feet 8 inches tall, and the large-brimmed hats always looked good on her; she wore hose and had a variety of dress and work shoes. Memories of her spiffed up or in her work clothes hold a precious and dear spot in my heart because she always gave everything her very best.

Because our family was rather large, we had to operate like a well-oiled machine. That took a lot of organization. Even as a young pre-school child, I watched carefully and was aware of how our household functioned. Probably the most precious yet unseen things we had were love and respect for each other and our neighbors. The most visible things for us, which included uncles and aunts and even my Grandpa and Grandma Starling, was the amounts and types of work everyone had to do to survive and provide for the needs of their families in the mid 1940s.

In general, throughout my community, life was simple and so very different back then; unlike today, very few women worked outside the home. When I was young, many homes didn't have running water in the house; water was carried in buckets from an outside well, some were lucky enough to have a pitcher pump inside the kitchen or on the back porch. Hot water heaters were almost unheard of; water was heated on top of the stove (ours was a wood burning cook stove) and that water was used for washing dishes and bathing. When I was about six years old, Daddy bought Mama a brand new *Home Comfort* wood-burning cook-stove that had a hot water heater attached. The coils running around the heating box of the stove heated the water. The stove also had a large heating cabinet for keeping food warm. Having the new easily accessible supply of hot water made it much easier to get a warm bath; even though baths were still not nightly, they were at least weekly. Daily baths didn't become routine for most rural folks until the late 1950s or early 1960s.

EVERYONE WORKED

In our family, everybody worked. No matter how old or young, there were always things which needed to be done that fit your age and size. Each day, after we came home from school, we changed clothes, got a snack (usually a biscuit with a hole punched in the top with cane syrup poured in the hole), and then went to the fields to work, if needed for the crops; otherwise, we had more than enough to do besides tending to agriculture. Whether we went to the fields or not, we each had responsibilities and chores to be done. One of my many responsibilities, even at five or six years old, was to be sure there was a good supply of stove wood for cooking, and during the winter months fire wood for the fireplace to last for the next 24 hours. I had to manually bring in the wood loaded across my arms, for both stove and fireplace. While that may not seem like much, our woodpile was about 100 yards from the house. Stove wood and firewood were separate kinds of wood, split differently. Each was stored in its own pile. And the amount needed for both fires required a lot of hard work—especially for a little kid, but for me, that was the beginning of learning responsibility.

My parents believed in teamwork. That taught us to trust and depend on each other as well as gave us the opportunity to negotiate the best way to cooperatively get things done. The six youngest children were boys; so we were paired according to age: Alfred and Pete, Billy and Sherwood, and Ronald and me.

Alfred and Pete primarily had responsibilities in the field. Both had dropped out of school to help Daddy on the farm. Pete's main job was to drive the John Deere tractor—he was the expert in the family with the tractor. Billy and Sherwood also worked in the fields, as all of us did, but they helped Mama in the house more than the rest of us; consequently, both become excellent cooks. Ronald and I jointly shared responsibility for some other chores, such as feeding the hogs, cows, horses, herding the cows from the pasture or woods and penning them up each evening and separating the calves from their mothers for the night. This allowed us to milk the cows the next morning and then let the calves suckle all day. Another one of my responsibilities was to feed the chickens and gather eggs each evening after school and it had to be done before the chickens went to roost. We had to hustle to keep abreast of our chores.

After supper each evening one of the four younger children that went to school every day would have to put away the leftover food and clear the dining room table, another would wash the dishes, and another would dry and put away the clean dry dishes. If there was time left, some would do homework before washing and getting ready for bed. Everyone went to bed early and got up early. Occasionally Daddy or Mama would allow us to stay up later, but we had to rise-and-shine like everyone else the next morning and not complain about being tired or sleepy—that kept us from wanting to stay up late.

About 5:30 a.m., Daddy would come to the door of our bedroom and say, "Boys, it's time to get up!" As soon as someone answered, he left; whoever Daddy spoke to was responsible to wake up the others. If Daddy had to come back to get us up, and I can only recall once or maybe twice when he did, he returned with a razor-strop and tore up all our butts. When he told us to do something, he only told us once; after that first instruction, he expected whatever he said to be done without further discussion or delay. If we didn't, the consequences could be quite painful on our backsides. When he gave any one of us a whipping, he gave a good one; and it still amazes me how that would cause all the rest of us to be very good for a long period of time.

After we rose from the nights sleep, Sherwood was responsible to start a fire in the wood stove so Mama could cook; if it was cold weather he also had to build a fire in the fireplace. After we got dressed, Billy and Sherwood would help Mama prepare breakfast. Pete, Ronald, and I would go to the cow lot to milk the cows. We always had in abundance fresh cow's milk, from which we always had fresh sweet cream, and Mama would use her *daisy churn* to make homemade butter. From the butter whey we would have buttermilk which was used to make fresh, hot biscuits every morning. We drank a lot of milk, and Daddy would frequently buy large containers of chocolate from the drug store for us to make chocolate milk. Many mornings for breakfast we had hot baked biscuits, fresh cow cream, bacon or ham, milk to drink, and cane syrup. We would use almost a gallon of syrup at one meal when there were eight children and two adults to feed. For variety, Mama regularly mixed things up at breakfast and would substitute fried or scrambled eggs and grits for some of the other staples. Breakfast at home is still one of my most pleasant memories.

After breakfast we had to help clean up the kitchen, again by washing, drying, and putting away the dishes. We also had to help make sure the floors were swept and all the beds were made before we walked down the lane in front of our house to catch the school bus at about 7:30 a.m., and there was no daylight saving time; so, in the winter, we would catch the school bus while it was still dark.

During spring, as soon as we got off the school bus we changed clothes, got a snack to eat on our way to the fields, and then we all worked until just before sunset. We were allowed just enough time to do our evening chores before it was pitch dark, if we hurried. Usually, the after school field work was to take care of corn, peanuts, tobacco, or whatever agricultural work was needed to be done— more often than not hoeing the weeds from the crops. Mama would usually have Billy or Sherwood go to the kitchen when we got home from school to help finish preparing supper. As a rule, Mama was in the field working and doing whatever we did. Her strategy was to out-work all of us; she made absolutely sure that no one loafed, goofed-off, or did sloppy work; Mama could be as tough as Daddy when it came to discipline. We could talk her out of more things, and she would ask us more than once to do something before resorting to punishment, but she didn't tolerate any of us being idle.

TABLE FARE

Most of the food we ate was raised in our garden, or in the fields, or from the farm animals we had. In fact, about the only food products that we purchased were salt, pepper, flour, spices, tea, coffee, flavoring, and a few other items we couldn't grow.

We always had a big garden with a wide variety of vegetables and grew what the season would allow. In the winter we grew mustard greens, collard greens, and turnip greens. The late spring was the time for the big garden; it contained string beans, butter beans, two to three varieties of peas, squash, okra, onions, radishes, tomatoes, eggplants, sweet early corn, new Irish potatoes, cucumbers, and rutabagas; these vegetables were all produced in abundance and shared with family and neighbors. This broad variety of vegetables lasted from late spring until well into the summer. Many of these vegetables, such as peas, okra, tomatoes, butter beans, and creamed corn, were ideal for canning. Many evenings after supper, Mama would sit on the front porch with Daddy and shell a bushel of peas to be cooked for dinner the next day. There was always a large supply of field corn which Mama usually cut off the cob and made cream corn; like most Southerners, we frequently had corn on the cob.

In the fields, Daddy would usually plant additional rows of field peas for canning, cucumbers for making pickles, and cantaloupes. Mama always made lots of jelly in the summer. She usually started in May by getting Mayhaw's from friends and making Mayhaw jelly, which has always been a family favorite. Mama would normally find time for us to pick blackberries; we had plenty of them, and she tried to make sure none went to waste. She made the absolute best blackberry jelly I have ever tasted. Since blackberries were plentiful and didn't require cultivation, Mama took advantage of them and made as much jam and jelly as she could. Besides blackberries, she made watermelon rind and fig preserves—more of my favorites.

Any vegetables in excess of our immediate need was never thrown away but was canned for use in the winter months. Canning was done the hard way by boiling the vegetables, then putting them in a pressure cooker in glass jars. Under pressure, and with *Ball* sealable lids and rings, the vegetables would keep for storage throughout the winter. Later, in the 1950s, we got a freezer, which changed how vegetables, and even meat, were stored for a long period. This made food preservation much simpler and a lot easier.

Daddy planted about 60 acres of corn each year in late March or early April for harvesting in the fall of the year. The corn in the fields would usually be dried out enough by early to mid-September and we would start the break-corn harvest, which was to break and slip-shuck each ear of corn off the stalk, toss it in a trailer, and then store it in the corncrib. Every ear was hand picked. Even though I hated this particular job, it didn't prevent me from having to do it. The corn in the crib was treated with *highlife* (a chemical) to kill beetles, rats, or anything else that might be in the crib; the crib had no windows, so as soon as the *highlife* was applied, the door was sealed for at least a week to give ample time for the chemical to act.

The crib kept our corn for cooking and for our animals—it was all the same. Every Saturday morning, without fail, we had to shuck and shell about 30 pounds of corn. After it was shucked and shelled, one or two of us would take it to Taylor's Store (about three miles away) to get it ground into grits and cornmeal. In those days, cash wasn't necessary because the mill would take a toll for pay (I believe it was about 10% of the net weight) so we usually returned home with about three pounds of grits, and about 24 pounds of cornmeal that would serve us for about a weeks worth of meals. You can see a picture of the corn crib in the back of the book—for farmers in our generation, a corn crib was about as important as a house because it kept food for the family and our farm animals.

HOG KILLING TIME

During the fall of each year, several annual events took place. But one particular affair always stood out more than others: hog-killing. Daddy would have a hog-killing in mid-November as soon as it turned cool enough so that the fresh meat wouldn't spoil; we usually butchered anywhere from 10 to 14 hogs at a time. That much meat would feed us for a year. We had a 60-gallon sugar kettle that was normally used to make cane syrup, and that kettle was an ideal size for scalding the hogs, after they were killed, so the hair could be scraped off. We always had from six to eight neighbors who came to help with the hog killing and meat processing. There was never any pay for the neighbors, only loads of fresh pork to take home for their families. Anyway, offering pay to a neighbor for lending a helping hand would have been an insult and just wasn't done.

We had fresh pork and fresh sausage (both patties and linked), for the next few days after our hog killing. Most of the pork (hams, shoulders, sides, and linked sausage) was placed in our smokehouse and hung from horizontal sticks on racks. A small pit, about six inches deep and about 24 inches across, was dug in the dirt floor of the smokehouse and a small fire of oak wood was kept slowly burning for about two weeks, which was about how long it took to cure and preserve the meat. The meat would hang there for a year and not spoil; it would often mold, and may have skippers or insects get into small parts of the meat, but we would just cut those parts off, scrub the mold off and the meat was perfectly fine. In fact, I think those things actually added to the unique country flavor of pork. You can see a picture of the smokehouse in the back of the book—you can't get hams or bacon or sausage today that compares in flavor to what we prepared in that rustic old building.

Late in the afternoon on a hog killing a good bit of time was required to cook the grease/lard out of the fat that was chopped up into cubes as large as two inches. Once the fat was cooked out, that left crunchy cracklings which were often used in making crackling cornbread—that is a Southern delicacy that was once very popular, but it has almost disappeared from our menus.

Pork was our main source of meat, but we did have other meats. Once a year Daddy would butcher a fattened steer and we would share it with neighbors. Unlike pork, beef wouldn't keep for very long and had to be eaten fairly soon after slaughter. If Mama decided we were going to have chicken to eat, which was usually Sunday dinner, we would catch the one she chose, ring its neck, cut off the head and drain the blood, scald it to pluck the feathers, singe the hairs with a fire made from a newspaper, and cut it up for frying or stewing.

Each year, during the first part of November, Daddy would make a trip to Steinhatchee to buy as much as 100 pounds of dressed mullet (fish) with the red roe. On the trip, we would usually cook out somewhere near Steinhatchee or eat with the Carmichael's who owned the fish house. Daddy would bring the fish home and salt them down in a wooden barrel which was kept in the smoke house. He would put a layer of dressed mullet then a layer of salt, a layer of mullet, and a layer of salt until the barrel was full and the fish were completely covered with salt. The fish would keep this way for several weeks. Whenever we wanted fish, Mama would get it from the barrel and soak them for several hours, usually all night or all day, to get rid of as much of the salt as possible before cooking.

RAISING CANE

Daddy raised about two acres of sugar cane every year. Like everything else, sugar cane had its season for harvest. When the days started to have a regular chill, around the first of November, we would strip the cane, top it, cut it down, pile it up neatly, and cover it up—all before the first frost. We used the blades (leaves) that we stripped off the stalks to cover the cane and protect it from the frost. The week of Thanksgiving was always a big cane-grinding week. We were out of school, and many business people, merchants, and other friends always loved coming to the cane grinding. It was never any fun to us because we had to do all the work. It took about four to five hours to cook a round of syrup. The sugar kettle held 60 gallons of cane juice, which produced about nine gallons of syrup. In my first memory of making syrup, the sugar kettle was fired with wood, but as progress and opportunity came available we switched to a small homemade hotshot kerosene burner to fire the kettle.

We squeezed the juice from the sugar cane for years using a horse walking a trodden circular path operating a rugged press. In the same manner that we improved our fire to cook the syrup, we got a mill with a big pulley that was about six feet across; our tractor provided the power using a large eight to10 inch belt connected to a smaller pulley. A lot of people in the neighborhood would come by when we were making syrup; it was, in a way, a community event. And just as certain as sunrise, Daddy and Mama made sure that our visitors took home a bottle of freshly made cane syrup.

We boys ensured that the syrup-making operation was successful; we brought in the cane from the field to the mill, fed cane into the mill (that was a long, slow job), and then disposed of the stalks of cane after the juice had been squeezed from them. The sugar cane industry calls the leftovers pulp, but we called them *pummings*. As soon as one batch was squeezed and another was delivered, we took the pummings to the field to rot, which helped fertilize the soil with valuable nutrients for the next crop—nothing was wasted, not even the seemingly worthless squeezed out stalks of cane.

November was also a time for digging our few rows of sweet potatoes, another crop that we planted annually. Each year we would build a couple of potato banks. They looked like small tepees. We used old scrap slab boards from the local sawmill to provide strength and rigidity, tar paper to wrap and keep out the rain and cold, and then lined the inside floor with tar paper covered with a thick layer of pine straw; a flap opening was left for access. We also used our tepees to store Irish potatoes as well. The potatoes stored this way would last for several months without spoiling.

SOAP

Mark Twain said that soap and education are not as sudden as a massacre but they are more deadly in the long run. He may have known about Mama's homemade lye-soap. Mama made laundry soap from animal fat, oak aches, and lye. In addition to using this homemade soap to wash clothes, we also used it to scrub the wooden porches and floors in our home. It was a very rugged soap that would burn your skin when used for personal cleansing, so we didn't use it for bathing unless we absolutely had to or we were so dirty that it took that extra cleansing agent to remove ground in dirt. Lye-soap was good for cleaning up grease or motor oil—things that regular soap couldn't dissolve.

KEEPING THE FIELDS READY

December was a time to clear new ground for planting tobacco. We had to weed our fences during the Christmas holidays, which meant hoeing out all the unwanted plants along both sides of the wire fence so that the wire was clear from any growth. Shortly after New Years when the undergrowth in the timber was most dormant and the moisture and wind was right, Daddy would set the woods on fire using a controlled burn. This was really intriguing to watch. All of us had to be there during the burn just in case the wind shifted and the fire line got out of control. If that happened we had to jump in and fight the fire using rakes and hoes, but the best tool of all was green pine tops—they worked like magic to snuff out a fire that threatened to get out of control.

Daddy always had upwards of 75 hogs and about a dozen cows that were not for our food consumption. He would fatten them up to sell at the livestock market. Even as young children, we observed the natural breeding of farm animals, and if necessary, assisted hogs and cows giving birth as just a matter-of-fact of life. I guess that was sex education as it was intended to be. We certainly understood how things worked, and we respected it, which is quite different from the learning and values kids get in today's modern and "enlightened" world.

Monday morning, rain or shine, was always washday. Mama got a washing machine shortly after I was born; before that, all her washing was done in tubs and with a rub board—it was some of the hardest labor that women had to do. I remember her washday practices all too well. They began early every Monday morning. We built a fire under the wash pot so Mama could boil our work clothes. She would then beat them clean on a battling block before running them through the washing machine. Then they were hung outdoors on a long clothes-line to dry. If our clothes needed pressing, as soon as we were old enough, we all had to iron our own clothes; Mama ironed her and Daddy's clothes, and if time permitted, she would sometimes iron a few of our clothes. But mostly, that was our job.

Mama was a great cook; she baked bread every day, hot biscuits at breakfast, cornbread for lunch (we called the noon meal dinner), and either fresh bread baked for supper, or left over biscuits or cornbread from earlier in the day. Mama didn't bake a lot of cakes or pastries. But she made great blackberry cobbler, blackberry pies, and egg-custard pies. She also made syrup and peanut-pull candy, syrup teacakes, and pear tarts. These tasty sweets were more than satisfying to all of us and we really loved them—I still remember them with great affection; at times, I can close my eyes and almost taste them.

MAKING CLOTHES

Mama was very industrious and made almost all the clothes we wore, but most women of that time and in our area did the same. She made our pants, shirts, and underclothes when we were younger, and many of our shirts as we got older. She would buy most of the cloth used to make her dresses and our shirts and pants, but some of the fabric came from the food staples we bought. From the mid 1940s to the mid 1950s, most bags of flour used for making bread and many of the bags of animal feed, such as chicken feed, came in cotton bags with printed designs and patterns; these products were packaged to supply fabrics for homemade clothing—it was a good marketing strategy. Some of the designs were better suited for females and some for males. Mama would always ask Daddy to carefully select the bags of flour or the bags of chicken feed to assure the dye patterns matched; he always bought at least two bags so there would be enough cloth to make a simple work dress or a boy's shirt, depending on the print of the material.

The only sewing machine Mama ever had was an old *Singer* treadle (foot-operated pedal) sewing machine; it was a second-hand machine when she got it. Mama could make three plain work dresses a day (nothing fancy), one in the morning, one in the afternoon, and one in the evening. She sewed for many of the ladies in our community. She had a real gift of going to town, looking at a dress in a store, then coming home and cutting the pattern for that dress out of newspaper; she was then able to adjust the pattern as she cut the material to fit a person of a different size. Mama never received pay for any of her work. Some aunts, or close friends, would actually come spend two or three days at our home while Mama sewed for them; that way it was much easier for her to have the person try-on a partially made dress so she could properly fit or adjust the dress for a better feel and appearance. The deal she made with all of them was they had to do what she was planning to do that day, whether it was just cooking dinner, washing clothes, ironing, or hoeing corn in the field.

Mama was always up at the crack of dawn and would still be going strong until bedtime; all of her work was manual labor—she didn't have any of the modern appliances to make her jobs easier or faster. She was always busy doing something; even when she was resting Mama would be shelling peas or butter beans, or working on some other task she could do while sitting—like some type of needle work.

MAMA GOT SICK

In the early 1950s, Mama learned she was a diabetic and had to take 40 units of insulin per day. She would give herself shots, but her eyesight was beginning to fail somewhat, and she would ask me to check the number of units of insulin in the syringe. By the time I was 11 or 12, it became my job to give her the insulin shots. The modern sterilization solutions and throwaway needles didn't exist at that time; I had to boil her needle and syringe every day to sterilize them, after a while the needles would get dull and I would have to sharpen them. With some practice, I learned to tell when I needed to increase or decrease the dosage based on what I knew Mama had planned for the day, but we always discussed it and I gained her approval before adjusting the dosage. I knew that too much or not enough of her medicine could cause her to go into insulin shock and when that occurred we didn't know if we should give her something sweet or more insulin; the wrong choice could have grave consequences. That was a good lesson for me in responsibility; I learned how to recognize a vital need and to have the discipline to provide a critically needed essential care. I continued preparing and giving Mama her morning insulin all through my junior and senior high school years.

In the coldest part of the winter, we would sit around the one heat source we had: a fireplace. Daddy sat on the left, Mama sat on the right, and we children would form a semi-circle around the fireplace. We would listen to the radio news with Daddy or some other radio show after the news. Frequently, as we sat around the fire, each of us had a pot or bowl of dried ears of corn to shell by hand. We saved the good kernels for seed to be planted in the spring and the poorly developed kernels were ground into corn meal. We would also shell dried peanuts to use as seed. The cracked or damages peanuts were put in a separate bowl and Mama would use them to make syrup-pull candy or peanut brittle. All our seeds for planting were always the best of the crop; that way, we hoped to ensure a better harvest and improve our seeds over time by always keeping the very best for planting. There was an old saying that said something like whatever seed you sew will determine your harvest—which meant that when you plant your best, you will reap the best.

TOBACCO

The main cash crop on our farm was about four acres of tobacco. Tobacco was a time-consuming crop to grow because the plants were very tender and required a lot of manual labor while they were maturing. Tobacco plants required poisoning to keep worms from eating the leaves, and we had to remove the suckers (deformed shoots that sprouted and took away needed nourishment from the healthy plant) that grew at the base of each leaf; we broke off the suckers to allow full development of the useable leaves. After poisoning, pruning, and dressing the plants, we cut the tops to allow the upper leaves to develop more fully. Every summer, from the time school ended until just a couple of weeks before school started back in the fall, we were either suckering or harvesting the ripe leaves that were ready for curing.

Harvesting the tobacco required a large number of people; about 14 working bodies were about the right size for a crew to harvest and prepare a full barn of tobacco for curing. During my growing up years, for the harvesting of tobacco, our family swapped work with C. G. Howell, his wife Ethel, and their three daughters, Patsy, Anetha, and Susanette; and with Mr. Milton Rye and his wife Delma. Children as young as five or six years old could hand the tobacco to the person stringing it on a stick as well as an adult. It wasn't hard work, just repetitive and boring—extremely monotonous. The three families together gave us 14 people, which was a complete harvesting crew. We would work one day harvesting Daddy's tobacco, the next day Pete's at Mrs. Hattie Ross's, the next day down at Mr. Howell's, and the next at Mr. Rye's. This totaled four full days each week harvesting the tobacco, and we repeated the process weekly for about seven weeks, depending on the yield of the crop.

Through swapping work, the adults received no pay from their neighbors; they simply traded their work for the work of the other adults. The cooperative effort was quite efficient; we all worked together and knew exactly what we had to do at each farm. The harvesting process required the cropping of the ripe tobacco leaves in the field, transporting them to the barn area to be strung up on sticks and then hanged in the barn to be cured or cooked for about six days and nights. The curing of tobacco starts at a low temperature and is gradually increased until it reaches about 180 degrees. A 20 foot by 20 foot tobacco barn would hold about 500 sticks of tobacco and each stick was about five feet long; we got maximum use out of minimum space. You can see a picture of the tobacco barn in the back of the book—it looks rough and insignificant, but it was a vital part of our living.

After curing the tobacco, we removed it from the barn early in the morning before daylight so it could pick up some moisture before we packed it in the corncrib where it remained until near the end of July. We took the cured tobacco off the sticks and placed them in piles of about 250 to 300 pounds each and then wrapped or sheeted it in coarse burlap cloth. The heaps of tobacco went on the auction block and sold to the highest bidder at the Live Oak Tobacco Market. I didn't like much of anything about the tobacco business, but it was still a job I had to do. I disliked tobacco because it was hard, dirty, and boring work.

DADDY'S BIRTHDAY PARTY

Perhaps one of my fondest memories of being raised in a large family was all the time we spent with each other, doing chores, working in the fields, or doing whatever we had to do. We were almost always with one of our siblings. I believe that companionship is a big reason we have always gotten along so well with each other and enjoy the company of each other. For well over 60 years, if possible, all my brothers and sisters have made it a family practice to get together at least twice a year, Thanksgiving Day and the forth Saturday in March, which is the time Mama always celebrated Daddy's birthday, and share the noon meal together. All the nieces, nephews, and their children and our more distant relatives are invited to attend, as many as can usually do go to the event, and it is always a great opportunity to visit a lot of different family at one time.

There were no telephones in the rural areas when I was growing up; the closest one to our house was 13 miles away in town. It was a common practice for friends or neighbors to just show up and sit-a-while. At times, this would be on a weekday night, a Saturday night, or on Sunday morning to spend the day. When this happened, the women would cook, the men would visit, and the children played.

Daddy and Mama were members of Patmos Primitive Baptist Church which was about eight miles south of our house, and about two miles south of Grandpa Starling's house. The church house had wooden plank floors, a wood exterior, and wooden windows that opened on hinges. The church had services the first Saturday and Sunday of the month. The men members sat on one side of the pulpit and the lady members sat on the other side; visitors sat facing the pulpit. Services would usually last a couple of hours. Children sat in church with their parents; there was no Sunday school provided. This also provided children with the opportunity to learn how to behave by mimicking the actions of their parents.

For regular monthly church, Daddy usually wore his work clothes; and Mama wore one of her nicer work dresses without the apron. She most always wore a hat, frequently one of the large brimmed hats, to church on Sunday or when attending an annual meeting at one of the churches in their church association.

Friendship and manners are how we show people that we care for them or have respect for them. Frequently, people from sister churches visiting our church would spend the night with the different members of the congregation. It was common for my parents to invite four to eight people, who were almost strangers, to spend the Saturday night at our house. When that happened, we children would give up our beds to the guests, make ourselves a pallet on the back porch or find a place to sleep where ever we could. We never complained about any inconvenience that a guest or company may have caused us. We children seldom attended church with Daddy and Mama on Saturday, but we usually did on Sunday. Following church we would typically come back by Grandpa Starling's for dinner. Often there would be other uncles and aunts and their children also visiting Grandpa and Grandma on Sunday and we had a great time playing with the many cousins we had. I think today's children are missing out on a lot of valuable family time by not having large families with several cousins to visit—unfortunately, that part of rural America seems to almost have vanished.

TABLE MANNERS

Mealtime was special. There was always plenty of good and usually fresh food to eat. We had a long rectangle-shaped dining table. Daddy sat on one end, and Mama sat next to him on the side closest to the kitchen. We all filled in around the table with the oldest sitting next to Mama and the youngest next to Daddy. On the side of the table to Daddy's right was a bench against the wall where we younger children sat. There were, as in most households, mealtime rules at the table: everyone had to be present before anyone ate, no eating later, or on the run; no one started eating until everyone was seated and the blessing for our food had been asked; as the dishes of food were passed around the table, each person helped his or her own plate, even the smallest child. Mama allowed us to take all we wanted from any dish; the only requirement was that whatever we took, we ate. If your eyes were larger than your stomach you had to eat whatever you put on your plate—no exceptions; we quickly learned to judge our wants carefully and accurately.

Children usually didn't talk at mealtime unless spoken to by one of our parents or older siblings. During mealtime, discussions generally were focused around happenings in the family, on the farm, about neighbors, or things that happened at school. Children are often spurred to laugh at the most inopportune times; mealtime was usually when that would happen. The problem would usually happen at the table when someone would tell a funny story. Then, we would all start laughing, but when it was time to break it off, Daddy could give us a stern look and all the funny went away instantly. Daddy had milk-white hair, a dark completion, and deep-blue eyes; those eyes and his countenance spoke volumes without him ever having to say very much. As I recall those times, I wonder just how much effort it would take to train a new generation to live that way—or if it could be done at all. I think America was stronger back then and certainly family values were held in higher regard.

MOTOR VEHICLES

I was eight years old before Daddy ever had a vehicle, other than a one-row John Deere tractor, which was used almost exclusively on the farm. Prior to Daddy getting a pickup truck, if he needed to go to town, he caught a ride with Uncle Clarence, his brother, or some other neighbor who had an automobile. Before we got the truck, we would go to church in a wagon pulled by the John Deere tractor. A couple of times I recall going to church, and going to visit Grandpa and Grandma Starling, in a wagon pulled by our horse, Nellie. That probably seems impossible today, but society has changed almost completely within my lifetime. Our necessities, luxuries, needs, and wants have all changed in one generation.

In 1940, Daddy purchased his first tractor, a John Deere model L; this tractor didn't have a starter and had to be hand cranked. In 1945,

Daddy traded the model L tractor for a newer one, a John Deere model LA; the model LA tractor had a battery with lights and a starter, it was a real trade upwards. In 1949 Daddy traded the model LA tractor for a John Deere model M. All the tractors he ever owned were one row cultivating tractors. The model M had a hydraulic lift system along with bottom plows, harrow, tiller, and the cultivator was much easier to attach, set-up, adjust, and maintain than the earlier models he owned. He kept his model M tractor until he passed away in 1969, and today, my nephew, RoAnn Padgett, owns it, has restored it and it is still operational even after almost 60 years since Daddy first put it to work in the fields. Like old family values, equipment that is well cared for can last forever.

In the fall of 1947, Daddy purchased his first family vehicle, a bright-yellow 1948 Ford pick-up truck with a state body. That was also the year that he learned how to drive; he never learned to drive too well, but neither did he ever have a wreck. I guess that speaks volumes for his attention to details and his concern for safety.

DISCIPLINE

There is no discipline in the world so severe as the discipline of experience. John Dewey.

Both of my parents were great disciplinarians and dealt with each child in a caring and unique way. While they were very loving and supportive, they also demanded from each of us the basics of honesty, integrity, hard work, respect, and courteous behavior. Above that, we were expected do what we said we would do, don't gossip, be supportive and helpful to each other, share with each other, take turns with chores and with things that were fun, and help those less fortunate than ourselves.

Both of my parents always supported the *wet* side in the periodic *wet–dry* elections to decide if the selling of whiskey was going to be legal or not. The reason they gave for voting wet was that they hoped we would not drink alcoholic beverages, but if we were determined to do so, then they preferred we not have to drive 35 miles to buy it and then drive 35 miles home, perhaps after having taken a drink—which was a potential opportunity for disaster. Daddy always kept whiskey in the top of the cabinet and never hid it from us. He never objected to us taking a drink of his whiskey or even chewing tobacco, as he did, or smoking, but we all knew better than to slip-around and do any of those things. We had to be open, honest, and above board in our activities; as a result of his teaching, Daddy never had to get even one of his eight boys out of jail. I don't mean to imply that we were perfect, we weren't; we simply knew what was expected and required in our behavior and we tried to always measure up to those expectations and not disappoint our parents.

We were, as most children, mischievous, but we never did anything that was destructive or defaced the property of someone else. We were always taught to ask before borrowing something from someone else and to return the item in as good or better condition as when the article or thing was borrowed, except for normal wear and tear, of course.

One time my brother, Ronald, had done something and Mama was about to give him a whipping. Ronald ran and climbed up the huge oak tree in the side yard; she didn't beg or plead for him to come down, she simply asked him once, but he stubbornly stayed up in the tree. It got dark and supper was served; and Ronald still wouldn't come down out of the tree. I was worried about him at supper, but Mama didn't seem to be too concerned. I reminded her he was missing supper, and she responded, "It's okay; sooner or later he'll have to come down out of the tree." Sure enough, later that night, he came down and the following morning he still got the whipping she had promised. Disciple was not ignored or forgotten simply because time had passed or there had been a measure of remorse displayed. Actions had consequences, and justice would always be served. That was a good process back then; it would serve us well in today's age.

GAMES

We didn't have any toys to play with. We had to create our own entertainment; it was usually jump-board, a sack swing, or swimming down at the pond, and occasionally we got to go to the fresh-water springs, which was a real treat. Pushing a syrup bottle in the sand was our *car* to play with.

Our yards had no grass and we had to keep all the weeds out of it; it had to be kept clean, plus it helped to keep snakes away, or at least you could see them before they tried to bite. Besides, the clean yard was good to play in.

Mama loved flowers and had several flowerbeds in the yard; she worked to keep the weeds out and watered the plants enough to keep them from dying. She also had benches on each side of the front porch and across the ends of the porch for potted plants. Her favorite was geraniums, and she had several colors and varieties in separate pots all across the front and sides of the front porch. She made us help keep them watered and fertilized using cow manure. Whenever we played outside near Mama's flowers, they always provided us with a pleasant smell. There's nothing quite like the aroma of freshly raked dirt mixed with the sweet fragrance of blooming flowers. Our yard blessed us with that for most of the year.

Once, when Daddy and Mama were not home, following a serious discussion as to whether the light in the refrigerator really went out when we closed the door, we decided to confirm our opinions. So we unloaded the refrigerator, removed the shelves, and Billy got in. We closed the door so he could be the one to tell us who was right. It may not have been one of our wisest scientific experiments, but it did show a reasonable amount of ingenuity and a pursuit of knowledge about the unknown. If our parents had known, we would have received another life-lesson, but we already knew that before our experiment.

FAMILY VALUES

When virtue is present, men use it for an example; when it is gone, they desire it. Wisdom of Solomon.

Socrates asked, "What is virtue?" That's something humanity has struggled with since the foundation of the earth. In its most simple form, virtue is an ethical code based on biblical standards—at least that's my definition.

We were taught values, morals, and principles; these are the fundamentals of virtue. The most serious offence we could make was to tell our parents a lie; this brought the most severe punishment. We were always taught to be grateful for what we had; to have a positive attitude; to be ready to help a neighbor or anyone less fortunate than us. I recall one year in the spring, a neighbor was dying of cancer and Daddy took all of us over to his farm several times and we worked to help make sure he didn't lose his crop that year. Neighbors did that for each other back then.

We were always taught that when an adult enters the room, if we were seated, to get up from our chair and offer it to the adult. We were taught to greet family, and neighbors, with a hug and it didn't matter if they were male or female. We never called adults by their first name.

It was always Mr., Mrs., Uncle or Aunt; and we had to respond to any adult speaking to us with yes sir, no sir, yes ma'am, and no ma'am.

We had to subject ourselves to the authority of any adult whenever we were in their care, or if we were simply away from the supervision of our parents and an adult happened to be present then we were subject to the adult's authority. That wasn't just in our family—it was a common community value; I think we could use more of that kind of neighborly service today. That was how I learned to respect seniority and authority; both of these attributes have served me well throughout my lifetime in public service and the military.

Another rule at our house was when we used anything, such as a tool, we were free to use it; but it better be put back exactly where we got it when we were through using it. By doing this, it would always be available for the next person, and they knew exactly where to find it. I learned to put things where they belong when I'm not using them. That is another value I was taught that has served me well through the years.

Still another rule at our home was that if we had work to be done, then the work always had to be done before we could play; in essence, rest after the work is done–not before you start. I recall late one afternoon when I was playing in the yard, Daddy walked by and asked if I had gathered the eggs. I said, "No sir, not yet." He went to the back porch, got his razor-strop, and gave me a whipping; he said, "You always do your work first, then if you have time, you can play." That little life's lesson left a permanent impression on me and enhanced my work ethic.

THE GOPHER HOLE

I remember one Saturday afternoon when Daddy told me to take the seed peas and go down to the small field in front of the house and replant any of the peas that hadn't come up yet. I carefully did the job on several rows and was getting tired when I came upon a gopher hole. That gopher hole seemed like a magical thing that just appeared out of nowhere to rescue me from planting peas. I looked at the gopher hole and figured that I could end my job by pouring the rest of the peas down the gopher hole; it worked, or so I thought. Daddy walked down in the field to check my work and quickly realized I didn't do the job correctly. He didn't say anything to me that evening, and I thought I had gotten by with doing my sloppy half-job. Early the next morning, Sunday, at the crack of dawn, Daddy made me redo the entire job. No whipping; I just had to redo the job. He said, "Son, if you don't have time to do a job right the first time, when will you have the time to redo it?" Boy, did that ever teach me a valuable lesson about work and life. These early lessons were probably the most important things I was ever taught. School has knowledge, college has even more information, but responsibility and reasonableness only come from the intense work of someone who cares enough to invest their own life into yours. That's what my parents did.

But the mercy of the LORD is from everlasting to everlasting upon them that fear him, and his righteousness unto children's children. Psalm 103:17.

PUBLIC SCHOOLS
1ˢᵗ THROUGH 12ᵗʰ GRADE

Children today are tyrants. They contradict their parents, gobble their food, and tyrannize their teachers. Socrates.

WORLD WAR II ENDED in 1945, a little more than a year before I started to school in September 1946. The nation was in a period of recovery from a wartime effort to one of economic growth and development. The prior six years had been very difficult for everyone throughout the nation, and it had been especially grueling for my family because of the capture and imprisonment of my brother, Tom, by the Germans.

PLANNING FOR SCHOOL

Daddy finished the third grade, and Mama went through the fifth grade; they attended schools that only operated for a total of three months each year. Daddy and Mama were always supportive of us going to school. They knew the value of getting an education and both of them sacrificed much to ensure that each of us was able to go to school as long as we could.

Before any of his children started to school, Daddy learned that the school board was drawing attendance zones for the Live Oak schools and for the many rural country schools that existed at the time. He met with the officials who were drawing up the attendance zones to get our farm included in the Live Oak attendance zone; we were in the farthest corner of the attendance zone, but still inside. The neighbor's children living next door on the south and west attended one of the nearby rural schools; no one in my family ever attended a rural school.

We had to ride the bus farther than most kids because we lived in the corner of the attendance zone which made our daily trip a lot longer. After I caught the Live Oak bus, it then connected with the rural bus at a designated point and each exchanged selected students to the designated bus going to their assigned schools. This change of buses took place every morning and afternoon. If one of the buses broke down, there was havoc, and we would be very late getting to school or getting home, depending on whether the breakdown occurred in the morning or afternoon.

I usually rode the bus a little more than 15 miles one way, but for one year in my upper grades, due to closing some of the rural schools and reassigning the buses, drivers, and redrawing some routes, I rode almost 30 miles each morning and afternoon; but, thank goodness, that only lasted for one year. I never missed a single day of school in all 12 years of my public school education; consequently, I have probably ridden more miles and have spent more time on a school bus than just about anyone in the state. If awards were given for time and distance traveled to school, I would certainly be a top candidate for the winners circle.

By the time I started first grade, my oldest sister had already been married for nine years and had three children. My two living oldest brothers were veterans of World War II; they had returned home, married, and started their families. Winifred, the second oldest sister, had just graduated from Suwannee High School in May 1945, and had finished one year of college in business education at Florida Southern College. Margaret, the younger sister, was a sophomore in high school and dropped out of school in late spring of 1947, which was the end of my first grade year, and got married in June 1947. By this time, Alfred and Pete had already quit school to help Daddy farm. Living in a rural agricultural area, children were like natural resources and helpful in supporting the economic benefit to the family simply because farm work was manually intensive labor and required a lot of able bodies.

The economic times of the 1930s and the national wartime effort of the early 1940s stretched the survival capabilities of each small farmer to the fullest. During the period of the Great Depression in the 1930s until the end of World War II, a very low percentage of students starting school in the first grade actually graduated from high school. Dropping out of school by the older brothers and sisters was a common practice for older teenage students back then because they were needed to either work on the farm or get a job to help support the family, or the young men joined a branch of the armed forces or were drafted into military service. Public education just didn't rank nearly as high or have as much priority as survival or freedom.

When I was in school there were very few teaching materials, no Xerox or copy machines, and reproduced materials were almost non-existent. I can't recall ever seeing a 16 mm movie projector, record player, or even a slide projector until I was in junior high school. We had a very basic set of textbooks and each classroom was self-contained. Our teachers always started the day by reading Bible verses. After the Bible reading we would stand and in unison repeat the Lord's Prayer; when we finished the Lord's Prayer we reverently placed our right hands over our hearts, faced the United States Flag, and recited the Pledge of Allegiance to the Flag of the United States, which had 48 stars at the time because Alaska and Hawaii were not yet states. I was in the eighth grade when, on June 14, 1954, the two words "under God" were added to the Pledge of Allegiance following the approval of President Dwight

D. Eisenhower. I believe that was a strong statement of our nation's spiritual foundation and our gratitude for our nation's freedom and prosperity. We could use some more of that thankfulness in our nation today; our country and our people would benefit from it.

Teaching was fairly straightforward in those days. We studied to learn rather than study to perform on a test. We learned to spell by memorization, not phonics. And we learned math, in part, by learning and reciting the multiplication tables, which of course helped with division, adding, and subtracting. While these things seem to have lost their luster in today's classrooms, we probably have suffered from their loss because now children use gadgets to write or make computations, and these devices, no matter how fancy they may be or how much information they contain, they just don't do a lot to teach the cognitive skills kids need for learning.

That's not to say technology is bad; on the contrary. Technology certainly has its place in our schools, but the real demands we should place on children is thinking independently and functioning based on raw mental abilities without relying on some sort of assistive device. Children first and foremost need to learn how to learn, and that takes concentration and practice instead of finger dexterity. I recall being assigned to reading groups, which was the innovative technique of the day, where children of varying skill levels were put into clusters and the students with better skills helped those who needed assistance and then the teacher provided overall instruction; it was a group dynamic that worked quite well. We were taught reading using the *look–say* method (which is a linguistic system); you look at a word and just say it, then eventually, through exercise and use, it became as well established as our knowledge of harvesting tobacco.

SCHOOL BELLS RING

I started first grade at the Nettie Baisden Primary School, and Mrs. Nettie Baisden was my teacher and the principal. Like most kids in that era, I carried my lunch to school—at least for the first few years. There was a cafeteria in the basement of the old junior high school building, but all they served was soup and a half-pint of milk in a glass bottle. About 45 years later, my first grade classroom became the School Board Meeting Room and that lasted from the late 1980s to the early 1990s.

In September 1947, I started second grade. Only the four youngest boys in my family remained in school. My new classroom was next door to my old first grade classroom; my new teacher was Ms. Verna Brinson. Both she and Mrs. Baisden were great teachers. They both knew my parents and each had taught many of my older brothers and sisters, so we weren't strangers.

The teachers didn't have a lot of teaching materials; they had a room, desk, reading and math books, crayons, paste, a limited supply of colored paper, and chalkboards—that was about it. The only things required by the state to be in the curriculum were reading, writing, and arithmetic. Each classroom was 100 percent self-contained for instruction, recess, lunch, art, music, physical education, and all other activities. Teachers were pretty much independent from supervision, they were expected to organize their classroom as they saw fit, and to teach how and what they wanted to teach. Classroom teachers were with their students almost every minute of the day—much like a parent; there were no aides or assistants to help with instruction or supervision.

It was during my second year of public school that I went to my first movie—it was a school sponsored project. We each paid a dime and we were marched by our teacher's downtown to the Alimar Theater to see the movie, *Song of the South*, which we all knew as *Uncle Remus*. Going to the theater was something special for us. Many of us were country kids who had never seen a movie before, and of course this was way before television, so seeing a movie was almost like going to heaven.

Not everything was perfect in what we call the good old days. There were some drawbacks to our school system. It was possible to go through grade school and never learn some of the necessary basic skills that would be needed later in school, like fractions. The reason this could happen was simply because many teachers didn't like to teach fractions (or whatever particular study skill or curriculum they may have been less than proficient in), and this would leave a gap in our learning and preparation for the higher grades.

DON'T GET SMART

During most of my primary school years, Daddy's brother, Uncle Clarence, was our school bus driver. It wasn't uncommon for me or my brothers to occasionally spend a night with Uncle Clarence, but when we did, we had to get up even earlier than usual and then ride the entire route from start to finish. Whenever anyone misbehaved on the school bus, Uncle Clarence would make the misbehaver either sit on a *Coca-Cola* crate to his left and work the stop sign or sit to his right on a wooden box and open the main bus door as punishment. Usually, there was a set number of days for the chastisement to last. After one of my misdeeds on the bus, I was disciplined by Uncle Clarence and made to work the stop sign. I knew one place on our route, the Hauley Touchton home, which had a cattle-gap that crossed the road where the opening was barely large enough for a school bus to get through with just inches clearance on either side. The cattle-gap was built over a two to three foot deep hole with the sides reinforced so that it wouldn't cave in under the weight of any vehicle that traveled over it. As we approached the gap, I asked Uncle Clarence, "How far away should I open the stop sign before we get to a stop?" He pointed to an object about 25 yards up the road, and said, "About that far."

A famous comedian used a punch-line for all the things he did wrong; he would purposely behave mischievously, and then say with a sly grin, "The devil made me do it." I didn't like being punished and I was waiting with a devilish motive for the bus to get to the cattle-gap. I plotted to operate the sign just before reaching the cattle-gap because there was a bus stop just after we crossed over it. Sure enough, as we approached the cattle-gap, I opened the stop sign and when the bus went through the opening, it bent the stop sign double and mutilated it. Without showing frustration or alarm, Uncle Clarence stopped the bus, marched me off the bus, took off his belt, and gave me a good whipping right on the spot; not only did I get physically hurt, my pride was injured because all the kids on bus watched as I got the living daylights beat out of me.

Uncle Clarence straightened up the bent stop sign, and extended my punishment for an additional two weeks. I dared not tell Daddy about what happened because I would have gotten another whipping from him—and it would have been far more severe. For a long time, I lived in horror that Uncle Clarence would tell Daddy what happened, and I would still get the whipping anyway. Apparently Uncle Clarence never told Daddy, but I sweated it out for a long time and that was a lot more punishment because I lived in fear and dread of what might happen. As I look back on things, I realize that uncles and aunts look out for nephews and nieces whenever they can, just so long as they don't have to hide dangerous or serious offences. In fact, they usually protect the little devilish acts because it creates a special bond that lasts forever.

NEVER LATE

During school days, missing the bus was a serious infraction around our home. Tardiness and laziness were not well tolerated. Daddy and Mama would say to us, if we were dragging at all in the mornings, they hoped we would miss the bus. They had a real incentive plan for us to go to school, and Ronald served as a prime example for not missing the bus.

One spring morning when Ronald was about 10-years old, he was easing around in one of his lazy moods, and missed the school bus; he was right at the bus stop, but he wasn't where he should've been. Sometimes even the bus drivers can be a little cantankerous; this one was. He pulled off and left Ronald; he may have been making an example of Ronald or he may have just been in an ornery mood—either way, Ronald missed the bus. Ronald's retribution for missing the bus was getting to work with Daddy all day. On that particular day, the wind blew hard all day long. Daddy made Ronald keep the fertilizer hopper full as Pete drove the tractor to add the granular chemical nutrients to the corn field. Having Ronald there made the job go a lot faster for Pete, but the work was punishing for Ronald. Every time Ronald dumped a bag of fertilizer in the hopper, the swirling wind would blow the dry fertilizer dust into his eyes and it would burn and sting. When I came home that night, Ronald said to me, "Don't ever miss the bus because working all day for Daddy is hell." I took him at his word and never once missed the bus in all 12 years of my schooling.

LESSONS LEARNED

In September 1948, I began the third grade, and for the first time I wasn't housed in the main permanent building. Mrs. Flossie Dennis was my teacher, and here is where I got my first taste of a wooden-framed relocatable classroom. The relocatable classroom was on the Nettie Baisden Primary School site, which was adjacent to Mizell's feed mill. Actually, it wasn't a relocatable as we know them today; what we had then were old army mess halls from the Camp Blanding Army Base that were no longer needed after World War II. The army base was being closed down and most of the temporary wooden buildings were declared surplus and sold or given away. Either way, they were available to school districts, and somehow our school district got several of them to use as classrooms. Each building was long and contained enough space for three adjoining classrooms. Each classroom had a freestanding kerosene heater with a smokestack through the roof in the middle of the room.

The third grade curriculum gave me a strong desire to travel. The reader textbook we used had a story about Norway, *As I Was Going To Saint Ives*. I read that story so many times that I daydreamed about living in a foreign country where they spoke a different language and had cobble-stoned streets.

Third grade was when students began learning to write cursive letters. Until then, all our writing exercises were simple printing. I could never print very well and my penmanship didn't improve when I started trying to form cursive letters. I also recall that this is the time when we began to get more deeply involved in learning math. Penmanship may not have been my most stellar attribute, but I enjoyed math and was pretty good at it. So good, in fact, that I would one day become a math teacher.

Mrs. Agnes Folsom (whose husband would serve as the school superintendent about 15 years later), was my fourth grade teacher when school started in September 1949. She was a great teacher; again, we were in another Camp Blanding surplus wooden relocatable building, just like the one we had in third grade, except this one was on the elementary school site adjacent to the old junior high school building. The teacher in the room next door was Mrs. Ina Gaston, another fantastic teacher. Because our classes were so close together, we collaborated on many of our activities. We always went to the playground together and one of the teachers would supervise the boys and the other girls.

One of the advantages of being a fourth grader (at least it was an advantage for my parents) is that I was big enough and mature enough to take on more responsibilities for home chores after school. Being a kid it seemed more like a punishment than a reward, but getting more responsibilities helped to increase my conscientiousness and my dependability. I think today's children are robbed of that opportunity to a great degree because of the relative ease of our modern lifestyle.

In September 1950, I started the fifth grade, and my classroom was located on the first floor of the old junior high school building and my teacher was Mrs. Mae Brannon. I can't recall the circumstance, but Mrs. Brannon either didn't teach the second semester, or was out sick a lot. Mrs. Brannon wasn't as strict as any of my other teachers had been. I really can't remember being taught too much that year.

During my fifth grade school year, Honorine, my oldest sister, and her husband, Alex, lived in the northeastern part of town. They didn't have a car, and at least twice a week I would spend the night with them so I could walk their two oldest children to and from school. I enjoyed the responsibility and got to spend time with my niece Dolly, who was seven at the time, and nephew Tommy, who was six. The additional double duty of serving as kind of a big brother and an escort only lasted one year. Nevertheless, I am glad that I had such an opportunity; besides, it helped my sister at a time when she needed me.

In September 1951, I started the sixth grade, and my classroom was located on the first floor of the old junior high school building and my teacher was Miss Virginia Green. Miss Green was from Madison County; she was a very caring and helpful teacher and I liked her very much. In fact, I think everyone really liked her. Unfortunately, she only got to teach a few years; she had cancer and passed away. Her death was a tragic loss for the school and for the students; Miss Green loved kids and was passionate about teaching.

BUS DRIVING NIGHTMARE

Ronald wasn't the only one to have a cantankerous bus driver. One year we had an older man as our bus driver; he couldn't hear very well and his eyesight wasn't too good either. He wore glasses that looked like the bottom of a soda-pop bottle. At one point in the regular route, the school bus would turn around by pulling up on the south side of Aunt Della Boatright's house, backing onto the road, and then heading back in the direction it had come from. One day our regular bus was out of service and we had to use an older substitute bus that had a manual lever by the gearshift that had to be lifted up in order to engage reverse, which the driver didn't know. So when he pulled the bus into the woods next to Aunt Della's to back up and turn around, he couldn't get the bus into reverse. Every gear he tried just got the bus deeper and deeper into the woods.

Before long, we were in the thick part with large pine trees and stumps surrounding us. Most of us children on the bus didn't know how to help the driver; a couple of the older boys did know what he should do but they wouldn't tell him. I think they were enjoying the adventure. After a few frustrating moments for the driver, laughter from the kids, and the aggravation of getting deeper into the woods, the driver decided to make a big circle and go through the trees to get out of the thicket. A small measure of good fortune was with him because he missed the big stumps that could have snagged us and kept us in the woods.

When we got to the edge of the woods, a two-foot deep drainage ditch ran alongside of the road. After missing the treachery of the stumps, he made a lurch to jump the ditch and get on the road again. When the rear tires jumped the ditch, all of us on the bus, along with the seat cushions, went flying into the air. When I came down, my teeth hit the metal framing on the seat in front of me and chipped parts of my two middle upper front teeth. The chips in these two teeth remained visible until they were crowned in 2006. No doubt, such an event could never happen today with all the modern safety features on school buses and the heavy emphasis that is placed on safety and responsibility. Still, that is a funny memory; albeit, I carried the memento for more than a half century. You can see the gap in a picture of me in the back section; look at the one where I am a smiling second lieutenant.

When I started junior high school, the seventh grade, in September 1952, the school operated on a block schedule; that is, all students in my class had the same schedule and we all were in the same classroom together each period of the day except for study hall. Study hall was kind of a free period where a student could take an elective course such as band or just use the period as a study hall to do homework or review lessons. The drawback to taking an elective course was that you had to give up your free period and then you had to make up the study time at home after school. That didn't offer much incentive for most students to add more coursework to their studies.

DAYDREAMS OF HEADING WEST

I recall daydreaming my time away in the seventh grade math classroom. The room was on the second floor on the west side of the old junior high school building overlooking the roof of the auditorium. The chalkboard was at the north end of the classroom and had large windows on the left side and steam radiators underneath the windows. I had math class about midmorning and I loved to look out the window to the northwest where I could see the Seaboard Coast Line trains and railroad tracks from just west of Houston Street and for a few hundred yards on westward. Every day of the week the Live Oak, Perry, and Gulf Railroad Company ran a combination train carrying passengers and freight. That old train was a steam locomotive and it was tailor-made to inspire kids into rich fantasy dreams. I enjoyed hearing the sound of the steam engine and the loud whistle as it would leave out in the mornings headed west. It usually carried some of my dreams of adventure along with it.

During the early 1950s, Live Oak had two walk-in movie theaters and one drive-in theater. One of the walk-in theaters was the Suwannee Theater and they would show serial Western Cowboy movies every Saturday; the serial movie, which you had to go to every week for about six to eight weeks to see the whole story, would always stop at a critical time and leave you hanging on the edge of your seat. The whole idea was to get you to come back the next week to see the story continue. I never had a chance to go but once or twice, but I remember the admission was nine cents, a coke was a nickel, a bag of popcorn was a nickel, and a piece of bubble gum cost a penny; so for 20 cents I could have an entire afternoon of entertainment. That wasn't necessarily a bargain in those days because 20 cents would buy more than a gallon of gasoline; it was also considered a luxury and we didn't get to splurge and frivolously spend that much money very often.

I believe it was during this period when Live Oak got its first radio station—WNER, 1250 AM; it operated at 1,000 watts of power and during daylight hours only. While radio offered some entertainment and the movies were an occasional supplement, most of our amusement came from our everyday lives. It seems like life was full of excitement and adventure; boredom from inactivity didn't happen because we had to work so much. And daydreams were our luxury.

MORE WORK

Our work was never done. The flue-cured tobacco market in Live Oak was the largest tobacco market in Florida; Live Oak had about eight or nine large warehouses. Usually during the last week in July and the first two weeks of August, the tobacco was auctioned off. During those days, farms filled most of Suwannee County; there were some large farming businesses, but most were small family-run operations. Tobacco was the main crop for practically every farmer, and when the tobacco market opened each evening, trucks would be lined up for ¼ to ½ mile waiting to get unloaded. Many high school students, especially boys, would get jobs working at the tobacco market, and I was no exception.

I worked several summers for the buyer for the Brown-Williamson Tobacco Company; my job was to tag the sheets of tobacco he purchased and make sure they were properly labeled and shipped out every day. Most of the tobacco shipping was done by rail, although some was transported by trucks. The Brown-Williamson Tobacco Company made the brand name cigarettes of *Viceroy*, *Kent*, and *Kool*. They paid me 75 cents an hour. That was a pretty good wage because during the summer I had been making anywhere from three to four dollars a day for harvesting and working in the green tobacco, and that work was much harder and the days a lot longer, so I felt fortunate to have the job tagging in the warehouse.

Prosperity and peace were bringing about enormous changes in all of society, both locally and nationally. In 1952, our nation elected a Republican president, Dwight D. Eisenhower, following 20 years of having a Democrat as President of the United States. The economy, at least for farmers, seemed to slowly but surely improve following World War II. The leadership of Presidents Franklin D. Roosevelt and Harry S. Truman had served the rural South quite well, and just about everybody was a registered Democrat. It was hard to find a registered Republican in Suwannee County during that period.

THE NEW AGE

Times were changing in ways that were hard for old-timers to understand in our rural Live Oak community. On an April Sunday morning in 1952, Ruby McCollum, a financially affluent local black woman, shot and killed her white lover who was a prominent local physician, Dr. Leroy Adams. He had just been elected to serve in the Florida Senate. She was convicted in 1954 and sentenced to death, despite her assertion that Dr. Adams had forced sex upon her and insisted that she bear his child. Later, her conviction and death sentence were overturned by the Florida Supreme Court, and she was declared mentally incompetent and incarcerated for 20 years in the Florida State Mental Hospital at Chattahoochee. I believe she was later set free under Florida's Baker Act. This whole ordeal was the talk of the entire county during my junior high school years. That kind of thing was something we would have expected to see in a movie or read in a novel; it seemed more like fiction than reality—but, tragically, it wasn't. Our sleepy little town had become seedy.

During my junior high school years, after the seventh grade, one of the things I remember most was never getting to play during physical education class. Beginning with the first day of school in the eighth grade, and since my name "Boatright" was first alphabetically in the class roll and listed first in the coach's grade book, I was designated to take roll for him each day. I was getting my first taste of classroom responsibility. In addition to keeping attendance records, I had to serve as the equipment manager for the balls, bats, and other PE equipment; it was my responsibility, at the beginning of every class, to check out and check in the PE equipment to my classmates. During the main part of the class period, I was assigned to stay in the coach's office and listen for the telephone, and to fill out his report cards. I was instructed to give everyone a grade of C, except for anyone who played on a sports team; they got an automatic A and he also told me to give myself an A—this was even more classroom experience as a teacher, but I didn't agree with the unfairness of his system or with the coach's lack of commitment to doing his own job. Still, he was the adult in authority and I was responsible to do what I was told; I didn't have to agree with him, I did have to do what he said.

Living on a farm and having parents that believed in work far more than play, I realized that if I was going to ever learn about sports it would have to be at school and certainly not at home. I missed getting to play all my eighth grade year because of my "teaching" assignment. That really didn't bother me because I knew that I still had four more years of required physical education classes in high school. To my great dismay and extreme misfortune, when I moved to high school in September 1954, my eighth grade coach moved up to be the high school coach and I had him for the next four years. Each year of high school, I continued to keep his roll book, check out and check in the PE equipment, listen for his telephone, and fill out his report cards giving all class members that played any varsity sport an A, along with me getting an A, and all the rest of the class got a C.

So, it would appear looking back at my grades that I was a real athlete, when in reality I was never taught, and never developed any of the common athletic knowledge, skills, or the athletic abilities most of my peers were able to accomplish by participating in the normal PE program. You may ask, "Why didn't you say something?" First of all, we were taught not to question the authority of teachers, bus drivers, or any other adult. The lack of being taught the basic physical education skills is perhaps my biggest disappointment of high school. Nonetheless, I went all through high school honoring the values I was taught at home, which I believe have served me far better than any athletic skills I may have acquired if I had fought against authority to change things. Additionally, I believed then, and I still believe today, that when younger people respect older people and act accordingly, everyone in the community is better off. While life may not always be fair, fairness will always prevail in the grander scheme of things. We need to learn to accept and deal with things that are not always fair—it balances out our personality, ethics, and the ability to judge things in a proper light.

HIGH SCHOOL

When I entered high school as a freshman in September 1954, there were only my brother, Ronald, and me to catch the school bus. Billy had graduated from high school in 1953, and was attending Florida State University studying Chemistry; Sherwood had just graduated from high school in May 1954, and was attending Aurora College in Illinois studying to be a history teacher. Ronald was two years ahead of me, and was a junior.

All during high school, Billy worked every Saturday as a cashier at the local Piggly Wiggly, which later became Lovett's, then Winn-Lovett's, and finally Winn Dixie. Sherwood worked every Saturday as a clerk in Creekmore's General Store; when he went off to college in 1954, Miss Creekmore hired me to take his place, which I did for the next four years. I made $3 every Saturday working from about 7:00 a.m. until closing time, which in the summer time may have been as late as 9:00 p.m.; it wasn't very much money for the hours I had to work, but it gave me a steady and regular income. For that, I appreciated her and the job opportunity.

The store was located in the heart of Live Oak on the main street and was owned by Miss Evelyn Creekmore, whose father had previously owned the store. The store was a typical 1920s and 1930s style general merchandise business. It sold everything essential for a mule farmer from bridles, to horse collars, to plow stocks, plows, plow sweeps, and garden tools. In the dry goods department there were overalls, brogan high-top work boots, light blue chambray work shirts, and felt-brimmed rimmed hats for men. A limited variety of grocery essentials were sold, mostly staples such as salt, pepper, flour, sugar, coffee, tea, a few spices, vinegar, and a small assortment of some basic canned goods. The grocery section also offered a limited selection of meats, such as ham, shoulders, sausage if it was in season, wieners, bologna, and a round hoop of American cheese was kept in the cooler display cabinet. All of the meats and cheese were sold by whatever amount the customer wanted or according to how much money the customer could afford to pay—scales were seldom used for the really small amounts of cheese and bologna that someone might buy just for a snack or a quick meal; a slice or chunk was just "eye-balled" for the sale. For those purchases in the old general-merchandise stores, the customer would ask for something like 10-cents worth of cheese or indicate the thickness of bologna between the thumb and forefinger and say, "About that much," and then leave the slicing and pricing to the store owner. Back then, there was a mutual trust between customers and proprietors that sustained a solid business relationship.

The store also sold eggs and vegetables that were in season; Miss Creekmore would buy fresh eggs and vegetables daily from the local farmers and then resell them in her store. She also sold soft drinks, which was always a favorite for kids. Soft drinks were kept in an ice box—a real ice box. At that time the store didn't have a refrigerated ice box and used real ice to keep the drinks cold. The ice man would come twice a day in the summer and re-supply the ice in the cold drink box. I spent a lot of my time selling cold drinks and draining and disposing of the water from the melted ice. Creekmore's was not a fancy store, but it was a real landmark in the community because it had endured for so many years and had been a functioning part of the neighborhood. Those kinds of places have all disappeared now; I think that is sad because community stores gave credit to those who needed it, bought locally produced goods, and quite often served as a meeting place and somewhere you could always get the latest news.

This was the time when all the boys kept their hair cut short, most sported a flat-top cut that was really popular, and just about everyone wore dungaree pants (blue jeans), with the cuffs of the pants rolled up so the underside of the denim would show, a button up shirt with the back of the collar turned up, and white buck shoes, like hush puppy shoes except they were white, or loafer type slip-on shoes. The girls wore both full dresses and skirts and blouses with lots of crinolines under the skirts to make them stand out. The poodle skirts were very popular, and were made from charcoal-grey felt, with a pink poodle design on the front to the side. These two colors, pink and charcoal, were very popular during the mid 1950s. The hit televisions series *Happy Days* captured some of this local charm, and I'm not aware of anyone who grew up in that era who doesn't have fond memories of it.

There were only a few high school students who had their own cars. Most rode the school bus, if you lived a good distance from school as I did, or walked to school if you lived in town. Several city students still rode bicycles to school, and three or four even had motor scooters, either *Cushman* or *Vespa* brands. In middle school, there would be 50 to 75 bicycles in the bicycle parking area. None were locked and I can't recall ever hearing of one being stolen. Theft and vandalism were not taken lightly; respect for others' property was held in high regard. The loss of that kind of innocence to the values we see today is a tragic indictment on the way our society raises children and the values we now hold collectively as a nation.

Lunch period was open for all high school students, meaning we were free to walk downtown or go wherever we wanted during the 30-minute lunch period. A hot meal in the school cafeteria cost 20 cents. The Suwannee High School building and campus was only a block from the county courthouse, and just two blocks from the main downtown area. There was a furniture store, a grocery store, a beauty shop, a bakery, and the snack shack directly across the street from the high school. This close proximity to downtown made it easy to run a family errand during lunch, such as go to the drug store to pick-up a prescription, or to any other business to get other needed items for Mama or Daddy. Our lunch break provided more than just an opportunity to eat. Quite often we had to use that time for family needs and that sometimes kept us from getting lunch.

NO MORE FARMING

When I registered for my ninth grade classes, I was told by the Vocational Agriculture teacher that because I was raised on a farm I had to take vocational agriculture. I reminded him that I had older brothers who finished Suwannee High and none of them ever took vocational agriculture and I wasn't going to either. I told the teacher that Daddy had taught me all I needed to know and wanted to know about farming. Daddy had been a pretty successful farmer and the teacher knew it, so I really didn't see any need for me to have to take his class. I think he may have been on a recruiting binge for students whom he wouldn't have to spend a lot of time teaching the basics of agriculture, something like my PE teacher. All my ninth grade classes were in the high school building except physical education which was in the basement of the old junior high school building.

During my freshman year I took Algebra I; this was my first real awakening to the fact that I wasn't prepared academically for any high school math other than general mathematics. But I knew I wanted to go to college someday, so I enrolled in the algebra class that was taught by Mrs. Medlock. She was a great teacher, but regardless of her skills, I struggled to stay up with the class; it was hard and I could only manage to be almost up with the students who were better prepared.

I made Cs which was a real effort for me. About the fourth six-week period the academic struggle began to really catch up with me and I made a D in algebra. We received a separate report card for each subject for our parents to sign and return to the teacher. I really dreaded showing Daddy that report card with a D. Trying a little ingenuity, I brought my report cards home and kept them through the night and waited the next morning until I thought there was just enough time for him to sign them before I ran down the lane in front of the house to catch the bus. Daddy signed all the report cards, except the one with a D. He handed the signed ones back to me and said I could return the one with a D the next day.

Needless to say, I had a long day at school, worrying about the consequences of making the D. I didn't dare ask Daddy for the report card. That evening before supper, during supper, and while chores were being done he never mentioned the grade or report card to me. I lived in dread during those few hours that seemed like an eternity. The next morning, just before leaving to go to the bus stop, Daddy handed the report card to me and simply said, "This will not happen again." He didn't have to say anymore than that. I knew exactly what he meant, and there was no question in my mind about the consequences if I should ever make another D. I suffered under a double load; one was that I knew just how hard that he and Mama had worked and how they had sacrificed to keep us in school and to provide for our essential needs, the other was the pure, raw dread of not meeting their expectations—which was the harder of the two horns of my dilemma. I did my best to reward their commitment. I can honestly say that I tried, academically, just about as hard as I could.

Suwannee High School didn't have a gymnasium. Basketball was played on a clay court and high school varsity basketball was played upstairs in the old National Guard Armory located on Wilbur Street in back of Mizell's Farm Supply and Feed Mill. The upstairs of the old armory was also used for the Junior/Senior Prom each year. This was the only place in town that had an open area large enough for the prom.

Driver education was first offered in my senior year of high school. At that time a family's automobile insurance rate was reduced if they could provide documentation that their children on the policy who were less than 25 years of age had successfully completed the driver education course.

I believe it was during my senior year that industrial arts was offered for the first time and I took that class. The teacher was Mr. Ken Wood; he was a great teacher and a master craftsman. Mr. Wood's class was rich with fresh ideas and his ability to inspire challenged me to learn about a lot of different things. A really good teacher will inspire as much as he or she teaches—Mr. Wood did that.

TYPING

In my junior year I took typing. During the fourth six-weeks of school I slipped and fell from an oak tree, while building a swing for my nieces and nephews, and broke my left arm midway between the elbow and wrist. Daddy and Mama carried me to the hospital and Dr. Hugo Sotolongo set the arm, and put it in a cast which I wore for about eight weeks. An immobile arm wasn't good for my typing, but I still passed the class alright because I had learned the keyboard and was daily exercising to improve my typing accuracy and speed. Practicing the locations of keys and the finger movements helped to keep me from losing too much in the skills I needed. One thing that made typing a little harder for me while wearing a cast was that the typewriters were all manual and the keys required a firm stroke with a reasonable amount of pressure to make the letters strike the paper. Electric typewriters were more sensitive to the touch, but we didn't have them. A good thing about typewriters, both manual and electric, was that there was no easy way to correct keystroke errors, so accuracy was more important than speed—which applies to most everything in life.

During my senior year we took the placement test on the mornings of February 12th and 13th, 1958; it was a required test for all seniors. To everyone's surprise, Suwannee County awoke the morning of February 13th to about 1½ inches of snow covering the ground. With that kind of oddity greeting us, that day wasn't a good one to finish our testing, so not much learning took place in the classrooms, and no testing was conducted until the following morning. Since very few students in my class had ever seen snow, this turned out to be perhaps the biggest highlight of our senior year.

BUS TROUBLES

When I was in school we still had many miles of dirt roads where the school buses had to travel, and even a few miles of three-trailed-roads through the woods that the buses sometimes used. Three-trailed-roads were the paths that have three ruts; one for a horse, and one for each side wheel on a wagon pulled by the beast of burden. Most all these roads vanished during the 1950s.

A part of our regular travel routine was that the school bus broke down every month or so, and based on where we broke down, it became a real effort to get to school or get home—depending on whether it was morning or afternoon when our travel disruption occurred. There were no telephones except in town; so if a school bus broke down in the morning and didn't arrive at school by about 8:30 a.m., then a mechanic took a tool box and a spare bus and back-tracked our route until we were located. We then would transfer to the spare bus and continue on to school and leave the broken bus with the mechanic to get it going; if the breakdown happened on the way home it usually took a little longer for us to be found because our afternoon bus ride didn't end at the school so we had to wait for a parent to pass the word that we were late.

On the morning breakdowns when a mechanic came to get us, before we left in the replacement bus, the mechanic would checkout the broken-down bus to see if he needed anything additional to get it going so he could tell our regular driver to relay the needs to the bus shop when he got to town so the necessary parts could be delivered back to him. Often we would be two to three hours late for school because of the breakdown. Still, without the modern conveniences in communications, we had a pretty good system to get everyone to school even when problems occurred.

I remember one particular time when our bus broke down. Just about the time our bus quit, a parent was returning from the livestock market. He had been delivering hogs and his truck was a mess and smelled awful. In spite of that, he felt compelled to offer his services to deliver us to school. It was either the day before Thanksgiving or Christmas holidays began, and we didn't want to miss the activities at school. The farmer's offer to take us to school was a mixed blessing. We took the ride so that we wouldn't miss the holiday festivities, but we paid for it by riding where the farmer's hogs had left several crude reminders that they had been there.

On another occasion during a very rainy week when many school buses were getting stuck in the mud, we got trapped and didn't get to school until lunch. We checked into school, and then school was dismissed at 1:00 p.m., due to the bad weather, so no one on my bus attended a single class that day, yet we spent the entire day trying to get to and from school. I guess that was the closest I ever came to missing a day of school—actually I did miss the classes, but kept my perfect school attendance record because I was giving it my best effort to be there.

During my junior year we had a school bus whose brakes failed from time to time, yet the bus driver would keep going anyway and just drive slow, down shift, and use the emergency brake to stop the bus. This same old bus sometimes wouldn't start if it choked down; when the bus stalled like that, we boys would get off and push the bus to get it started. For several years most of the school buses serving the southwest part of the county would stop on the way home from school at Howland's Grocery for those with any money to buy a soft drink or candy bar. At that time soft drinks and candy bars were a nickel, later the sodas went up to seven cents. I think there was a lot more caring about people at that time, and it showed through such simple courtesies as stopping the school bus at a store so kids could get a snack. That couldn't be done today.

While the buses weren't always dependable, they ran well enough to get us to and from school, even when students had to push the bus to get it cranked, which was a part of the learning experience and a part of the community service we were expected to make. Today, if a bus were to break down, radios or cell phones would get another bus dispatched and likely parents would rush to get their children. Somehow this new attitude seems, to me, to break down the community rather than build it up.

SENIOR TRIP

We had 100 seniors in my graduating class. There had been a tradition for the past several years for each senior class to take a class trip to Washington, D. C. Our class trip was planned for the first full week in May with approximately 35 seniors making the trip. The trip cost each student about $125, which included the round-trip train fare from Live Oak to Jacksonville, to Washington, D. C., and on to New York City. The cost also included our hotel rooms with four students to each room, our sightseeing in Washington and New York, and most of the food. Again, for many like me and my classmates who had never ridden a train before, this was quite a trip.

Always being a jokester and prankster, I told jokes most of the night on the train ride up to Washington, D. C. I was finally living out the adventures I had imagined back in my seventh grade daydreams when I watched the Seaboard Coast Line trains leave going westward. Traveling was every bit as grand as I had imagined, and I wanted more of it.

COLORED SCHOOLS

Experience is a brutal teacher, but you learn. C. S. Lewis.

Up to the time I was in high school, our few black neighbors had no public transportation to and from school. There was a one-room colored school about five miles from their house, and when they went to school they had to walk. In the 1940s and 50s all black schools were called *colored* schools, they weren't called *black* until sometime in the late 1960s when we started to aggressively integrate the schools and reframe our language.

One day I was talking to some of the black neighbor boys who were about my age; they told me that during the colder months they had to pick up wood along the way to school for the wood-burning heater they had, if they wanted to be warm at school. I went into a couple of the one-room colored schools, Hillman School near Arch Starlings, and the Bakersville School near Hosea Smith's house; both of these schools had very few materials for teaching. Everything was old and either worn out, or almost worn out, and the whole teaching and learning environment left just about everything to be desired.

Even when I was a young teenager, I realized how unfortunate and deprived the colored students really were, and how difficult it would be for them to get even a semblance of an education, because even if they wanted to go to high school their parents had to pay someone in town to provide room and board for them. The vast majority simply didn't have the financial means for that. The one-room rural schools I visited didn't have electricity, but they did have a hand pump for fresh water, and an outdoor toilet. The schools certainly weren't comparable to the all-white schools I attended.

IN THE ARMY NOW

During my senior year, the local Florida Army National Guard Unit, Company A, 1st Battalion, 187th Armor, needed additional recruits. Since the high school was right beside the Guard Armory, the most convenient and logical place for finding new recruits was where the most boys were: next door at Suwannee High School. Our school principal was agreeable to let recruiters talk to any students who wanted to hear about opportunities available for young men in the military service. The principal usually let them use a vacant room or office most any time during the school day that was suitable for either small groups or individual conferences.

Captain Paul Crews was the Company Commander, and Chief Warrant Officer Lawrence W. Lee, his official military title being Mr., was the full-time Administrative and Supply Technician for the local National Guard unit. Captain Crews and Mr. Lee met with about 20 of the senior high boys, and 13 of us joined immediately. We were all sworn into the National Guard on March 3, 1958.

I was extremely proud of my new uniform and all the things that went with it; the crisp, clean and matching garments were a lot different from blue jean work clothes and they looked sharp too. At the time I joined, I had three other brothers in the National Guard, two in the unit I joined in Live Oak, and one in a unit in Jacksonville.

My enlistment in the National Guard started a long and wonderful dual career for me that took me from a simple enlisted recruit all the way to Brigadier General; I'm still amazed today that such an opportunity was ever available to anyone like me. I went from a kid feeding hogs, selling soft drinks to supplement what little money we had, and harvesting tobacco to become a soldier nominated by the President of the United States to our Senate for promotion to the rank of Brigadier General. That a boy raised on a farm in rural backwoods circumstances could become a General Officer truly emphasizes that the old adage isn't just a cute little catch-phrase but a genuine fact, "America is the land of opportunity." I firmly believe that if it could happen for me it can become real for anybody.

I graduated from Suwannee High School in May 1958, and worked that summer in the tobacco fields until leaving for Army Basic Training on July 13, 1958.

ARMY AND COLLEGE

There is no security on this earth, there is only opportunity.
General Douglas MacArthur.

AFTER HIGH SCHOOL graduation, I worked in the tobacco fields as usual until time for me to leave for Army Basic Training at Fort Jackson, South Carolina, which is located near Columbia, South Carolina. It had just been a couple of years earlier when the regulations changed and required National Guard and Army Reserve soldiers to go on active duty for training for six months and to complete the required Army Basic Training and Advanced Individual Training (AIT). My high school classmates who joined the National Guard when I did were shipped off for Basic Training at three different times. The four in my group entered active duty for training on Sunday, July 13, 1958. Early that morning we boarded a train in Live Oak and headed for Fort Jackson; we changed trains in Jacksonville for one headed to Columbia, South Carolina. The train from Jacksonville to Columbia was very slow, and didn't arrive in Columbia until late in the afternoon. Members of the basic training unit met the train with military buses to take us on to Fort Jackson.

ARMY DISCIPLINE

There is an old Jewish proverb that says a man who can't endure the bad or difficult things in life will not last long enough to see the good. Army life also teaches that kind of lesson. Our Army discipline started immediately after we stepped off the train with hollering, push-ups, sit-ups, and a constant correcting of every little mistake anyone made—whether the infraction was real, imagined, or just made up to have something to yell about (which was at least fifty-percent of it). Many of our drill sergeants had served in World War II and/or the Korean Conflict of the early 1950s. They were all combat veterans who demanded perfection and were not forgiving for any mistakes we made. It took us, as most troops, about one week to in-process, which means to get fitted with a complete issue of military clothing, including the new Army Dress Green uniform that was still the standard dress attire when I retired 39½ years later. One of the uniforms we were issued was two sets of Bermuda shorts and long knee socks. The socks came almost to our knees, and the Bermuda khaki short-sleeved shirt had a flat collar. The regular dress khaki uniform required a tie which had be tucked into the shirt between the second and third buttons—to me, that always looked smart and snappy.

Even though I was new to the Army, the Army wasn't totally new to me or to my family. My seven brothers all served in the military: six in the Active Army and/or Army National Guard, and one was in the

Navy. Basic training was routine for me because I was in fairly good physical shape from working in the tobacco and watermelon fields, and having all the older brothers and sisters, in addition to Daddy and Mama giving me orders, I had already learned to follow instructions and to do what I was told. I liked the Army. For the first time I wasn't competing with my classmates where I was silently classified as one of the country kids; the ones that lived in town were city kids, and most of them pretended to have an air of elitism when any of us from the rural areas were around.

The Army placed me on a level playing field with everyone else; I could choose to make of myself whatever I wanted. I truly believed that the opportunity was there for me to prove my worth as either a poor soldier, a good soldier, or an excellent soldier. I made up my mind, the day I joined in March 1958, that I would do everything I could to be an excellent soldier and to take advantage of all the Army had to offer. I didn't talk to anyone about my thoughts, because I was concerned that if, for some unknown or unforeseeable reason, I failed somewhere along the line, I would be teased or kidded about it for years to come. As a result, I chose to be silent, and just performed my best in every assignment, and I never flaunted a competitive spirit toward my fellow soldiers, nor did I shirk away from any assignment or opportunity. That potential-seeking outlook ultimately would make a long-term difference in my career options.

I wanted to go to college someday; so, on the few weekends that we had the liberty to go off base or downtown, I always chose to stay on base and pull kitchen police (KP), or guard duty for someone else to make the extra $4 or $5 per day from those who wanted to go but had duty and were willing to pay someone to take their place. Many soldiers without a vision to the future were willing to pay to get someone take their duties. I was willing to take their responsibilities and their money; then, I saved all the money I could. Back then, an Army Private was paid $78 a month. Even at that salary, and with my extra work, I was able to bring home at the end of the five-month period over $350 in cash. At that time, it seemed like a small fortune—and to me, it was.

I completed basic training in September 1958, and was shipped to Fort Knox, Kentucky, on a chartered bus to start Advanced Individual Training (AIT), at the Armor School. I learned soon after joining the National Guard that the local unit had been converted to an armor unit about two years prior to my joining. Since basic training had not been required for very long in the National Guard, there was a critical shortage of Military Occupation Specialty (MOS) trained personal in the operations and maintenance of army tanks. The Live Oak National Guard Unit, Company A, 1st Battalion, 187th Armor, had the older version M-47 battle tank. The armor school was instructing all new trainees on the newer M-48 battle tank. Although they weren't the same, there was a lot of similarity between the two tanks. One of the main differences, though, was that the older M-47 tank had an assistant driver who sat on the right front of the tank while the newer M-48 tank only had one driver who sat in the middle in the front of the tank.

I worked and studied hard in armor school, and picked up as much information as I could about the M-47 tank to take back to my National Guard unit. I really enjoyed learning, training, and firing the M-48 tank. At the end of the three months of armor school, I graduated on December 12, 1958, from Armor AIT. During graduation, I learned that my efforts had paid off when my name was called as the Honor Graduate in my class. This graduation tribute only whetted my appetite to continue to improve and to always give my best to the United States Army and to the Florida Army National Guard. Right after graduation, I was separated from active duty at Fort Knox on December 13th and headed home to see what the future might hold.

THE LOAN

I had been home for just about a week when Hosea Smith, a colored friend of our family, walked about three miles to our house; he wanted to see Daddy. I told Hosea that Daddy wasn't home but asked if there was any way I could help him. Hosea told me that he wanted to borrow a little money from my Daddy. I trusted Hosea and told him that I would be glad to loan him whatever he needed, if I had enough. Hosea said he needed $300 until he could fatten and sell some hogs, which he planned to do in May, and would repay the money to me on May 20th, which was about six months away. I told Hosea that would be fine, and I loaned him the $300 I had saved by taking on extra duties and carefully managing the soldiers pay I had received over the past few months. Hosea reemphasized that he couldn't pay off the loan until May 20th, which was an easy date for me to remember since that was my birthday.

I knew that Hosea was as honest as the days were long, and my money was secure. Interest was never charged on a loan and nothing was ever written down or signed by Daddy or any of us if we loaned a little cash to a friend for a short period of time. Hosea walked back home and I never saw him again until the first Saturday in the following May. On that day, Hosea walked back to our house to ask me if he could wait one week longer to repay the loan since his hogs weren't quite ready to sell and he wanted to continue fattening them for another week so that he could get a better price for them. I said it was fine with me. Hosea said that if I needed the money at the time promised, he would go ahead and sell the hogs anyway because that was the deal we had made. I assured Hosea that waiting another week wouldn't be a problem for me and, as expected, on May 27th he walked back to our house again and paid me every penny he had borrowed. For me, this was a real-life demonstration of the highest level of trust, honesty, and integrity that can be displayed by some people. Sadly, there are very few individuals today who have that same quality of trustworthiness. I wish we had more men like Hosea Smith; America would be a better place if a man's word and his handshake were his bond as it was between Hosea and me.

PREPARING THE FIELDS

Following the Christmas holidays of 1958, I began working in the fields every day, plowing, tilling, and harrowing the land using Daddy's John Deere Model M tractor to prepare the fields for planting later in the spring. By this time, Pete had bought a two row Massy-Ferguson tractor with a three-point hitch. In addition to farming Daddy's land, he was also farming several acres down the road at Mrs. Hattie Ross's. He planted the same basic crops for her as he did for Daddy, including her tobacco. Pete and Mrs. Ross had something like a share-cropper's agreement where, in return for him doing the work on her land, the profit was shared between the two of them.

Even though I had saved enough money to begin my college education, being on active duty with the Army for the last six months had not afforded me the opportunity to register or make housing arrangements to start classes in the spring of 1959. As a result of not getting enrolled in college, during that spring, I was challenged with being a full-time farmer. With both Pete and me running tractors every day, we were able to have a highly successful planting and harvest that year. We could never work in the fields at the same time, especially when planting or cultivating the crops, because the two tractors were set to plant and cultivate different row widths. But that, like all organizational challenges, was just a simple scheduling issue we had to manage. I enjoyed my stint at full-time farming for that year, but something inside kept calling me away and I knew I had no future as a farmer. I guess knowing that I was going to do something other than farm helped me to enjoy it for that season.

ARMY OPPORTUNITY

During the same period of time, my involvement with our local National Guard unit continued to grow. In the late 1950s, and until the mid 1960s, local National Guard units drilled for two hours one night a week; my home unit drilled every Monday night. Drilling on weeknights made it very difficult for me to work or go to school and then drive long distances one night a week for Guard drill.

In about 1965, the National Guard switched from drilling one night a week for two hours, to one full weekend each month. This new weekend schedule made it much easier to live farther away from the Guard unit and still actively participate. Many of my high school classmates who had joined at the same time I enlisted had started work or were going to college. Several lived out of town and had transferred their membership in the National Guard to other units closer to where they were living.

I was promoted to Private First Class, and because of my formal military schooling at Fort Knox, Kentucky, I began to teach the more difficult tank related subjects such as tank gunnery, tank maintenance, and armor tactics. I enjoyed teaching these classes, even though I was just a private, and there was so much I didn't know, yet to the people being taught, I probably knew more than anyone else in the class. I was soon recognized as one of the tank experts in our unit. Commitment, dedication, study, and hard work were paying off.

Our unit attended annual training at Fort Stewart, Georgia, that summer; I was heavily involved in all the unit training activities. My military occupational specialty during that summer camp was loader, which meant placing the 90 mm shells into the breech block of the main gun. Everything I did gave me more knowledge and increased my value to the Army. Being valuable at one skill made me want to learn more things, and that improved my worth to the Army.

NEIGHBORLY HELP

In the late spring of 1959, Oliver Hingson, a cousin and neighbor that lived about two miles away, was diagnosed with terminal stomach cancer. He suffered intensely for many months, and in about July or August, he was given morphine to relieve the constant and severe pain.

Many of our neighbors helped the family with their farm, but very few in the community could or was willing to administer the morphine shots to him. Usually, there was someone visiting during the day who would give him the shots, but there was no one at night to do the job, and that was when he needed it the most. I offered to help; I spent almost every night on a small cot in his room. Oliver would wake me whenever he needed a shot. I would get up and dispense the pain-killing drug and then go back to sleep. As the end approached, I would sometimes have to give Oliver a shot up to five or six times a night. It was the right thing to do; and something that I considered both a reasonable and Godly help to someone in need. It wasn't easy to watch Oliver suffer, but not helping him just so I wouldn't have to witness his pain would have been terribly wrong.

I continued to help Daddy and Pete on the farm during the daytime, and I spent the nights with Oliver doing whatever I could to help him through the pain and suffering caused by cancer. I had planned to start college in the fall of 1959 at North Florida Junior College in Madison. As time approached for me to begin classes, I realized that I was really needed by the family and postponed starting college again. My next attempt to go to college would be in the spring of 1960.

COLLEGE BOUND

I helped the family all through the fall of 1959, and then started college in January 1960. Oliver passed away just a couple of weeks after I started classes at North Florida Junior College. When I began my college education, I had been out of high school for a year and a half. By the time I began my formal studies, it seemed like I had lived a completely different life. I guess maybe I had.

Attending NFJC proved to be quite a challenge for me. It didn't take long for me to realize that my academic skills weren't what they should have been. The classes I took, and most especially the English, math, and science courses, were very difficult for me.

When the attendance areas had been originally established for NFJC, which was a way for the school to provide transportation to those who needed it, Suwannee County was part of the college's attendance area. If population were considered, Suwannee County would have been the largest county in the attendance area for NFJC. Unfortunately, due to a lot of politics and selfish actions by a few powerful people, Suwannee County chose not to be a participating county, and that was both tragic and foolish because that meant no transportation was provided for students from Suwannee County to attend the college. We were left to get to school on our own, if we wanted to study at NFJC. But for those of us who were determined to further our education, transportation was just another obstacle to overcome. And most of us did.

I rode to school with my older brother, Sherwood, on Monday and Tuesday mornings; he taught at Suwannee High School in Live Oak and it wasn't a problem for me to ride with him. From there, I caught a ride to NFJC with Ellsworth Carroll. Jimmie Meeks and I shared the gas and expenses for riding with Ellsworth. I came home every Monday night to attend National Guard drill. I was met by Sherwood, who had joined the National Guard in November 1958. Sherwood and I would go home to change into our uniforms, and the three of us, Sherwood, Pete who had joined the National Guard in May 1950, and I would attend the Monday night drill. Tuesday, Wednesday, and Thursday nights I stayed in Madison and shared a rented room at a local elderly couples home. Staying in Madison saved valuable time that I needed for my studies; it also helped reduce the wear and tear of so much traveling.

NFJC wasn't a large institution. The semester I started was when the college had just moved into the science building, which was overlooking a lake; the library was opened as well, and a small room just east of the library was used as a snack bar and student center. The total enrollment was probably less than 75 students. One way I know it wasn't very big is because my student ID number was 63, which made me almost a founding member of the college.

Junior college was designed to be affordable; the tuition was $60 a semester for a full-time student whether taking 12 or 18 semester hours. Having already served in the military exempted me from having to take a physical education course; I probably would have done very poorly in a PE class, considering my lack of physical education training in junior and senior high school. But then military training and boot camp might have tipped the balances in my favor if I had been forced to take a PE class.

In my first semester of college, I got the only F I ever made; it was in biology, which I retook in the fall and made a B. That singular F was a real wake-up call for me. Since I was paying my own way to attend college, I realized that while I thought I was trying and studying hard, I had to apply myself to an even greater level, which all my future grades reflected as they improved over time. Getting a poor or even a failing grade can sometimes be the best grade we ever got—if we learn from the experience and change our ways to improve our study habits. F doesn't have to mean failure; it can mean foundation if we will build on it. That F was a great incentive; much like the D I had made in Algebra and tried to hide it from Daddy. Only, I didn't have to hide the F from anyone; I just had to overcome study habits that had led me to the poor grade just like I had done in that high school algebra class.

SUMMER CAMP AND HEARTACHE

By the time my unit went to annual training in the summer of 1960 at Fort Stewart, Georgia, I had been promoted to specialist fourth class, and my military occupational specialty was tank gunner. My unit had received the next generation of tanks, M-48, which I had trained on at Fort Knox, Kentucky, and knew the most about. Annual training was successful and I continued to be as involved as possible in the training and operation of the unit even though I had a low rank; but then rank isn't everything, it can change. The National Guard was good to me. I would make about $35 during the two weeks of active duty for training. During this time we were paid for our National Guard drills quarterly in March, June, September, and December; my quarterly check was about $28. Twenty-eight dollars probably seems small today, but it was my only stable and sure source of income; and as small as it may have been, it enabled me to attend college.

The fall semester at NFJC was uneventful and I continued to take only the mandatory classes to meet requirements for receiving an Associates of Arts Degree; with an AA degree, I could transfer to Florida State University. Paying my own way through school didn't provide me the opportunity to take any enrichment or frill classes; if the course didn't count toward a degree, I didn't take it. Extra classes were a luxury I couldn't afford. Today, a lot of young folks go to college at their parent's expense and take as many unrelated classes as they can to extend their time in college. I think that is an abuse because it fosters, if not teaches, irresponsibility.

The summer of 1960 brought suffering to a new level for my whole family. On July 1, 1960, our oldest living sister, Honorine, passed away from complications with her heart and asthma. She left behind a mourning husband, Alex, and three heart-broken children who were 17, 16, and 13. Two days later Grandpa Starling, Mama's father, died at the ripe old age of 94. We buried Honorine the day after Grandpa died; she was only 39. Those deaths were numbing to our family, but the loss of Honorine at such a young age was the most devastating.

ARMY OFFICER

During September 1960, Warrant Officer Four Mr. Lawrence Lee, the full-time administrative and supply technician with the local National Guard unit, talked to me about my future with the Guard. He said I had scored high enough on the battery of tests I had taken upon entering basic training that I could qualify to attend Officer Candidate School (OCS) at Fort Benning, Georgia; if I wanted to. He said there was an awful lot of paperwork, and the number of attendees from Florida would be very limited. I had to have endorsements up through my chain-of-command, which Mr. Lee could get for me if I chose to follow the idea. Mr. Lee told me to think about it for a couple days and let him know what my decision was.

I did as he suggested and pondered the opportunity that lay before me. After waiting the couple of days as Mr. Lee suggested, I stopped by the Armory and told him I would like to pursue the opportunity and I asked for his counseling and help. He told me the next class would begin on February 3, 1961, and Florida had a quota of four slots in the class. I had no idea of what my chances were for being selected, especially since I had slightly less than three years of enlisted time and was only 20 years old. At that time I weighed 112 pounds and the minimum weight requirement for entering OCS was 120 pounds; 21 was the minimum age. So I was missing the mark on both requirements.

Just before getting the required physical examination to determine my physical fitness and my potential for completing the course, I ate all the bananas I could force down and drank all the water I could hold; when I stepped on the scales at the physical exam station I weighed in at exactly 120 pounds. Since I would turn 21 years old in less than a month after OCS graduation, I was granted an age waiver and approved to attend the Reserve and National Guard OCS class.

It was a severe culture shock when I reported in at the 51st Company for the OCS class. We were subjected to intensive verbal in-your-face screaming, extreme physical harassment of push-ups, sit-ups, and running that never let up during any waking moment of the day from the time we arrived until graduation. I knew the course was going to be difficult; I had been told to expect it to be extreme. Still, having been forewarned and knowing the harsh reality were two different things.

During our first formation, the Tactical Officer said there were 40 soldiers in our platoon; as we were mustered in ranks he told us to look to the person on the left and to the one on the right and to notice who they were, because in eight weeks only one of us would remain. Two out of every three would either quit or be washed out due to the physical and mental stress we had to endure. Sure enough, in May, our platoon graduated 13 out of the 40 officer candidates that started in February. One soldier never even unpacked his bags; he simply quit after less than two hours of verbal and physical harassment. I could quickly tell these eight weeks were going to be like no other; it was going to be the most difficult, grueling, and challenging experience I had ever faced. I made up my mind when I decided to go that I wasn't going to quit, I was going to apply myself academically, physically, and mentally, and I was determined to finish. I wasn't a quitter, had never been, and this was certainly not the time to start. Even though the regimentation of the course was very tough, I grew physically, academically, and mentally stronger in that short period of time.

The school taught me the great leadership skills of decisiveness, assuming responsibility, being technically proficient, and tactically knowledgeable. We were taught to always take care of the troops in our charge and that we were privileged to lead; we always had to put the mission first. I grew in other ways during that short period of my life; I gained a great deal of confidence in my abilities not only as a soldier and as a potential leader of soldiers, but in my civilian endeavors as well. Having the opportunity to be selected to attend and then to graduate from Officer Candidate School was a big win–win situation for me and the lessons I learned have lasted and made an impact on every facet of my life since then. The class graduated on May 2, 1961; my brother Carra brought Daddy and Mama to Fort Benning to attend my graduation ceremony. That was a very proud time for me and for my family. I had gone from a dirt farmer to a ground soldier, and now I was an officer in the United States Army and a member of the Florida Army National Guard.

Events, opportunities, and life in general had intervened once again to hinder, but only delay, my college education. I had to drop out for the spring semester of 1961 while I attended the National Guard OCS program. I had completed exactly 30 semester hours of college with a satisfactory grade point average. I had also been promoted to Sergeant just before attending OCS, which increased my pay and was a big help toward meeting my financial needs during the next fall semester.

Following OCS graduation in May, I returned home and worked on Daddy's farm and in the tobacco fields through the summer until college started; I did, however, leave the farming for my two weeks annual training period at Fort Stewart, but that was my only break in farming.

At the time of my National Guard drill weekend in May, I was still technically an officer candidate even though I had met all the military requirements for a commissioned officer. I appeared before the Federal Commissioning Board on June 3, 1961, and was commissioned a Second Lieutenant, Armor, in the Florida Army National Guard, with assignment back to my home town unit, Company A, 1st Battalion, 187th Armor. There was a pinning ceremony at the Live Oak Armory on Sunday afternoon during the June Drill. Lieutenant Colonel George H. Dale, who lived in Live Oak, but was the Battalion Commander with Headquarters in Lake City, was assisted with the pinning by Mama.

I was the only one in my family to be a commissioned officer in any branch of the military; my brothers certainly had the skills, knowledge, and ability to do the same, but for their own personal reasons, they chose not to seek that opportunity. All eight boys in my family served in the military. Thomas Lee, the oldest, served from 1942 through the end of World War II in Germany where for one year and seven days he was a Prisoner of War. Carra, the second oldest brother, served in the Navy in the Pacific Theater during 1943 through the end of World War II. Alfred, my next older brother, served in the Florida Army National Guard from October 1949 through the late 1950s in the Live Oak unit and in a unit in Jacksonville. Pete, the next brother, joined the Florida Army National Guard in May 1950, and served over 20 years and retired from the Guard. Billy, the next brother, was drafted into the regular Army in about 1958, and served two years in military intelligence before being honorably discharged. Sherwood, the next brother, joined the Florida Army National Guard in November 1958 in Live Oak, and served about eight years before being honorably discharged. Ronald, the brother just older than me, also joined the Florida Army National Guard in Live Oak, but after serving just a couple of years joined the regular Army for three years and served in the Army Security Agency in Germany. I joined March 3, 1958, and was separated on October 2, 1997. I rendered to the United States of America 39½ years of continuous military service. For that, I am very proud to have served.

DIFFERENT ASSIGNMENTS

In the year I was commissioned, we attended annual training in the summer. Since I was a green Second Lieutenant, I got all the crappy officer assignments, but that was fine with me. With every challenge came an opportunity; and I was determined to meet every challenge with the same vigor regardless of its relative importance in my own eyes. It is in the nature of man to put people in their place, either rightly or wrongly. And when anyone is new at a job, they usually get the jobs that others don't want and can pass off to another. The Spanish have a saying that if you want to be respected, you must respect yourself; to me, that means do what is asked of you and to never pass off a bad job simply because you can or because it is distasteful. I have tried to live to that standard.

Our unit arrived by convoy at Fort Stewart late Sunday afternoon, after which we had to set up camp, draw our army tanks and related equipment from the equipment pool, and move them to the tank firing range in preparation for starting the several qualifying gunnery tables required on the tank gun during the following week. My first big assignment and challenge came Monday morning; I was the safety officer on one of the tank firing ranges. We were scheduled to start firing at 9:00 a.m., and about 10 minutes before 9:00 a.m., I heard a two place (pilot and one passenger) small observation helicopter preparing to land in our area.

One of my duties that day was to meet, greet, and brief visiting dignitaries. Our Battalion Staff was on site to observe and evaluate our organization and operation of the tank firing range. As the helicopter landed, it was the Commander of the 48th Armored Division, Major General Maxwell C. Snyder. I had been pre-warned of his terrible reputation for chewing and spitting out every junior officer he came in contact with, and he was reported to especially have a taste for green Second Lieutenants. He was noted as a habitual destroyer of morale and he used the Lord's name in vain with about every sentence he spoke—something I didn't like but had no control over. General Snyder always carried a small swagger stick with him; he used it to point out things and he was prone to strike you on the chest with it while he was chewing you out. I don't think anyone ever looked forward to being visited by General Snyder.

I was very tense as I saw the General approach. The senior battalion officers that could get away, scattered when they saw the red two-star plate on the front of the helicopter, but they all wanted to position themselves to watch me get my first big chewing out by General Snyder. I had no place to go except to meet and greet the Division Commander as I was directed. I saluted him and introduced myself as Second Lieutenant Boatright, Company A, 1st Battalion, 187th Armor, from Live Oak, Florida. He put his arm around my shoulder and asked me if my Daddy was Joe Boatright from Live Oak. I said yessir, and he asked me about Mama, and then he asked about my brother Thomas Lee—he wondered how Tom was doing and made small talk around my family. General Snyder had served with Thomas Lee when Tom was captured and became a prisoner of war in Germany. The General had been the Battalion Commander over the Live Oak National Guard unit during World War II. He was very friendly to me and talked to me for several minutes one-on-one before we moved to the briefing tent; General Snyder never once hit me with his swagger stick as I had expected him to do. I was both relieved and thankful that I didn't have to endure what all the other officers were assuming was awaiting me.

Once we got into the briefing tent, all hell broke loose on the few poor officers that remained as part of the Battalion Staff. He chewed out every officer around that was a Captain or higher; nothing they could say would soften his verbally abusive attacks. After a few frustrating minutes, he was given the typical military briefing, and then the firing of our tank guns started. Shortly thereafter, when he was ready to leave, I escorted him to his helicopter, saluted him, and he boarded and left the area. The joke about him chewing me up and spitting me out turned, and the joke wasn't on me at all but on my superior officers. I got the last and biggest laugh after all, but naturally I never let them know it. Several of my superior officers were curious about what we had talked about privately, and they were dumbfounded about how nice and cordial the General treated me. I feel sure my oldest brother, Thomas Lee, being under his command and their serving in war together had something to do with it. But that was my secret.

BACK ON THE FARM

The fall of 1961 and the spring of 1962 were spent working with Pete and Daddy on the farm. I continued to save money so when I started back to college I could hopefully finish my AA degree and immediately transfer to Florida State University. I planned to go straight through until I finished my Bachelor of Science degree in Education. Even though stopping and working caused me to fall behind my peers,

I had a clearer direction and a plan for finishing college using just the money I had saved along with whatever I would earn during my junior and senior years at FSU. My time away from school had been well spent and wisely invested.

MORE ARMY TRAINING

As soon as practical after being commissioned, I enrolled in the Armor Officer Basic Course (AOBC), at Fort Knox, Kentucky. The two ways to complete the course were in residence at Fort Knox or by taking sub-courses by correspondence. The sub-course route was the one most Army Reserve and National Guard officers took. This required hundreds of hours of study and digging, because the only way to get the information needed was to simply excavate it from the materials and books sent with each course. Over the nearly four decades of my career in the military I have spent untold hours working, studying, and completing these kinds of required courses. I finished the Armor Officer Basic Course within two years of being commissioned. It was a lot of hard work, but well worth it.

In the summer of 1962 when my National Guard unit went to its annual training at Fort Stewart, Georgia, I was still a Second Lieutenant and a platoon leader in Company A, 1st Battalion, 187th Armor. Again, as soon as our convoy arrived at Fort Stewart late on Sunday afternoon, we had to set up camp, draw our army tanks and related equipment from the equipment pool, and move them to the tank firing range in preparation for starting the several qualifying tables during the following week.

UNIVERSITY

In the fall of 1962, I started my first semester as a sophomore at NFJC. I used the same routine that had served me as a freshman; I drove over to college on Monday morning, back home Monday evening for National Guard drill, and back to college on Tuesday morning. I stayed in Madison Tuesday through Thursday. For my sophomore year I rode to and from Madison with Inez Boatright; she was taking the Licensed Practical Nursing course at the Vocational Technical School which was operated by the college. I also got involved in taking drama, not as a class, but as an enrichment activity where I played the lead male role in the play *Bus Stop* in the fall, and Polonius in *Hamlet*. By then, the college had built a student union and a cafeteria to serve the growing student population. Since an increasing student body meant there were more things for the college to do, I got a job washing dishes; it paid

35 cents an hour, but I also got free meals, so this was a very good deal for me.

The spring of 1963 was my final semester of junior college. After washing dishes during the fall semester, I moved up to being cashier during the spring semester. I worked diligently, finished all requirements, and graduated from North Florida Junior College in April 1963. I was proud to be a farmer, a dishwasher, a cashier, a student, and a second lieutenant—I wasn't afraid of work or responsibility; hard work and dedication were learned traits that I would use throughout my lifetime.

I transferred to Florida State University, and immediately started the second trimester in May 1963. FSU had recently changed from the semester system to the trimester system. Their new course organization would allow me just enough time to finish in December 1964 if everything went well and all my required courses were available and could be scheduled during that time.

The summer trimester had courses that ran the full 12 weeks, other courses ran in A or B sessions only, each having 6 weeks. I lived in the college dormitory in Kellum Hall, room 702, and shared that room with a couple of different roommates during my time at FSU. Occasionally, maybe once or twice a week at the most, I would splurge and eat at the McDonalds about two blocks from Kellum Hall on west Tennessee Street. At that time a hamburger cost 25 cents, French fries 15 cents, and a coke 10 cents; so for 50 cents I could buy a full McDonalds meal. I enjoyed McDonalds then and still do today. I had never seen a McDonalds until I was in college; and I had never seen or eaten pizza until I was at FSU in 1963. I'm sure my rural raising had a lot of influence on the things I was exposed to. For instance, I was through college and teaching school before I heard about drugs such as marijuana. I guess I still hold to those old-fashioned values because when I grew up about the worst trouble anybody ever had was an occasional drunken binge, and that usually left enough misery in the hangover to serve as sufficient punishment to moderate regular pursuits of miscreant behavior.

A DIFFERENT BUS

I didn't have an automobile, and didn't get my first car, which was a white 1964 VW Beetle, until December 1964. I would catch the Greyhound bus to Tallahassee each Sunday afternoon then walk the 1¼ miles to Kellum Hall. I had Guard duty every Monday; so on

Monday afternoons I would walk to the bus station carrying some textbooks with me to study on the bus. The bus would leave about 4:00 p.m. from Tallahassee and arrive around 6:15 p.m. in Live Oak, where I would be met by my brothers, Pete and Sherwood. They would have a snack for me to eat and my uniform. I would change into military dress at the armory just before drill. After drill was over, about 10:15 p.m., I would change back into civilian clothes and Pete and Sherwood would drop me off at the Greyhound Station before they headed home. They always had to get up early the next morning and go to work and I always had an 8:00 a.m. class that was all the way across campus, so I had very little time for rest.

The round trip bus fare was about $4.20 and I would make two round trips a week: one for the weekend at home, and one for National Guard drill. That was rather expensive travel because I had such a limited budget, but that was part of learning discipline and responsibility while staying committed to those things I wanted to pursue.

I did the same weekly/weekend and National Guard routine for over a year and a half. Mr. Edmonds, the Greyhound bus driver who was usually driving when I was picked up about 11:00 p.m. in Live Oak as I headed back to Tallahassee, soon realized I was a student and we started passing the time on the trip with a little friendly conversation. After a couple of months, when Mr. Edmonds found out I was a Second Lieutenant and was traveling back and forth weekly to attend National Guard drill, he told me not to buy any more round trip tickets. He told me that as long as I was in school and making the trip back weekly, he would let me ride free on the return trip. That saved me about $2.00 a week per trip, which was a big help.

Since we always got in really late at night it was always dark; sometimes it was cold, and during the rainy seasons it was usually wet. One night Mr. Edmonds told me that his bus route ended in Marianna and he suggested that rather than walk the 1¼ miles back to the dorm, if I would wait for about 15 minutes while he unloaded passengers who had reached the end of their trip and loaded the new passengers, he would drop me off right at my dorm. I was really grateful to Mr. Edmonds, he helped me a lot.

A DEBT REPAID

I was able to repay his kindness when I learned that Mr. Edmonds enjoyed quail hunting. I told him Daddy had a farm and he would be more than welcome to hunt there. I drew him a map to our home, and he came to quail hunt. Of course, my parents were gracious to him for all the kindness he had shown to me. I wasn't at home when he went to hunt, but he told me how much he appreciated the opportunity to hunt quail on the family farm.

CRAMMING CLASSES

When I started school in May of 1963, I was able to get classes for the full summer trimester, which spanned sessions A and B. I knew I wanted to teach, but I really didn't have a specific interest in any particular subject. I kept remembering my sixth grade teacher, Miss Green, and how she somehow inspired me to want to teach sixth grade. So I planned to major in Elementary Education. I thought if I developed an interest in one of the subject areas I could switch and become certified in that subject. That never happened though, and I really enjoyed not only learning a little depth about all the subject areas, but I soon found out the 11-year-old student is a great age to teach. At that age the kids still usually have respect for authority, they usually still want to learn, and the boys are not deep into sports, motorbikes, and automobiles. Most of the girls haven't yet discovered older boys; that combination makes for a great teaching environment. I did very well my first trimester at FSU and my grades improved a little with every trimester.

In the summer of 1963, when my National Guard unit went to annual training at Fort Stewart, I was still a Second Lieutenant, but earlier that spring on March 31st I was assigned as Commander of a separate federally recognized unit. The unit was the Armored Cavalry Platoon Headquarters, and Headquarters Company, 1st Battalion, 187th Armor, with the command center in Live Oak. This was one of my most enjoyable annual trainings ever. As an Armored Cavalry platoon, our mission was to seek out the enemy. We still had to draw our equipment from the equipment pool on Sunday afternoon upon arrival at Fort Stewart, and move it to the training area, in preparation and support of Monday morning training requirements.

It seemed like the mission we had in that annual training was more real, more intense, and focused on what soldiers prepare to face—an enemy. General Douglas MacArthur was a great commander, one of the greatest ever, and he understood the enemy quite well; in a war both sides have a common goal, and that is to win at all costs. One of General MacArthur's best quotes was, "In war there is no substitute for victory." If you think about it, there is no logical response against his reasoning. And that was one of the main reasons why we trained every year.

On October 15, I was reassigned back to Company A, 1st Battalion, 187th Armor, as Tank Platoon Leader.

ROOMMATE IN TROUBLE

In the fall of 1963, I was able to get a good schedule of classes. During the fall I had a very bright roommate who was also enrolled in the College of Education and majoring in history. He was from Thomasville, Georgia, and he came from a fairly affluent family. He and I got along well enough and we became friends, even though he considered me to be just a rural north Florida country boy—a country bumpkin.

After some time lapsed in our friendship, I noticed things weren't going well with him for some reason. He seemed a little depressed and would go home quite frequently, even in the middle of the week. Of course with Thomasville being only 45 miles away that didn't seem too strange to me since I made two weekly trips that were more than twice that distance. At the time, I didn't realize that his grades had already deteriorated to the point he had received a letter from the College of Education dismissing him from school.

I came back to the dorm room about noon one day and he was almost in tears. He showed me his letter from the College, and was preparing to pack up and go home. He then told me the reason he had been acting strange was that his parents were in the middle of an ugly divorce, and he was trying to work and deal with both of them through the tough and strained situation. I told him that I thought I could keep him from being kicked out of school if he'd promise to work hard and get his grades back up. We talked for a while and then he asked how I could do anything that would help. I didn't directly answer his question, and I continued to encourage him to let me have the letter and give me his commitment to salvage the trimester if he had the opportunity. Reluctantly, he did; I got ready to leave and told him I would be back soon.

I took the letter and went to see the Associate Dean of the College of Education, Dr. Samuel T. Lastinger (my mother's first cousin). Fortunately, I got in to see him and handed him the letter. As Dr. Lastinger reviewed the letter I asked if he would help get my friend reinstated into the College of Education. As the Associate Dean read and reread the letter, I assured him that my friend would work extra hard and make respectable grades in spite of his currently low grades.

Dr. Lastinger believed what I said and restored my friend back to full status in the College of Education. With a knowing and satisfied look, the Associate Dean scribbled a handwritten note for my friend to give his instructors. I never told my roommate the whole story behind his reinstatement, but he always let me know how he appreciated my help. Whenever possible, I believe that people should get a second chance because we don't always know what may have caused them to falter or struggle for a while. Even God offered mankind a second chance; should we do any less? I do believe that when we help others, the kindness is returned to us someway. In my case, the second trimester also went well and my grades continued to improve.

PROMOTION

Throughout the spring trimester and summer trimester session A, I was focused on finalizing my required academic classes and preparing for interning in the fall. During the summer trimester session B, I worked on the farm helping to harvest the tobacco crop and attended National Guard annual training at Fort Stewart. The National Guard promoted me to First Lieutenant and assigned me as the Executive Officer (XO), in Company A, 1st Battalion, 187th Armor, in Live Oak—my home unit. I enjoyed annual training as the XO, but my primary responsibilities were mostly administrative and logistical in nature. I spent most of my time making sure the unit mess hall, supply room, motor pool, and company headquarters section functioned well and that we conducted and delivered support functions consistent with military standards. I got to spend some time in the field doing the unit operational functions, which I enjoyed most.

ALMOST THROUGH

Back at FSU, all my class schedules worked out just perfect for me and I planned to graduate in December 1964. I had the opportunity to intern at Pine Dale Elementary School, which was located adjacent to the railroad yards on the west side of Jacksonville. My intern experience was positive. My directing teacher allowed me plenty of opportunities to teach and develop my classroom management skills. However, he was what I would call quirky. He was like an old maid, very precise and exact, every student had to wipe each foot exactly two times each on the doormat before entering the room. As a teacher, I wasn't impressed with his petty rules, but again, it was his classroom and certainly not my place to question his procedures or his authority. I did appreciate the fact that he was kind enough to allow me the opportunity to teach under his supervision. Again, as with all my experiences and opportunities, I learned some good ideas, techniques, and methods for the various subjects I would teach, as well as a lot of ideas, techniques, and methods I didn't want to take with me to my own classroom. As I served my teaching internship I realized that you not only learn what to do as a practicing teacher, but also what not to do, which is about as meaningful and important as knowing what you should do.

During my fall internship semester in 1964, I was able to stay with my brother and sister-in-law, Alfred and Annette. Alfred allowed me to use his pickup truck to travel to and from school; and he let me use his car to drive back to Live Oak on Monday nights for National Guard drill. He or Annette never permitted me to pay for room, food, gas, or anything. They provided me with everything I needed to survive, just as if I was their son. I will always be grateful for all their help and support during this critical time in my life. Again, I was being rewarded for something and didn't know why.

Realizing I would complete my internship and be eligible to start teaching on my own, I applied for a teaching job in Live Oak starting in January 1965. I was fortunate; one of the sixth grade teachers went on maternity leave starting with the Christmas holidays and the Suwannee County School Board hired me to fill the vacant position starting in January when classes resumed.

A NEW CAR

I knew ahead of time that I was going to need transportation of my own; so while staying with Alfred and Annette, I decided to buy my first automobile in November 1964. They carried me to the Volkswagen dealer where I purchased a brand new 1964 white VW Beetle for $1,595. I was very proud of that car. It was the first time in my life I was not solely dependent upon someone else, or the Greyhound bus, to get me from one place to another—if my destination was farther than I could walk.

I graduated from Florida State University on December 19, 1964, with a Bachelors Degree in Education. Both my parents attended the graduation ceremony in Tully Gym. I felt blessed beyond measure to have a permanent teaching job, a new car, and a regular monthly paycheck. And having my parents witness the results of their labors through me was especially rewarding. I know they were proud, but I was bubbling over.

TEACHING, MORE COLLEGE, SUPERINTENDENT

Hide not your talents, they for use were made. What's a sundial in the shade? Benjamin Franklin.

IBEGAN TEACHING at Pine View Elementary School when school resumed after the Christmas holidays in January 1965; my new job was in Live Oak. I taught a sixth grade self-contained class for the spring semester. I was single at the time and had the small luxury of spending a lot of extra hours preparing lesson plans for what I would teach the next day. Since I was having so much fun, personal satisfaction, and reward for my efforts, I never felt like what I was doing was work. Every day I got up early and looked forward to the new and exciting experiences each dawning day would bring. My students and their parents were a pleasure to work with, and the practice I got was a great start to my career.

My teaching style was to maintain control of the classroom; I believed in discipline and a solid routine to follow. I have always believed that you cannot teach students if you don't first have their attention. Both experience and research have convinced me that if you don't have control over the classroom and create a learning environment where all students can learn, you quickly lose those with less ability. I have always liked humor, and as a result, I was prone to joke around with students, but never in a degrading manner or a way that would cause them to lose respect for authority. I wanted my students to feel that I was human and approachable and they should not be afraid or reluctant to ask me questions or request my help whenever they needed it.

In January 1965, I was still serving as Company Executive Officer of Company A, 1st Battalion, 187th Armor, in the Florida National Guard. The Guard was a serious commitment for me and it took its fair share of time, but it didn't hinder my teaching; likewise, my teaching was a serious and important part of my life and I kept it compartmentalized so that my teaching didn't bother my Guard duties. Sometimes it could be a juggling act, but so is anything that requires a commitment of effort and time.

About a year before I started teaching, a study of the old Suwannee High School determined that it was unsafe to use; the district abandoned the school and quit using it. The entire southeast corner of the main building had fallen into a sinkhole; sinkholes are not too uncommon in Florida because of the landscape and our normally large amount of rainfall. Underground streams wash out caverns, and when the caverns drain, sinkholes appear. Today, we have soil borings on all proposed school sites to help avoid potential disaster from schools being swallowed up by the earth. Anyway, our school, at the time, was at the old Pine View School site until the Christmas holidays in 1965 when we moved to the old Suwannee High School location after the new year started in 1966.

GOING AFTER SCIENCE

The sixth grade teachers had agreed to departmentalize by subject matter for the 1965-66 school term and they selected me to be the science teacher. I had no science equipment personally, and neither did the school. I did my best to assess what our science needs were. Once I had an idea of our needs, I went to the school board's Supervisor of Instruction and asked if there were any Federal Title III science grants available. There was, so I offered to write a proposal for science equipment to furnish a sixth-grade science lab. The county supervisor agreed that writing a proposal for a grant to meet our science needs was a good idea. In a sense, I was asking for more work when, in fact, I had plenty to keep me busy without pursuing other opportunities. Nonetheless, it was a genuine need and I had an idea about how I could help. As a result, I spent my entire spring break studying and writing in hopes of securing some much needed equipment and materials. To my pleasure, and a little to my shock, the proposal I wrote was funded for about $3,000—almost the annual salary for a beginning teacher, which was a decent amount to support our science department.

My teacher's contract was for a salary of $4,200 per year at that time. Unlike the science grant that was a supplement with no bills or living expenses, I had to spend my summer working in the tobacco fields, cropping tobacco, just as I had done while in college in order to make ends meet. The summer, as uneventful as it was, came and went and then school started back in August. I was excited, happy, and felt most fortunate at having been selected to teach science to all sixth graders. We were assigned to teach a six-period day, and my classroom was in the old Suwannee High School home economics cooking laboratory. The room was subdivided into six individual small cooking areas, which I turned into group learning centers. In each newly classified learning area, I placed a table and six chairs, which gave me a classroom capacity for 36 students. For some periods, I had the full complement of students that my cooking-lab-turned-science-lab could hold.

My military training helped me with organization. I assessed what I had and then reviewed what I needed to teach. There were six periods, six learning centers, and six subjects: biology, botany, physical science, meteorology, earth science, and health. Even before school started,

I had developed a six-week's plan of instruction for each of the six subject areas. The plan included hands-on experiences for each of the six areas, and then I had the students rotate every six weeks to another area. This enabled me to provide a study and hands-on experience for every student in each of the six different content areas. I would circulate from group to group providing instruction and guidance as each cluster worked through the six-week syllabus.

Each Friday, I prepared and demonstrated an extensive science experiment for the entire class. I developed individual tests for each of the workgroups, and I tested the students individually. At the same time, I assigned each group a six-week group project in which the entire group received a grade for the project based largely on each individual's involvement and contribution to the project. Again, military training helped me to stress the importance of the individual and the significance of personal effort to the group's performance. I didn't seek perfection, nor did I try to make each student a scientist; I did try to tweak the imagination of each student to have a love and fascination of science itself, and I wanted them to develop the ability to share with each other and to work together as a team. I was hoping to form life-skills that students could use as they entered the world of work; not just have them go through a routine or mundane academic exercise that had no long-term goal or value.

I formed a Science Club for any student who wanted to join, and then I asked the superintendent and board to authorize an overnight field trip to Saint Augustine in early May 1966; they did, and I drove a school bus for the trip and had several mothers as chaperones.

That trip was a great learning experience for all our students, not only in science, but also in English, composition, economics, and even civics because I required each student to write the superintendent and school board to gain approval for the trip and the use of the school bus. As we planned the trip, the students contacted the various sites we planned to visit and learned what prices were for all the things we would do and then we compared costs to make the most economical decisions. They contacted several motels and selected the one where we would stay, and then they reserved the rooms. As a part of our planning, they got menus from different restaurants, and the group had to select one restaurant and then everyone had to agree on a common meal, which made it easier for the restaurant and less hassle for us. Organizing this way saved time and taught a life-skill of give-and-take. The economic side worked out because the restaurant complimented us on our organization and then gave us very good prices. The trip was a huge success, and I gained a lot of support from the chaperones that would serve me well in later community activities.

I probably worked harder that year, in terms of physical effort and learning on my part in order to stay ahead of each group, than any other year in my teaching career. I felt then, and still feel today, that classroom instructional time is one of the most valuable commodities for students because they have so much they need to learn and a limited time is all that is available in the classroom. I determined to make every hour of every school day a memorable and meaningful learning experience. By doing that, I gave probably more than I had to give, but that's a part of teaching that only teachers can know. I wish that everyone could know the pleasure and excitement of sharing knowledge and then watching as some students carry on the lamp of learning and become teachers themselves—all because a teacher inspired them by setting a good example. That year, and the science project, were two of the most rewarding experiences I have had in all my life.

JAM-PACKED WITH STUDENTS

The following school year of 1966-67, I moved with my sixth-grade class to the seventh-grade and taught mathematics five periods per day. This too, was another highly rewarding experience for me as a classroom teacher. My classroom was the southwest corner classroom on the top floor of the old junior high school building. It was a very small room that only had about 600 square feet for me and all the students. In one class period, I had 39 students, so the room was wall-to-wall with student desks. We were packed in there like sardines; for the largest class, there was only about 15 square feet of space per person, which by today's standards would be unacceptable and prohibited by the Fire Marshall. There was only about 12 inches of aisle space between the rows of desks, and the front desk in each row was less than two feet from the chalkboard, which allowed me just enough room to walk and write on the chalkboard. The desks were so close to the chalkboard that some of the students on the right front side of the room couldn't see what was written on the left side of the chalkboard, and vice versa.

At any time when I was at the chalkboard or explaining or demonstrating or sharing information with the students, I always required that the classroom be quiet and that students pay attention. If the noise level of the students went up, I spoke softer, and always the noise level would go down. Without regard to the size of our space, we were able to have a valuable learning environment because our focus was on acquiring knowledge—and that is what school should always be about, accommodating learning.

Our class periods were 50 minutes long; I usually taught for about the first 35 to 40 minutes, and then used the remaining few minutes for students to complete their class assignments. By allowing some of the class time to reinforce the skills that had just been taught, students could apply the information while it was fresh on their minds and they could also ask me for help, which would also reinforce the information in the lessons. Not only was this technique a good way to get students to concentrate, it developed their skills for listening and applying learning.

Since I was raised on a farm, I was always aware of the fact that many of my students were, in many ways, just like me. Most afternoons, my students had to go home, get off the school bus and go into the fields and work; they simply didn't have time to do homework and meet all their responsibilities at home. I felt compelled to give to the school system what it deserved and to the kids and their families what they deserved. There always needs to be a balance. I always made sure that students from my classes who applied themselves wouldn't have studies to complete at night. I assigned the amount of homework or practice that could be completed within the 10 to 15 minutes I provided at the end of each period if the students applied themselves and used their time wisely, plus I was available to offer individual help as needed. Another technique I employed during this practice period was that I allowed a reasonable level of movement and sharing between students. Sometimes students need to discuss their assignments with each other, and the classroom is the most appropriate place for that to happen.

THE BIG LOSS

On February 4, 1967, Mama passed away at the age of 69. Her passing brought a period of sorrow and sadness that could only be compared to when my brother Tom was a prisoner of war, or when my sister Honorine had died so young. Losing Mama was worse because we knew for certain that she wouldn't return to us, as Tom did, and our matriarch was gone. We knew her health wasn't good, but overall she seemed to be doing fairly well given that we had insulin to treat her diabetes, which was a major health issue, but we didn't see it as life-threatening. Mama and Daddy awoke early in the morning as they usually did and had just lain in bed talking for a few minutes—sharing the simple chatter of a couple who had a lifetime of memories to thoughtfully ponder. After a few minutes of talk, Mama told Daddy that she should get up; then she moved to a sitting position and slipped on one of her bedroom shoes. After sitting briefly, she lay back down, and left us with an angel escort. Apparently a heart attack took her. An ambulance came and the medical help tried to revive her, but they couldn't get her to respond. We lived about 13 miles from town and by the time anyone could get there, it was too late. Mercifully, Mama was ushered into Heaven without the suffering and pain so many have to endure in their passing hours.

GRADUATE SCHOOL

I enrolled in a course offered by the Suwannee County school district during the spring of 1967. It was *Teaching Algebra in the Middle School* and taught by The University of Florida. I needed that class so I could build up enough college credits to renew and extend my professional teaching certificate. Dr. Jack Foley taught the class. After the first couple of weeks of class, Dr. Foley asked if anyone would care if he visited their classroom just prior to our class the next week. No one volunteered; I was eager to volunteer but didn't want to make it so obvious, so before he gave up on getting a volunteer, I raised my hand and extended the offer for him to visit my class. After class, I gave Dr. Foley the directions on how to get to my classroom; I added that he was welcome to come visit and observe at any time; to my surprise, he did. The next week Dr. Foley again asked for volunteers to allow him to do classroom observations. Again, no one responded, so once more I volunteered, to which Dr. Foley accepted my invitation. This same series of events happened three or four times. Finally, Dr. Foley started visiting my class every week before our regular class.

After Dr. Foley's second or third visit, I invited him to teach my class, and he did. None of our students had ever been taught by a university professor with a Ph.D. in mathematics—we all considered it both an honor and a privilege to have had such an opportunity.

As a side note, Dr. Foley was born and raised in Gulf Hammock which is in Levy County, Florida. He is the most gifted and natural teacher I have ever observed in public schools, community colleges, universities, or in the United States Army. He is a master teacher, and one I would call *A Teachers Teacher*. He possessed the unique ability to take a very complex subject or mathematical formula, explain it, and break it down in detail to where it seemed so simple that as a student you would think, "Gee, I should have known that just by living."

After Dr. Foley had visited and observed me teaching several times, he stayed one day after the students left and asked me if I had ever considered going to graduate school. I told him I had thought of going many times, but was in no position financially to go back to school full-time, or even part-time, because the nearest university was 65 miles away, and I just didn't see the possibility in the near future for me to pursue higher education studies. Dr. Foley said he was impressed with my teaching ability and the way I communicated and worked with students; then he told me he had received a federal grant to write a whole series of mathematics teaching materials for remedial studies. His grant was to be managed and housed in the Palm Beach District School Board offices; then came the offer—he said that if I would come to work for him, he would get me a job teaching in the Palm Beach School District and help me get enrolled in Graduate School at Florida Atlantic University. Dr. Foley said he could arrange for my work schedule and classes to not conflict with each other. He didn't ask me for an immediate answer but told me to think about it and let him know my decision within a couple of weeks. That was going to be a long two weeks with a lot of soul searching.

A NEW CHANCE

Still being single and not having many responsibilities or obligations, I struggled with the possibility of leaving a comfortable and secure work environment, a community that was very familiar to me, and then go into a world of unknowns. If I took the offer, I would go to an unknown school system, and an unknown work environment with an unknown set of requirements. I secretly feared that I didn't have the academic ability to perform competitively in graduate school; I guess I was secretly suffering under the burden of the meaning of the Jewish proverb, "Don't look for more honor than your learning merits." Yet, I realized this might be the only opportunity I would have to try it; at least for the foreseeable future. After weighing the options, I decided to cast off my fears and accept Dr. Foley's offer.

Dr. Foley extended his offer in early April, which meant the school year would be ending soon. I went to see the school superintendent, Mr. Henry Folsom, and told him I would like to request a one-year leave of absence from teaching to go to graduate school. He asked what I would major in and I replied Education Administration and Supervision.

Then I added that some day, perhaps 20 years later, I would like to be an elementary school principal. Superintendent Folsom told me the school board couldn't give a leave of absence for anyone to go back to school to major in Administration and Supervision; he said a leave of absence could only be approved for a teaching subject in one of the content areas.

Aristotle said that we should judge men by their actions. Superintendent Folsom didn't seem to be supportive of my idea of pursuing a higher education in administration. I think he immediately judged me to be a threat to him. So, I thanked him for his time and resigned my teaching position effective at the end of the school year. Once I had voiced my desire to have a leadership role in the Suwannee County school system, a different atmosphere developed in the superintendent's office. I could sense it and somehow I knew that if I succeeded in getting a graduate degree in Education Administration and Supervision, I would not be welcomed back to my home county. Suddenly, just because I was pursuing a better education, I somehow became a potential threat to the current administration.

COMPANY COMMANDER

On January 27, 1966, the National Guard raised me to the position of Company Commander. Less than five months later, on June 4, 1966, they promoted me from First Lieutenant to Captain. Commanding Company A, 1st Battalion, 187th Armor, in Live Oak, was the fulfillment of a long-term military goal.

I joined the Guard as a Private and served my entire career in that unit with the exception of about six months of training. Command of a military unit having about 75 soldiers and millions of dollars worth of equipment at the age of 26 gave me plenty to do to keep up with the major commitments and responsibilities I had assumed. During annual training at Fort Stewart in the summer of 1966, while conducting combined arms training with the 124th Infantry Regiment, I met Captain Ronald O. Harrison. He was a senior Captain and an Infantry Company Commander; I was a junior Captain and an Armor Company Commander; we became friends. Our friendship brought on discussions about how the military improves everything you do in life. The discipline, organization, and structure of a military operation can't help but to carry over to civilian occupations.

During 1967, civil unrest plagued many of the major cities throughout the United States. Strife existed because of several reasons.

There were race riots in major cities, the Viet Nam war was going on, marijuana and other drugs were fast becoming a stumbling block for the college-age crowd, and popularity for the Flower Children and the peace movement was on the news at every turn.

My unit had prepared for the exercises during annual training at Fort Stewart; however, due to the increased level of civil unrest throughout the country, a command decision diverted my unit to Camp Blanding for two weeks of intensive riot-control training. At that time, Camp Blanding had a very limited number of barracks and wasn't equipped to handle the large number of personnel that were suddenly thrust upon the camps limited full-time staff. We all slept in pup tents the entire two weeks; we had makeshift showers, and field latrines. It wasn't comfortable, but it was a military exercise and the conditions were actually beneficial for self-discipline and training. Not that there is anything wrong with being comfortable, but military discipline often requires soldiers to push beyond coziness or ease and perform under the most demanding and adverse circumstances. The simple training exercises where we slept and lived without the modern conveniences were good teaching tools.

FAR AWAY

In 1967, the Florida National Guard had a policy that required all company-size commanders to live within 50 miles of their command post. Since I was about to move for the next 15 months to West Palm Beach, which was more than 340 miles from the Live Oak Armory, I contacted Lieutenant Colonel Floyd Kennon, Commander, 1st Battalion, 187th Armor, headquartered in Lake City and talked about my near-term plans for attending graduate school. I told Lieutenant Colonel Kennon that I understood the policy of not living more than 50 miles away while commanding a company-size unit, and I was prepared to be relieved of command and even resign from the National Guard, if required, because there were no available officer slots where I could be reassigned. He understood my dilemma; since he was satisfied with my performance as commander, Lieutenant Colonel Kennon requested that I continue to command even though I would be living farther away than was recommended for maintaining charge of my unit. I was allowed to have a long-distance command; I felt rewarded, and I guess I was. I had invested a lot of time and energy to the command and those who were in positions of authority over me undoubtedly appreciated that effort.

Once I had made the decision to go to graduate school and move to Palm Beach County, I immediately began to make plans for a place to live. I knew one of our neighbors, Mrs. Hattie Ross, whose daughter's mother-in-law, Mrs. Clement, lived in Palm Beach in an older two-story Spanish-style home that was directly across the street from the old Palm Beach High School. Mrs. Ross had said that Mrs. Clement had a couple of rooms that she rented and gave me her telephone number. I contacted Mrs. Clement, told her who I was and that Mrs. Ross has recommended I check with her for a room. She graciously let me rent from her and she charged me a reasonable price for an upstairs, one-bedroom flat with a private bath and a private entrance—if I used the outside stairs.

The room was big enough for me and had a small closet; but ultimately, it was just an efficiency unit where I could cook on two burners, keep a few groceries in its small refrigerator, and I could wash the few dishes, pots, and pans in its tiny little sink. Mrs. Clement was a very good and decent person; she didn't require a deposit, lease, or anything other than my spoken word as a commitment, and I simply showed up on the date I said I would and moved into her home as a boarder.

In the middle of my graduate school studies, on January 20, 1968, my National Guard Company was reorganized as Company C, 3rd Battalion, 124th Infantry. The unit was split between Live Oak and Apalachicola, with the Company Headquarters and two platoons located in Live Oak, and two platoons located in Apalachicola.

Starting with my February 1968 Guard drill, and lasting through the remainder of my graduate school program, I would leave my teaching duties each Friday afternoon, around three o'clock, then drive 340 miles and arrive in Live Oak late that night, get a few hours sleep, and be at the armory by six o'clock the following morning (Saturday). I would spend a reasonable amount of time with the Live Oak unit, usually until about three o'clock in the afternoon, and then drive 165 miles to Apalachicola, spend the night, be at the Apalachicola unit early Sunday morning, visit the unit until about noon then drive another 165 miles back to Live Oak. After attending to the official and required company commander duties and responsibilities such as answer correspondence and signing various required reports and documents, I would change to civilian clothes and drive my VW bug back to West Palm Beach, another 340-mile drive, arriving just before midnight. After a few hours sleep, I would get up and drive 12 miles to

John I. Leonard Senior High School before the mandatory arrival time for teachers of 7:45 a.m. It was a grueling schedule, but my National Guard unit was split between Live Oak and Apalachicola, and my graduate studies were all the way down in south Florida.

The Germans have an adage that says whoever begins too much accomplishes little. In a way, I felt like I was doing too many things, but since I was young, single, and all these opportunities were falling my way, it seemed foolish to let them go. The only way to meet all the obligations was to simply commit to the schedule and never second-guess why I was putting myself through such a demanding pace.

WHO IS SHE

I had National Guard duty on the weekend following post planning for teachers in June of 1967. As soon as National Guard duty was over, I went home to change clothes before driving down to West Palm Beach to begin my new job working for Dr. Jack Foley the next morning. When I got home, Mrs. Jean Meadows, the previous County Home Extension Agent, was visiting Daddy. She had the new Home Extension Agent with her, JoAnn Newton Kirkland, whom she was showing around and introducing to a few of the local families. I looked at JoAnn and something rang a bell; I didn't recognize it at that very moment, but what I was hearing was wedding bells—and I was in an Army Fatigue Uniform; not exactly the kind of clothing you would expect for someone who was about to meet a real life dream.

I think I was smitten from first sight and wanted to impress her. Somewhere along the conversation after the formal introductions, I said to JoAnn, "I know Paul Crews, the County Extension Agent. He was a Lieutenant Colonel in the Florida Army National Guard." I guess I thought my uniform, Paul Crews Guard membership and County Extension Agent status, and JoAnn's employment as County Home Extension Agent somehow gave us common ground. After a little more chatting, I added, "I'll come see you some time." Since she didn't say no or offer any discouragement, I felt pretty good—the bells were still ringing, but I still didn't know what they were just yet. My time was slipping away, so I changed into civilian clothes, loaded my few belongings, and headed south again in my VW beetle, arriving really late Sunday night as usual at my little bachelor flat.

ON THE NEW JOB

On Monday morning I made my way to the Palm Beach County School Board district offices. Dr. Foley's project was housed upstairs in one of the three surplus World War II two-story wooden barracks. Tending to first things first, I got all my required paper work filled out for employment with the Palm Beach County School Board. When the paper work was done, I immediately started helping to write the math teaching materials. After just a couple days of work, my respect for Dr. Foley more than doubled. He taxed my abilities to the limit, while accommodating my shortcomings. Dr. Foley knew I was not a math major; but since he had observed my teaching, he knew that I organized my work skillfully. I guess Dr. Foley's mathematical skills encouraged me because before my graduate school was over I completed more than five graduate courses in mathematics. During the first summer, I completed two graduate courses and made an A in each course. I earned those hard grades as a full-time student and also working on the math project for Dr. Foley.

I served as a graduate assistant for the courses Dr. Foley taught, and I performed all the normal tasks that the position required; whenever needed, I would usually do additional things to help organize or make the project run smoother. On the occasions when Dr. Foley had to be out of town, he asked me to teach his graduate classes for him. The summer work went well and I learned a lot of new and intriguing things about mathematics including set theory, number theory, mathematical games, mathematical patterns, mathematical puzzles, and a whole host of varied and effective teaching techniques to present mathematical concepts that could be easily understood by students in remedial studies. By the end of summer, I had gained a renewed and deeper understanding and knowledge of mathematics; but even better, I had also completed the summer session of graduate school.

About the middle of the summer of 1967, Dr. Foley introduced me to Mr. William Hegstrom who was one of the leading high school math teachers in Palm Beach County. In addition to Mr. Hegstrom's teaching duties, he managed a grant that provided a math resource teacher and a full time secretary to the math teacher. As my good fortune continued, Mr. Hegstrom recommended me to the school board and I accepted the job as a Palm Beach County math resource teacher.

MATH TEACHER

When school started back in August, Dr. Foley no longer employed me on his project, but I was a full-time teacher for the Palm Beach County School Board. I also had the enviable position of having the full-time secretarial help of Mrs. Roberta Walden; she was a former court stenographer and a great typist. Mrs. Walden had an outstanding work ethic; I could dictate thoughts or ideas to her and she would produce work quickly and accurately with almost no supervision at all.

I taught remedial math the first period every day at John I. Leonard Senior High School. After the first period at the high school as the district's math resource teacher, I was usually scheduled to teach at other schools and would travel to wherever Mrs. Walden had placed on my agenda; and my students varied from kindergarten through 12th grade with all kinds of different needs. Mrs. Walden was a great organizer and kept my schedule planned with enough advance notice for me to put together teaching materials and lesson plans; she also would prepare any handouts that I might need and organize whatever support materials I needed based on which teachers had asked for remedial assistance. We worked really well together and I enjoyed traveling around the county visiting and teaching in the schools.

The remedial teaching project was a success and gained popularity. During early December 1967, some of the local administration asked if I would like to be a television teacher of mathematics for the elementary grades. Instinctively, I asked if the job would be actually interacting with students in a classroom or if it would be me alone teaching before a television camera. The television class didn't have students, so I declined the offer. I believe that the best teaching is done through interaction with students in a classroom. That doesn't mean that other teaching models are not effective; on the contrary, other models serve a good purpose, they just are, in my opinion, inferior to the face-to-face learning that a teacher with students provides.

In addition to my full-time job as a resource teacher, I enrolled in my second quarter of graduate school. Again, I took 20 quarter hours (four five-hour courses), which was a full load; I had a five-hour class load each evening from 5 p.m. until 10 p.m.—which meant I wouldn't get home until around 11 p.m. The drive from Florida Atlantic University back to my room in West Palm Beach was about a 45-minute drive. Working all day and then going to class so late was difficult and tiring.

But the worst part was always the morning after when I had to get up, get dressed, and then drive about 45 minutes to my school in Lake Worth for the first period class. Compounding the problem was the teacher reporting time of 7:30 a.m.

The long days and burning the candle at both ends made for some very exhausting times. Quite often I thought about quitting, but there was a driving force in me that wouldn't yield to the temptation; besides, I really wanted to complete graduate school studies. Anyway, regardless of the difficulty and stress, this was the only way I could make it work financially. Adding to my commitment was knowing that Dr. Foley had given me this opportunity because he had confidence in both my abilities and my loyalty to stay with it. I was also smart enough to know that if I did quit, then I would throw away a golden opportunity and then I would have been an even bigger loser. Such opportunities are rare and another wouldn't likely come my way again. I toughed it out and earned an A in each of the four courses; and I made those good grades in spite of my teaching full time.

A FULL PLATE

If teaching full time and going to graduate school full time weren't enough, I still had National Guard responsibilities at least one weekend a month. I was the Commander of Company A, 1st Battalion, 187th Armor, for the first half-year while I was in graduate school, and then I was Commander of Company C, 3rd Battalion, 124th Infantry, and my duties were split between Live Oak and Apalachicola for the last half of my graduate school program. On the weekends when I didn't have National Guard duty, I stayed in West Palm Beach and studied. Usually, when I stayed in West Palm Beach, I never left my room from the time I got home on Friday night until it was time to go to work on Monday morning. All of my available time, when not working at my teaching job or in class at graduate school, was spent reading, writing papers, and studying for my graduate program.

There is an ancient Arabic proverb that says a man should make his bargain before beginning to plow. When I went to work for the Palm Beach County school board, I wasn't familiar with all their policies—I don't think anyone is ever aware of all the intricacies of board, or any employer, policies. Most people just accept a job and go to work. In this case, the school board had a policy that discouraged teachers from taking more than one class per quarter or semester. Since the university had a policy requiring permanently affixed parking decals for all vehicles on campus, I found myself with a slight dilemma because I had to display a decal to park at FAU for classes, and if I did that, the decal would blaringly show that I was a full-time student to the school district. I never thought about being in the double bind, but I was. As a work-around, I used Scotch tape every night and put the decal where it was supposed to be displayed and made it look like it was permanently in place. As soon as I got out of class, I stuffed the decal back in the glove compartment so I could park on school board property without advertising my full-time student status. That was something I did for the whole time I was in graduate school. Neither the school board nor the university suffered any harm or loss because I worked and went to school; I was the one suffering, but I was committed to them both and working and studying myself crazy.

THE QUESTIONNAIRE

Even though I had a rigorous schedule and nearly all my time for thinking was consumed by lesson plans or college studies, I still had flash thoughts that sparkled pleasant memories. The most enjoyable memory was about the young lady I had met at my Daddy's house back in June. As September drew to a close and I was taking a break from my studies, I wrote a letter to Ms. Jean Meadows. Ms. Meadows was living in Monticello at the time and she had introduced me to Ms. JoAnn Kirkland. Whenever I had a free moment, it seemed that thoughts of JoAnn filled it. I wanted to know more about her. Since Ms. Meadows had been the way I had met this woman whose impression intrigued me, I decided to intrude on her kindness and pry out a little information. I had a whole string of questions I wanted answers to, so I just listed them on a yellow legal pad. While I don't remember every question, I do remember the ones that were most important. Given that JoAnn was introduced to me as *Mrs.* I wanted to know what had happened to her husband, was it a divorce, death, or maybe something else—even though I didn't know what a something else might be; does she drink or smoke; what church does she attend; where did she go to college, when did she graduate, and what was her major. These were just some of the things I wanted to know; I figured the rest I could ask myself when I got to meet her again.

About two weeks after I sent my letter of inquiry to Ms. Meadows, I got a return note. And, to my surprise, it answered all my questions. I was glad to get the information because I had thought about all those things and wondered where any action on my part might lead us. As a side note, I wasn't the only interested party nor the only one asking questions. I learned, sometime later, that Ms. Meadows and Ms. Kirkland prepared a joint response to my questionnaire. So while I was wondering about JoAnn, she was thinking about me. It almost makes one wonder about destiny or predestination!

THE DATE

When I came home to Live Oak for National Guard duty during the second weekend in October, the community was preparing the Coliseum and livestock area for the annual Suwannee County Fair that was to open the following Monday. While I was at the National Guard Armory on duty Saturday morning, JoAnn, in her role as the County Home Extension Agent for Suwannee County, was at the Coliseum (which was less than a quarter of a mile away from the armory) helping to decorate some of the exhibits. We met rather incidentally and struck up a conversation. As we talked, JoAnn was rather bold and asked if I would help her with some of the exhibit decorations when I got off duty. That seemed like the opening I needed to get to know her better, so I said that I would help her if she would agree to a date that night. To my great pleasure, she said yes.

For our first date, we drove to a quaint little place called *The Dutch Pantry* in Lake City. There is a Latvian proverb that says a smiling face is half the meal—I enjoyed the smiles and the company; I can't remember what we ate, but I distinctly remember the best half of the meal. That little restaurant has fond memories for me. Sometimes I go by the exchange on Highway 90, just west of Interstate 10, and every time I flash a victory smile there.

As we made small talk, JoAnn said she worked for the Suwannee County Board of County Commissioners through the University of Florida. A few minutes later, she told me that she had a pair of tickets for the Florida—Florida State football game and asked if I would like to go with her to the game. Of course, not being a fool and trying to be coy, I said yes. It was about six weeks until the game and I used every opportunity I had to learn more about her. She was like a puzzle or a mystery that I wanted to solve but didn't have all information I needed. I used that time wisely, but I doubt that she was surprised since she and her friend had provided all the details to my questionnaire.

While I enjoyed the game, and especially since FSU won 21-16, I was more excited about the company I was keeping. I remember it well, that date was on November 25, 1967, in Gainesville. Some days are special; some dates are special—that one was.

THE BALL

Since our football date had gone so well, before our evening ended I asked JoAnn to be my date for the Annual National Guard Military Ball at the National Guard Armory, which was the first Saturday night in December. She accepted. The Military Ball was always a large event. In view of the fact that the ball was a community affair, military personnel and civilians were there and we usually had upwards of 100 couples. The event included a live band, wet bar, set-ups, and heavy hors d'oeuvre's. Along with entertainment, the armory was always decorated artistically and special lighting effects were brought in to enhance everyone's enjoyment of the festivities. All the officers wore their formal military uniforms, the enlisted men wore their dress uniforms, and civilian men wore suits. The ladies usually wore formal evening gowns, typically with a corsage. JoAnn was dressed in high fashion, and I was more than just proud to be her escort—I was excited beyond even my own expectations. When all these things were blended, it made a showcase event much like you would see in the movies. And for me, I suppose I was more aware of everything, even the little details that were probably insignificant, because I was the Company Commander at the ball with a date. That evening put both of us in the social spotlight. It was JoAnn's first introduction to a lifetime of meeting military leaders and it began her indoctrination into military protocol.

There was a rather intense line in the tender love story *The Notebook* where the lead character says to the woman of his dreams, "When I see what I want, I've just gotta have it." The character in that story was smitten at first sight and acted totally out of impulse asking for a date. That night when I took JoAnn back to her apartment, I acted on that same kind of fancy. It was brash, probably too bold, but it was true; I said, "If you're not going to marry me, don't date me anymore." Since I had blazed the trail that far without being run off, I asked her for another date on the following weekend. She accepted. I wasn't sure if she was accepting my proposal for marriage, or my invitation for another date. I had made my intentions perfectly clear, and I assumed her acceptance was too.

From that point forward, our relationship continued to grow and things moved rapidly. JoAnn did accept my proposal; we became engaged during the Christmas holidays. JoAnn had been a widow for about six years when we met. I guess that bruise on her heart made me even more drawn to her and then I wanted to take care of her and do things for her. I was a teacher, a graduate student, a company commander in the National Guard, and I didn't have enough money to buy her an engagement ring. At least I didn't have it immediately.

About a month later, I surprised her with an engagement ring and made the moment a little more special by presenting it on her birthday, February 3rd. The little, thoughtful things make a lot of difference in a relationship. I knew what I wanted in my future, and I felt like it was my destiny. Shakespeare said that it is not in the stars to hold our destiny but in ourselves. I disagree to some extent because I think that God Himself intervenes in some cases, and His dwelling place is in the stars.

I had to spend most of my time between West Palm Beach, Lake Worth, and Florida Atlantic University in Boca Raton. Both of my jobs, one as a resource teacher and the other as a graduate student, were going well. The only drawback was that I stayed busy about 18 hours a day, always on the move, always tired, but being successful in both endeavors was rewarding and also provided the incentive for me to keep going. My coursework remained top-notch and I made all As during the fall term.

The Christmas holidays arrived; since my mother had passed away about 10 months earlier, I wanted to go to Live Oak and spend as much time with Daddy as possible. Mama's passing had left a hole in all our lives, but more especially in Daddy's and I wanted to fill a small part of that void—if I could. And I wanted to spend as much time as I could with JoAnn, the new lady in my life.

When I got home, on the Saturday before Christmas and met JoAnn, she told me that she had been invited to Jacksonville for a visit with her sister-in-law, Barbara, and Barbara's husband, Tom Poston. JoAnn extended the invitation for me to join her on the trip to Jacksonville where we would spend an afternoon and then go out to dinner. I gladly accepted her offer because I really wanted to spend as much time with her as I could, and I didn't really care where we were or what we were doing. And since we were getting seriously involved, it was time that everyone had a chance to meet me.

THE OFFER

Politics is not a bad profession. If you succeed there are many rewards, if you disgrace yourself you can always write a book.
Ronald Reagan.

During those Christmas holidays, Mr. Louis C. Wadsworth, the owner and publisher of the local weekly newspaper, the *Suwannee Democrat*, called and asked if I would meet with him at the newspaper. He called in the afternoon on Friday; since JoAnn and I were planning to make our trip on Saturday to visit her in-laws, I figured that I could meet Mr. Wadsworth in the morning and still make our afternoon trip to Jacksonville.

Mr. Wadsworth was more than just the local newspaper publisher. He was also a Brigadier General in the Florida Army National Guard, a well-respected civic leader, and a political power-broker in our community. Mr. Wadsworth and I discussed a wide range of topics that included our common ground in the military. When the topic moved to education, I was a little surprised to learn just how knowledgeable he was about the local school system. After I thought it over, I shouldn't have been amazed about anything that he knew because information and knowledge are the mainstays of the newspaper business.

We rounded out our talk on local education by discussing all the issues facing the school system in the next year or so. Since it was a conversation, I shared my take on the major issues and I even ranked them according to priority. As I saw it, the first major issue facing Suwannee County Schools was school desegregation; the second thing I considered a major issue was the district-wide lack of maintenance and repair of the educational facilities. We agreed on the first two issues so I continued reciting my view. The third issue, from my viewpoint, was the poor financial condition and unbridled fiscal management of the entire school system; fourth, we had seen an alarming increase in the number of non-certified teachers, and a large number of teachers were not teaching in their certification areas. I saved the last issue to drive home the point of our poor performance in Suwannee County: the Southern Association of Colleges and Schools didn't accredit a single school in the district.

I was Captain Boatright; he was General Wadsworth. Within the community, we may have been fellow citizens, but that would always be overshadowed by our military allegiance. Besides, I held Mr. Wadsworth in high esteem as a community leader and someone with insight into our local needs and the ways we needed to improve; and that was beside my deep admiration of his military capabilities. So, I was caught off guard when he asked me if I had considered seeking the office of Superintendent of Schools in Suwannee County. He made it more specific and wanted to nail down whether I was interested in campaigning for the upcoming spring primary.

I was flattered that a General would consider asking a Captain to take on the local political challenge of running for public office. Inside, my heart was racing; outside I tried to show the normal military image of always being in charge and never having any emotions. I suspect that General Wadsworth knew what was inside of Captain Boatright, after all, that is part of being a general officer.

As I prepared to leave, Mr. Wadsworth asked me to think about our discussion during the holidays, and if I decided to seek the office of Superintendent of Schools, he would contribute to my campaign and help as much as possible, considering his position in the community. I thanked him for his confidence and told him that if I ran, I would do it on my own and that I would not accept campaign contributions from anyone. I didn't want any real or perceived political obligations to tie my hands if I were to run and then be elected. It was a lot to think about; running for public office when I already had a good juggling act to keep in graduate school with good grades and hold my teaching position, and these obligations didn't consider my commitment to the Guard. I consented to think about what I might do and give further thought to seeking the office. I also wanted to discuss it with my Dad, get his advice, and then let Mr. Wadsworth know my decision before the beginning of the New Year.

The meeting I had with Mr. Wadsworth probably led to my first romantic blunder with JoAnn because the conversation about politics and the future of education in Suwannee County made us about two hours late in leaving for Jacksonville. I was almost certainly more anxious about disappointing JoAnn than she was about my being late. She wasn't upset and, as I have learned over the years, she wanted to be supportive of my decisions and choices—which can sometimes be difficult when a lot of career choices are weighed in the balances. Fortunately, our visit was very pleasant and I felt accepted by JoAnn's extended family. I enjoyed meeting the Poston's and we had a really good time during our evening out.

By the time I returned to my Dad's home late that night, he was already asleep. The wear and tear of life after Mama was taking its toll on him.

When morning came, it wasn't long before we broke into the issue of my potential bid for public office. I wanted to know Daddy's thoughts, both the pros and cons, of running for school superintendent. Daddy had some insight into running a campaign, and being elected by the voters. About 14 years earlier, Daddy had been elected to the Board of County Commissioners. In a sense, he discouraged me from running but not in a negative way. He told me about the pressures you get from everyone who wants to influence your decisions to meet their own personal agendas, and how no matter what choices you make you also make enemies. Ultimately, Daddy told me to think about it carefully, long and hard, and if I decided to run then he would do everything he could to help me. He gave me a knowing grin and said that together we would beat their a**. I liked that humor in Daddy; he hadn't given up, even though he was lonely without Mama.

The holiday season offers more time to do more things than usual. Since we had the opportunity, JoAnn invited me to spend a couple of days with her parents and get to know them, and her brothers and their families. I appreciated how JoAnn was treating me and involving me in her life. Meeting her family was a good thing, but it was also broadening my responsibilities. I didn't know exactly how to cope with so many decisions and so much change. Trying to sort it all out, I spent a lot of time alone, thinking, pondering, evaluating what my new life with JoAnn would be like, and also weighing the pros and cons of running for public office. Just getting elected would be a miracle in and of itself. But after that, the real work would start because I would be faced head-on with the list of priorities I had enumerated to General Wadsworth, plus I knew from life's experiences that a whole other set of issues and problems would surface and challenge everything in me. Suddenly, I wasn't sure which idea was best. I was torn between my own desires and I was trying very hard to face reality—could I actually do it? If I could, was it really worth it?

PRAYER TIME

One afternoon, under the heavy burden of indecision, I drove down to Charles Springs on the Suwannee River. I needed to be alone, and I wanted to have a quiet place to think. I found a secluded spot on one of the huge rocks along the river's edge and sat down for some old-fashioned soul-searching that was covered with a lot of praying that I would make the right decisions. Whenever life has presented me with opportunities and big decisions, I have always relied on prayer for guidance. I was taught as a child, and it has carried throughout my life, that God answers prayers. It was always easy to believe in prayer, learning how to pray was a little harder; trusting that you have heard from God takes a lot more faith. But that's what faith is—trust.

After praying and pondering, then pondering and praying some more, I made a decision to run for office. I didn't *feel* like it was the right thing to do; I *knew* it was the right thing. Making such a lofty decision cannot be a half-hearted venture. Sure, I wanted to win the election once I made the decision. But I didn't just want to win it like it was a prize or something; I wanted the job because I felt in my heart I was seeking the office for all the right reasons. I had no other motive than to do the best job possible for the people of my home community.

I was raised in a big family, so I knew something about group dynamics. I had been committed to studies and never missed a single day of school in 12 years—that had to be worth something in public education. My dedication to our community, state, and country was evident in my service with the National Guard. Considering these things, I reasoned through all my motivations for why I should be superintendent of schools. First, I would lay aside political party affiliations and surround myself with the best and smartest people I could find and afford regardless of their political past. Second, I would operate the schools as a business and not as a political post. Third, I would retrace the issues as I had prioritized them to Mr. Wadsworth.

When I considered these things, I also wanted to reanalyze my strengths so that I could clearly and succinctly defend my position on all the issues that would have to be addressed. I felt my strengths were clearly tied to the things we would face; first and foremost, I was a hometown boy from a well-respected family. Second, I had no political baggage that I would bring into a campaign. Third, and something I considered one of the high points, I was well respected as an effective teacher. Last, but certainly not least, I was a product of the system and had earned the credentials to qualify me for the office. Adding to my strengths were the values taught to me by my parents: honesty, integrity, commitment, dedication, and loyalty. I had also learned from the military to have a positive attitude, and that would serve me well. I was convinced that all these things would give me the winning edge over any potential candidate I might face. If I were to run an unsuccessful bid for office, then I would have to chalk it up to the will of a power higher than me—but after so much prayer, I didn't believe that would happen.

GOING FOR IT

I was determined to be successful, and with Daddy's help and political skills, I felt a lot more comfortable. I met with Mr. Wadsworth again, briefly, and told him that I believed it was the right time for me to run for office. He wrote an article and publicly announced my intentions to seek the office of Superintendent of Schools. The story appeared in the *Suwannee Democrat* the first week of January 1968.

On New Year's Day, I had to go back to West Palm Beach to continue my teaching job and start the winter quarter of graduate school at FAU. On January 3rd, I notified Mr. Bill Hegstrom, the administrator to whom I reported at the Palm Beach District School Board, that I would be resigning from the project at the end of the quarter, which would be March 21st. I gave him the main reason for leaving my job, which was to return to my home county and seek the elective office of superintendent of schools. He didn't seem surprised that I was running for public office; I was probably more surprised that he wasn't surprised. Mr. Hegstrom and I continued to have a very good working relationship. We discussed the project and both of us were pleased with our success. Since I had already made my decision, I felt that it was only fair to give him as much notice as possible so he could select my replacement at his leisure. Whenever someone gives a long advanced notice of leaving a job, there is always an opportunity for tensions to build. Anxiety on both sides can sometimes cause difficulties, but our relationship remained good right on through my last day of work.

TEACHER STRIKE

During that particular winter quarter, tensions were building up state-wide among Florida teachers and there was a threat of a statewide teacher strike. I told Mr. Hegstrom that I wouldn't participate in a teacher walkout if there was, in fact, a strike. I do not believe in unions or negotiations with them; I believe that, as teachers, our first responsibility is to our students—and that means staying on the job even when you are not satisfied with the social or political climate.

As I feared, the tensions came to a climax and the leadership of the Florida Education Association (FEA), the state teacher's union, called for a statewide teacher walkout on February 19, 1968. That divided the teachers between those who walked out and those who didn't. The rift was worse than it would seem. On the surface, it was a work stoppage by some teachers versus about an equal number who kept teaching. Families were divided because in some cases there were husbands and wives who were both teachers and on opposite sides of the strike. Then there were brothers and sisters, children and parents, and the whole range of relatives and friends who shared mixed feelings on the walkout. It was a serious problem for every school district in Florida. I believe the core crisis lasted about two weeks, but the feelings and tensions lasted for several years in some cases. Both my teaching job and graduate school studies went about as smoothly as they could during the spring quarter, in spite of the teachers strike.

HOLD MY PLACE

About the same time as I tendered my notice to the school system that I would be leaving, I also informed my landlord that I planned to leave at the end of the quarter; again, I believed in being open and honest and letting those who were depending on me have as much advance knowledge of my circumstances as I could give them. I said that I wanted to come back and finish graduate school during the summer quarter. I guess my early warning, and I hope my business dealings, with Mrs. Clement were valuable to her. She offered to hold my room during the 2½ month's absence—and she did that at no charge to me.

The day after my FAU classes were over and my teaching duties ended, I returned to my Dad's house. That was March 22nd, and I immediately went to the Supervisor of Elections office and paid the qualifying fee to run for office. I can't recall how much the qualifying fee was, but I believe it was about $175. Since this was my own pursuit, and I wasn't taking any contributions, I was my own campaign manager. Normally, that's not the way political office is gained; but then, I wasn't running for the normal reasons. I believed I was pursuing a higher calling, not just trying to get ahead politically.

I went to a local printer and had about 4,000 pocketsize campaign cards embossed so that I could give one to everyone I spoke to as I asked for their vote. By this time, I had moved up in the automobile world from a 1965 VW bug to a used 1960 Ford, four-door sedan. The first evening of my campaign was spent with Daddy. We discussed our strategy on how to make the most contacts and how to divide the county geographically so as not to duplicate our efforts; there were six full weeks left before the May 7, 1968, Democratic Primary. Daddy suggested that the best thing to do was for us to make every effort to meet everybody personally; it didn't matter whether they voted or not, I wanted to let everyone in the county know I was serious about being superintendent. If I met and spoke to everyone, then that should speak volumes about my commitment to them.

MEET EVERYONE

We each, separately, rode door-to-door and spoke to everyone who would greet us. We met farmers in their fields, in their pigpens or barns, or where ever we could. I walked all the residential areas of the town of Branford, the communities of Wellborn, O'Brian, Dowling Park, Houston, and Suwannee Springs meeting all the homefolks.

People running for office can sometimes be a bother if they happen to show up at suppertime or whenever someone is really busy. I made it a campaign point to keep my comments short and sweet unless I was asked specific questions, then I would give my very best response— nothing designed to sway one person one way and then another answer to the same question that someone else might want to hear. I gave everyone an honest answer. Besides offering courteousness, I didn't want to be a nuisance so I was always cautious with everyone's time. I wanted to meet all the merchants in the county at their businesses, which I tried to do, and I always kept the interruption to a bare minimum necessary to ask for votes and let them know just how serious I was about being their school superintendent.

The campaign began to heat up after I got in the race. There were four people trying to get the job of superintendent: the incumbent, the high school principal, the elementary school principal, and me. My three opponents were all good men with excellent credentials for the job; all of them had a Masters Degree in Education Administration and Supervision, each one of them had several years of experience as a school administrator, and they all had the financial means for running an aggressive campaign. We all were making campaign speeches; some were, I believe, unrealistic and made only in hopes of getting elected. We all had good support backing our efforts, all of us campaigned hard, and each one of us was determined to win.

Although I was a product of the Suwannee County Schools and had been a teacher for the district, I wasn't employed by them at the time, which in a sense made me an outsider. But I was an outsider in a good way; I didn't have an interest in either holding my job in the district or getting a higher job in the district. My intent was to offer a different and better approach to running the school system. There was only one way I knew to achieve that goal and that was to work harder, longer, and make absolutely no campaign promises that were empty words. What I offered was honest, caring, leadership, and to prove it I operated on a shoestring budget and wouldn't accept campaign contributions; that way, I couldn't be perceived as a bought candidate. I spent less than $750 on my entire campaign; that included the qualifying fee—which was the bulk of my financial investment. I only bought campaign cards, newspaper advertisement, radio advertisement, and gasoline for me and my Dad to go around personally meeting as many people as I could—and I did it all at my own expense. Political campaigns can be expensive; but if candidates paid their own way, then there wouldn't be nearly as much corruption from political paybacks for campaign support, and the vote-seeking activities probably wouldn't be quite as mean-spirited. You can see a picture of my campaign cards in the back of the book—this one is from my re-election campaign.

By election time I had been Company Commander in the local National Guard unit for three years and had demonstrated my leadership abilities to the 125 soldiers in the unit, most of them lived and voted in Suwannee County. As with other vocations, most of the soldiers had wives who were eligible to vote, and all of them had other family members and friends they might influence in the election. I kept those facts in the forefront of all my dealings with military personnel and their families because military ethics don't allow the mixing of personal gain with politics. I never mentioned nor discussed politics while I was in uniform or on duty—that would have been a breach of trust on both the military and political fronts. However, since I was running for public office and was the company commander, I'm sure the soldiers discussed my political goals and ambitions among themselves; that would only have been natural. As citizens, I did discuss the local political issues with many of them and I asked for their vote and support, but I did that while not at the Armory, or in uniform, or on military duty. I was pleased to learn through discussions with civilian/soldiers that I had an extraordinary level of support from the National Guard community.

WHO TURNS OUT THE VOTERS

One of the biggest grass-roots support groups I had could not vote—my students. The sixth and seventh grade students I had taught in the Suwannee County schools were excited to know that I was running for superintendent. As I worked on the campaign trail, I met their parents, grandparents, and other family members and learned that my students had asked them to vote for me. I guess that was about the greatest feeling of all: knowing that my students believed in me and were so well pleased with my teaching that they asked their families to vote for me for superintendent. I had the trust of children; that was even more special than having the support of the military troops who were under my command. I have always believed that we should trust whomever children trust; they usually have a pretty good insight when it comes to picking out the good guys from the bad ones.

JoAnn and I continued to date throughout my six-week campaign for the office of superintendent of schools. It was probably somewhat unfair to her because it was like dating in a goldfish bowl. Our dates weren't the normal kind either because every Friday night we attended a political rally in a different community. The rallies were at church grounds (not in the churches), or at some private or public area where there was plenty of room for people to park and congregate. The local Democratic Party arranged the times and locations. The Party would serve as the master-of-ceremony and usually had a flatbed truck or some kind of platform for the candidates and there would be loud speakers and a microphone. Each group of candidates seeking the same office usually drew straws to determine the order in which they would speak. Most rallies gave each speaker five minutes to make his or her case to the crowd.

Those rallies were grand opportunities to meet prospective voters and solicit their support. Dad, being the better politician, attended all the rallies and he worked the crowds for me. He had a real gift for remembering the names and faces of people, even if he hadn't seen them for years. I guess that is a personal talent that could be developed, but I look at it as more of a gift that he had and something I didn't have. To this day, I'm still amazed at his uncanny ability to put names on faces.

The critical issues facing the school system were brought up at every campaign rally with each of my three opponents always providing their proposed solutions. I never offered a single solution to the district's problems in a campaign speech. I believed that making off-the-cuff assertions that any of us had the answers to the districts problems was just an empty shell game of trying to buy votes. Besides, if I made those promises I would, in effect, tie my hands to something that couldn't be done. What I offered at every rally was my commitment to hard work, honesty, and integrity. I may have sounded like a broken record at times because I stated and restated that I had no answers, but that I would carefully study each problem, seek a solution or solutions to that problem, and then actively and aggressively go about fixing the problem.

POLITICAL ONE-UPMANSHIP

Seasoned politicians look for ways to demean their opponents; it's a cheap tactic that has become well-entrenched in American politics, but sometimes it's effective. In my case, they chose youth and inexperience inferring that since I wasn't married with children I wasn't qualified to run the school system; it was a lame argument and the points were moot, but that was all they could come up with. Fortunately, their shameful and petty ruse was one of those ineffective ones because people knew me.

The final community campaign rally was held in Live Oak at the football stadium on Friday night before the election. I got the luck of the draw and pulled the longest straw, which gave me the opportunity to make some parting comments without my opponents having a chance to rebut anything I had to say. They all spoke and each one had their barbs for the others. I gave my standard comments and then spoke briefly off-the-cuff. I used my cute little, "Vote Right and Vote for Boatright." With this being the last stand before everyone cast their vote, I used my competitions arguments against me. I reiterated their statement that I wasn't married and had never raised a child. I looked over the crowd and gave a brief pause to let that sink in, and then I added that no doctor in our county had ever gone through labor, but they all knew how to deliver a baby. That seemed to really work in my favor; I could feel my opponents bristle as I got a big round of applause. The last few days before an election is the most critical part of any campaign. The last rally was a pretty good steam roller for me, but that was on Friday night and I had to leave on Saturday morning for National Guard annual training at Camp Blanding.

At Camp Blanding, my unit moved straight to the woods and set up bivouac because there wasn't enough barracks to house all the troops. My unit had to bivouac in the field the entire two weeks. On Monday, Lieutenant Colonel Howell, Battalion Commander, offered to let me go back to Live Oak after lunch on Tuesday for the vote tally that night. Prior to leaving for Summer Camp, I voted absentee and I encouraged the soldiers in my unit to do the same. I think most, if not all of them, cast absentee ballots.

There were about 30 voting precincts throughout the county, and all of them used paper ballots. Paper ballots required manual counts and then manual tallies. Once each precinct did the count and tally, the precinct's tally, ballots, and ballot boxes were taken to the Supervisor of Elections Office for final certification of the precinct totals. As the Supervisor on Elections certified the returns, they were sent about a block away and posted on a very large chalkboard that was attached to the wall of the *Suwannee Democrat*. Lights and loud speakers were set up, the street was closed off, and a festive, almost carnival, atmosphere surrounded the entire area.

THE TALLY

There was back slapping, back stabbing, and every candidate had their circle of supporters awaiting the final results. It was an anxious time because win or lose, this was it—the decision point was at hand. The anticipation and excitement was high, and so was my expectation to win. I didn't just want to win; I wanted to win by a big margin so that I could know the people were behind me, but with four candidates, the most likely scenario would be a run-off election between the two top vote getters if no one got a majority of the votes that were cast. As the first precincts results started to filter in, my vote count was ahead. The rural votes started to trickle in later that night and early in the morning hours. As those results were posted, it started to look like I might win without a runoff. But even after counting the votes cast during the normal election, we would still have to wait on the absentee votes to be counted the next day. I felt like I would get the advantage there because many of those absentee votes would be from my soldiers.

Sure enough, when the final votes were counted, I won by 62 percent of the vote and didn't have to face a runoff election in the second primary; even better, I didn't have any Republican opposition in the November 1968 general election. So, for me, the race was over and I had won. I was jubilant, but didn't have time to celebrate with my family or friends because I had to be back at Camp Blanding before breakfast to return to my military duty.

The National Guard annual training ended on May 19th about noon on Saturday. As soon as the equipment was cleaned up, stored, and secured, the unit was dismissed. The first thing I wanted to do was see JoAnn; we had arrangements to make for our wedding, which was to be June 1, 1968—the earliest possible day to be the mystical June Bride. It seemed like everything we did had to be reduced to fit into small amounts of time, just as concentrated milk or soups are condensed to take up less space. Not only were we getting married, I had to complete my last quarter of graduate school during the summer term. The only freedom I could see was that in the fall I had no known responsibilities, and I could use that time to prepare for assuming the office of superintendent and start establishing myself as a husband in my new life as a married man. But that kind of free time was not only elusive, it wasn't meant to be.

FAITH AND MARRIAGE

Faith is something we all have. And we all need a measure of faith. I had to have faith to step out and run for public office, and I had to have faith that I could be successful. I had learned to develop faith throughout my life, and when I earned a commission in the Guard that had taken a lot of faith. Getting married was a leap of faith as well. Now, I was facing faith from a different angle—religion. Love is not just looking at each other; it's looking in the same direction. JoAnn was a member of the Church of God; I was a member of the Southern Missionary Baptist Church. While these are both Christian and share a lot of common ground, some of the minor doctrines are different, but as with all Christian denominations, there usually isn't enough doctrinal difference to really matter. Since we were starting a new life together, it seemed that we should have a common doctrine—even though our faith was the same. It seemed good to us to begin our spiritual walk together in a new church, one where neither of us had an affiliation. We wanted to look in the same direction.

So, by agreement, we joined the First Presbyterian Church of Live Oak. We were married in the church so that made our House of Worship even more special to us. The pastor, Reverend Jim Walkup, performed the ceremony for us and Mr. and Mrs. Randy Wilkes were the only others in our wedding party—she was the bridesmaid and he was the best man. After our wedding, we had a reception in the fellowship hall that was hosted by the ladies of the church. We were welcomed as a couple and as members of our new church. You can see a picture of us on our wedding day in the back of the book—I'm the happy one with the big smile.

Once the formal wedding festivities were over, we had a short two-day honeymoon in Atlanta. During the spring, we had made some plans for our new life together; JoAnn bought us a home in Live Oak. We lived there for the first 10 years of our marriage, and that place still holds a lot of fond memories. When our all-too-short honeymoon was over, we came back to what was now our home. I only got to spend one night at home, and then I packed and went to West Palm Beach for my final quarter of graduate school.

BACK TO SCHOOL

Graduate school was very busy. There was the normal stress of studies, and the abnormal pressure of being newly married, recently elected to a public office that I would assume in a few months, and a growing military responsibility.

As I resumed graduate studies, once again I worked for Dr. Foley. When my professors learned that I had been elected as the school superintendent in Suwannee County some of them joked around about it. Most of my professors were excited for me and wanted to make sure my studies were successful, but not all my professors shared that same enthusiasm. The professor of Public School Finance told me that he would make sure that I didn't have straight As in graduate school; he lived up to his word in that regard. Even though, in his class, on my graduate research project, on each test in his class, and on all my class assignments, I made an A. When the final grades were posted, he didn't assign the grade I made, he lowered it to a B. But then, life isn't always about fairness. Sometimes we have to take unfair and even unethical treatment simply because those who have authority over us don't use wisdom or good judgment in their position over us. In the grand scheme of things, dealing with unfairness and injustice probably helps us to grow and mature; these things may even serve to help us be more conscientious in our business with others. This lone professor could have advanced his own cause more if he had heeded the Oriental proverb about acknowledging the merit of other people in order to let your own merit be known—he only damaged and diminished his own reputation by such foolish and arrogant actions.

The College of Education was adamant that each graduate participate in the graduation ceremony. I didn't want to go through the ceremony; I had earned my degree and that was what I had gone to school to do. As required, I paid my fees to rent the cap and gown, but on the last day of class I decided to forgo any further delay in returning home; I had met all the requirements for my degree so I simply left. A few weeks later, my diploma and transcripts arrived in the mail, but my grades were sent the week following graduation. That was when I learned that I hadn't made all As in graduate school. The lone professor exercised his ill will and reduced the grade I had earned, which was an A, to a B. I didn't appreciate it, but then I looked at all the things that were going right in my life and shrugged it off with a "so what?" After all, I had my degree and all he controlled was a single letter grade, a simple symbol, not of my success but more so of his inept or poor attitude. Whatever his personal problems were that made him behave so unreasonably, he still didn't change anything in my life or probably in anyone else's life where he exercised the same actions.

FACE THE FUTURE

With graduate school behind me, and JoAnn beside me in our new home, we began to plan our future lives together; we took a careful and deliberate approach to our strategy. JoAnn continued her job as the County Extension Home Economics Agent. One of our first projects together was to remodel our home. The kitchen was of the late 1940s vintage and needed an upgrade. We put in a central heating and air conditioning system, installed carpet, and repainted the house inside and out. I wanted a sprinkler system in the yard. As with all big home improvement projects, we did them, but they weren't done overnight. We planned together and did them as time and resources allowed. I guess the best thing about our remodeling was the joint effort in planning, having a plan and then following it seems to be a good way to get things done—planning adds structure, something we all need.

It was still about five months before I would take office. Mr. Henry Folsom, the incumbent superintendent whom I had defeated in the primary, was kind enough to recommend, and the school board approved, me to be employed as Assistant Superintendent beginning in August 1968, and continuing until I took the oath of office as Superintendent on January 7, 1969. That was a good gesture on his part; commonly, incumbents who have lost an election use their remaining power to subvert their successor. Sometimes they do that out of spite and sometimes it is for future political gain. Mr. Folsom was gracious in his defeat, even though when I had asked him for a leave of absence to pursue graduate studies he was less than supportive. However, after the election, he took a more tactful approach.

I was grateful to Mr. Folsom and to the school board for providing me the time to learn more of the details of the system and to better prepare for taking office. To his credit, Mr. Folsom wanted me to get involved in making many of the difficult decisions facing the opening of the schools in August 1968, and the challenges we would have throughout the fall semester. I discussed the issues with Mr. Folsom and respected his position because he was still the duly elected chief school officer in Suwannee County; I never privately or publicly assumed the senior leadership role or took responsibility for the decisions he made. I knew from experience and from Daddy's advice that sometimes when things go wrong, the next person in line could be used as the fall-guy if any decisions he may have made were the wrong ones. I didn't want or need that; I was going to have plenty of opportunities to make my own decisions and mistakes after I officially took the office.

SUPERINTENDENT

Lord, grant that I may always desire more than I can accomplish. Michelangelo.

W HEN I WAS ELECTED superintendent, 49 of the 67 counties in Florida held a public vote to select their chief school officer; 18 were appointed by the local school board. Since I was elected in May of 1968 but had to wait until January 7, 1969, to take the Oath of Office, I had a long time to prepare for the challenges ahead. And since Superintendent Folsom and the Board approved my employment as assistant superintendent during the fall and prior to my taking office, I had the opportunity to be involved and gain an in-depth understanding of the struggles and complex issues I was going to face head-on.

PREPARATION

During the years, and more especially in the fall, before I took office, Superintendent Folsom and the school board had struggled with several issues. Throughout that fall, and in my first year as superintendent, I became acutely aware of the two immediate issues pressing against the school system. First, there was a lot of deep-rooted unrest within the teacher ranks because of the strike in March of 1968; the intensely held feelings in both camps just wouldn't let go. Second, we, like all other schools, were under an ever-increasing federal pressure to fully integrate. As the newly hired assistant superintendent, and soon to be superintendent, I was involved in the discussions of how the board was dealing with these two issues.

THE STRIKE

On February 19, 1968, when the statewide teacher strike began, I was teaching in the Palm Beach County school system. But I chose not to walkout and join the striking teachers. I always considered myself to be a professional person and didn't need the union to act or negotiate on my behalf. I felt strongly that walking out only hurt the children and did nothing of any real consequence to the state or the school district—at least such actions did nothing that I considered to be a positive influence.

I wasn't in Suwannee County during the walkout, so I didn't have any firsthand knowledge, other than conversations with friends and family, about the strike and its influence locally. However, I did read the school board minutes and learned there were 66 classroom teachers and three school principals that walked away from their jobs and joined the strike. While it wasn't noted in the minutes, a heavy blanket of discord smothered school faculties, the community, and families because of the strike. The statewide teacher walkout was the result of a promotion by the Florida Education Association (FEA) to protest the working conditions and inadequate state funding for schools. It wasn't as if the conditions and funding were unknown or unrecognized; they were. Moreover, the strike only caused further agony around the state without providing any real measure of relief. So ultimately, we only got heartache on top of dissatisfaction.

As the strike neared its end, teachers who had walked out were asking for reinstatement to their teaching positions. On March 22, 1968, the School Board voted to honor the requests of striking teachers who had not already returned to work, but only on the recommendations of principals. As a condition of their return, the teachers would be reinstated to their contract and granted personal leave without pay for their absence. Sixty-five teachers returned with full contract reinstatement; the lone holdout was granted a leave of absence for the remainder of the year and then allowed to return to duty. For the returning teachers, their strike had only lasted four weeks; they lost pay for that amount of time and didn't get anything comparable to a *quid pro quo*. It was a futile effort, in my opinion.

Even though the conflict between the school board and the teachers had been resolved for the most part before my election, high tensions continued to linger. All during my campaigning and throughout the election period, the teacher walkout had left a spillover effect that permeated everything in the school system. The teachers at every school were in a nerve-racking environment. There were strained personal feelings, professional working relationships were damaged, and faculty meetings were always nail-biting in the aftermath of that very divisive event.

Two of the three school principals that had walked out during the strike had been candidates for school superintendent. Many of the best teachers in the county had walked out during the strike and generally they had supported one of those two principals as their candidate for superintendent. Times were difficult. The strike left everyone edgy, the incumbent superintendent was preparing to leave office after losing his bid for reelection; two principals who wanted to be superintendent were now working for a 28-year-old assistant superintendent who would soon be the chief school officer and just happened to be the victor over them in a landslide election.

As the assistant superintendent, and later as superintendent, I got firsthand experience into the long-term strained feelings whenever I dealt with some of the teachers that had walked out in the strike. Working with the principals who lost the election wasn't exactly a bed of roses either. But then, every job has its challenges. An ancient Chinese saying reminds us that a gem cannot be polished without friction, nor man perfected without trials. And if we don't want to deal with problems, we shouldn't seek or tackle the big jobs.

DESEGREGATE

In April 1968, a report was given to the school board addressing racial segregation in the Suwannee County schools. The report was prepared by a Technical Assistance Committee from the State Department of Education and stated that O'Brien School (all colored) was too small and should be closed. The committee also recommended that half of the Douglass faculty should be white. In August 1968, Superintendent Folsom presented a list of teachers recommended for transfer to Live Oak Elementary, Suwannee Junior High, and Suwannee Senior High from Douglass School (a colored school for grades one through 12); Superintendent Folsom also gave a list of teachers in the various Live Oak Schools who, upon board approval, were to transfer to Douglass School.

Each teacher scheduled for transfer to another school was given the opportunity to meet with the board and offer a reason to oppose the proposed move. I personally talked with many of the teachers about their transfer, and while most weren't eager to move, most accepted their transfer as a professional decision that made the best use of everyone's talents and skills for the good of the school district. Some teachers offered reasonable justification for exemption from the proposed transfer and the board, to their benefit, accommodated the teachers; for all others, the new classroom assignments began in the fall of 1968.

On December 3, 1968, about a month before I took office, I was asked to speak about my thoughts and plans at the school board meeting regarding school desegregation. Superintendent Folsom and the board had delayed, hesitated, and stalled for months; they didn't want to make the decision to integrate schools. But as painful as it was, decision time had arrived and there was no sidestepping it. The school board members were all present, though I feel certain none of them wanted to be in that particular meeting. The members were L.

C. Davis, Jr., Chairman; L. H. Gill; Eustace Collins; Dr. Clyde Bass; and L. M. Crews, Jr. As the meeting got underway, a lengthy discussion evolved about school desegregation and a required response on the matter by the School Board to the Federal Office of Health, Education, and Welfare. This was a politically and socially sensitive issue that I was going to inherit from the departing superintendent. Since I would have to implement any plans and deal with all the consequences, I was asked to give the board my ideas. I knew at this point I was preparing for the proverbial *baptism by fire*; I was going to be engulfed in the fiery blazes of racial turmoil—both sides of it.

I made it clear from the start that I would recommend that all schools in the county be fully integrated when the next school term began, which was August 1969. I explained to the board that it was inevitable and that we were facing total integration one way or the other—voluntary, or by force. I explained that we needed to develop a desegregation plan we could live with, and implement in a timely and fair manner. I pointed out that we, as a community, would best be served to avoid even the appearance of further delay or any procrastination in meeting the changing social order of integration. I noted that we wouldn't want to be placed under a court order, which would take all desegregation decisions out of our hands and put every choice into the lap of a federal judge in Jacksonville. My final reasoning was that I thought we, the superintendent and board, could do a far better job of managing the desegregation issue than any federal judge—after all, it was our community and since we lived together, we should work together as a community for our own common good.

When I closed my remarks, the room became chillingly quiet. Mr. Collins, the longest serving member of the board, I think he had been a member for about 20 years, leaned way back in his chair and looked at me straight and hard. It felt like he was trying to drill right through me. Mr. Collins was the most conservative member on the board and many of the colored people in our area thought he was a racist. Perhaps he was; but then, maybe not. He did possess insight. As the quiet became deafening, I wasn't entirely prepared for his response, "Son I don't like what you are saying but I think you are right." He was honest to say he didn't like what I said; he was shrewd to agree. After a few rustles and mumbles, Mr. Davis made the motion to fully integrate the schools in all grades when school started again the following August.

I'm not sure who seconded the motion, but as discussion was called for, I spoke up once more and acknowledged that how the members voted was their business. I told the board that my personal hope was that they would be unanimous in their vote to integrate or be unanimous in their vote not to integrate. I told them I felt one of the worse things that could happen at this critical stage was to split the board and have divided factions; at least a unanimous vote would keep the board working together through this explosive and divisive issue. The question was called and the vote was unanimous to totally desegregate all grades when school started back at the beginning of the following school term. When I asked for a unanimous vote, I had a pretty good idea that the motion to desegregate would carry since it was moved and seconded. What I hoped to accomplish was uniting everyone behind the vote and avoid the unnecessary friction of a divided board, especially on such a critical issue. Fortunately, we passed that test.

I worked with Mr. Folsom and Mr. Leroy Bowden, the Supervisor of Instruction, to finalize the district's integration plan we would submit to the Atlanta regional office of the United States Department of Health, Education, and Welfare. It was a demanding and tedious effort to flesh out, and it considered far more than just racial integration; it was a plan for harmony within our entire community. Our plan was approved and integration of faculty, staff, facilities, transportation, and students was accomplished at the beginning of the 1969-70 school year. The last segregated class to graduate Douglass High School was in May 1969.

DUMP TRUCKS

On November 30, 1968, the National Guard reorganized my unit into the 269th Engineer Company (Dump Truck). The unit was authorized to have 42 five-ton dump trucks but we actually only had about 22 trucks that were available. Reorganization of a military unit takes an enormous amount of time and energy to transfer out all the equipment unique to a particular type unit and its mission, and to receive all the equipment matching the new type unit and its mission.

The equipment and materials transfer is not nearly as difficult as the retraining of soldiers for new military occupational specialties (MOS), or their new military jobs. Except for the administrative, supply and mess personnel, all other soldiers had to be reassigned and retrained in their new military jobs. Based on the types of military equipment assigned, and the complexity of the military unit and its mission, reassignment can be one of the most demanding and intense actions any military unit will face. But for a change, commanding the Engineer Company was the easiest command I ever had; I can attribute the relative ease of command to having one basic type of equipment, the five-ton dump truck, and the mission was simply hauling rock, sand, gravel, and asphalt. In view of the fact that I was about to assume the role of chief school officer for Suwannee County, having the work and stress load reduced for my Guard duties was a real blessing.

THE OATH

At the December 21, 1968, board meeting, Superintendent Folsom was assigned to the Vocational Agriculture Department at Suwannee High School beginning January 8, 1969, which was the day after I was to take over as superintendent.

The big day finally came; it had been a long time since that early talk with Mr. Wadsworth and the grueling intensity of the campaign. It seemed like a dream, but it also seemed right as I took the Oath of Office as Superintendent of Schools on January 7, 1969. The school district had an annual budget of over $3 million, and I had an annual salary of $14,500. At that time the school system had 4,473 students in grades one through 12; there was no kindergarten in our school system back then. There was 238 professional staff, including teachers and administrators. The salary for a beginning teacher with a four-year degree was $6,000, which was roughly $115 per week for the year.

I was 28 years old, which was young by most standards for the position of authority that I held. Now, I was challenged with bringing order to the school system where a long-established tolerance for mediocrity had reigned alongside of the unwillingness to tackle some of the hard problems that were bearing down on the district. On the same day I was sworn into office, the school board was reorganized and Dr. Clyde Bass was appointed chairman; the other members were L. C. Davis, E. A. Collins, Claude McMillan, and Alvin Brown. Mr. Alfred Airth was the school board attorney. The school board met twice a month: the first Tuesday after the first Monday in each month, and on the third Saturday; our regularly scheduled meetings were at 9:00 a.m. We kept that schedule for a while, but then dropped the Saturday morning meeting and held one regular board meeting a month. One meeting a month was more than sufficient to cover the board's duties for the school system.

School boards hire attorneys for legal advice; that's a good thing. The Suwannee County School Board had employed Mr. Airth for a long time. He was one of the more prominent lawyers in town and was an older gentleman who was well established in the community. Since I was the new superintendent, I wanted to make a few changes immediately. Replacing Mr. Airth was one of the changes I wanted; however, the board employs the attorney and not the superintendent. The board has sole authority to choose and hire their legal counselor. The reason I didn't want Mr. Airth was that I had watched him perform in our board meetings. To me, he appeared to give a lot more personal advice than legal guidance. He seemed to be pushing his personal preferences about how the board should act on the different issues they faced, and not providing pure legal advice only when asked—which his job was supposed to do: give an opinion on request. At the reorganization meeting the day I took office, I asked the board to terminate the services of Mr. Airth and I recommended Mr. Arthur Lawrence as his replacement. The school board unanimously approved my recommendation; I think that was a good show of support and solidarity. I recommended Mr. Lawrence solely on my belief that he would serve us better than any other attorney would. He did what we expected and attended all meetings and gave counsel only when he was asked. Mr. Lawrence and I, over time, expanded our professional relationship into a personal friendship.

After being in office less than two weeks, I became the recipient of legal action by both the White Citizens Council, and the local chapter of the National Association for the Advancement of Colored People (NAACP). One suit was brought because I supported integration and immediate desegregation; the other was because I was not allowing the NAACP to be a partner in the who, how, and process of integration. I was elected to do that job along with all other administrative functions of the school district; the NAACP was not an elected body chosen by the voters to make those decisions. I was willing to listen to them as well as the White Citizens Council, I even sought their advice, but I was not going to be tied or confined to anyone's timetable for hiring new or placing existing colored teachers where the local groups requested. I was trying to serve all the children in the county without mistreating anyone, and at the same time I was being sued by those whom I was trying to protect and serve—it was a thankless job to say the least.

As soon as my reign at the helm of the school system began, I started to address the critical issues facing the school board. These issues, as I saw them, were never published but I discussed each of them privately with the board members. Once the board and I had an understanding of the critical issues, I systematically set out to address them publicly. As the first order of business, I called the staff together and said that politics was over, operating Suwannee County schools was the largest business in the county, and we should run it like a business. I was well aware that no one in my lifetime had served more than two consecutive terms as superintendent and my chances of doing so were no better than any of my predecessors. Being a product of the school system, I understood the thinking of the community and what it would take to move the school system forward. My hearts' desire was to see the system operate based on superior standards and values, impeccable morals, and the highest principles.

Our Finance Officer, Mr. Bill Airth (the brother of the former board attorney), had previously owned an accounting firm in town. Since I was now the accountable party, I regularly asked, "How are we doing financially?" His standard reply was, "You have so many other problems to deal with, you take care of those and I'll take care of the finances." That seemed reasonable to me, knowing the considerable amount of experience he had. I thought that he was good at his job and served the school system well—I was wrong in that assumption.

One day, in late March or early April of 1969, I repeated my question to Mr. Airth about our finances; he said he needed to talk with me. The way he said it raised a flag and I immediately said, "Okay. Let's talk now." We went into my office, behind closed doors, and he said the school district was over $159,000 in the red. Our total operating and capital budget was just over $3 million; that deficit represented a very large chunk of cash relative to our budget, especially since the vast majority of our total budget was tied to salaries and other similar expenditures that left no wiggle room for other expenses. I asked him why he didn't tell me about the deficit earlier, and his reply was that I had too many other major issues to have to worry about this. To him, that probably seemed like a good reply. But to me, I was very disappointed and upset that I hadn't been told earlier about the financial problem. I curtly advised Mr. Airth that bad news doesn't get any better with time. During that meeting, I told Mr. Airth I would assume the finance officers responsibility and work out a solution to solve our fiscal problem. I told him that I had lost confidence in him and he had until June 30th to find himself a different job as he would no longer be employed by the school system after the fiscal year ended.

MONEY MANAGEMENT

Somehow, I found the time to immerse myself in the budget for the next three weeks. I had to learn every detail I possibly could about the district finances. I also made an appointment to discuss my financial dilemma with the Commissioner of Education and a couple of his key finance people; I urgently wanted their advice regarding my options and alternatives. The Commissioner and his staff were extremely helpful; they explained ways to transfer money between discretionary accounts and other accounts, and they suggested ways for tightening our belts to ease the economic stress. Their suggestions were solid in their logic and covered small things, much of it simple, which added up to make the deficit go away. Their ideas included things such as using retread tires on the back of the school bus, reducing or eliminating field trips, and only purchasing the absolute essential items we had to have to keep the school system functioning. Fortunately, the school system ended the year in the black. We had no reserve or contingency fund, but all debts were paid. In the wake of that fiasco, I informed the board that my intentions were that we would never have to borrow money again, short of an unforeseeable emergency. I added that if we couldn't manage the public business and live within our means, neither of us deserved to be in public office. The board agreed and we never borrowed money again.

In April, after being deeply absorbed in the budget woes of the district, I asked some of the school principals about their bookkeeper's qualifications, and if they thought their bookkeeper had the knowledge, skills, and abilities to perform the duties as District Finance Officer. I called a couple of the people suggested as possibilities to come by my office to talk about the job. After talking with everyone, I felt Mrs. Madelyn Baucom, bookkeeper at Suwannee High School, could do the job. She had a lot of experience, but didn't have a college degree. I didn't care, what I needed was someone who was honest, ethical, had a positive attitude, and would work hard. She said she was committed to those things and I told her she would need to organize the office in such a way as to maintain an audit trail, have solid checks and balances, and build a school district finance department that would be recognized as one of the best in the state. I offered for Mrs. Baucom to take a college class in Public School Finance at the University of Florida in the summer; she did. Mrs. Baucom did an outstanding job as a finance officer; thanks to her help, I never again had to worry about where we stood, financially, as a school district.

Soon after Mrs. Baucom became the finance officer, she broke her leg. The timing couldn't have been worse for her, it was the end of a school budget year, but she worked every day. During the June, July, and August time period is when school districts are required to complete the annual financial reports for the prior year, and develop the operating and capital budget for the following year. Mrs. Baucom was a real trouper, she worked through discomfort and pain; there aren't very many people who have that kind of dedication.

BUILDING BUDGET STRENGTH AND OWNERSHIP

During mid-spring of my first semester as superintendent, I asked the strategic administrators to select a week during the summer when everyone would be available to meet at the Suwannee High School library to collectively develop the entire district budget for the following year. Involving everyone worked like a charm because then all the major staff members knew about every line item in the school district budget and why things were or were not in our financial plan. By having the principals involved, when the community or school staff would fuss about something in (or not in) the budget, the principal's knew the facts and shared some ownership for the budget's development and priorities. That budget building process worked well for me and I used it every year I was in office.

Shortly after becoming my finance officer, a frustrated Mrs. Baucom told me that purchasing throughout the district was out of control. She said that school principals, coaches, maintenance staff, transportation workers, and others were buying things at-will, signing a sales receipt, and charging things to the school district. That was disturbing news, but something we could fix in short order—even though it had been a longstanding practice in the school district.

We had staff meetings every Thursday afternoon at 4:00 p.m. After Mrs. Baucom broke the bitter news of our purchasing practices, I used the next staff meeting to change those bad procedures to sound business practices. As my first order of business, I informed the staff that all purchasing would be done using an authorized, serial-numbered purchase order signed by the finance director or myself; I followed up with a memo restating the district policy and noting there would be no exceptions to this rule. I sent a letter to every vendor we had on file and reiterated the policy and let them know that the school district would not pay for any items purchased without an authorized purchase order signed by the finance director or me. There were some anxious vendors and school employees ensnared by the policy, but it was a sound business practice and it worked. It didn't take long to get our spending practices under control once the policy was in place, understood, and rigorously adhered to.

As with all policies that require several people to cooperate, there will always be those who buck the system—especially if the policymaker is new and the old standards have beneficially served the longstanding staff. One principal, in particular, didn't like the new purchasing system. He continued making purchases just like he always had, signed the bill, and sent it to the district office for payment. The first time it happened I tried to be lenient, so I paid the bill and gave the principal a stern warning and reminded him that our policy had changed and his freelance purchasing had to stop. It wasn't long before he did the same thing again, still trying to give him the easy way out I paid that bill and said that I wouldn't assume responsibility for his inability to follow directions and the next debt he incurred without a purchase order, would be his to pay.

Sometimes the best lessons are the expensive ones. Within two weeks, the rebellious principal made a purchase for almost $400 and sent the bill for the district to pay. In keeping with my word, I refused to authorize payment. I called the principal and told him that what he had bought was not a school district purchase, it was now his personal acquisition and he had to arrange for payment, not from the school internal account or any other public account, but from his personal resources. After talking to the principal, I called the vendor and told him that he was partially responsible because he continued to sell items to a school district employee without a valid purchase order in violation of the instructions I had given both the employee and the vendor. The principal paid the bill; the vendor found the fortitude to comply with our purchase order system, and the problem of random, unauthorized purchases ended.

Schools and the various district offices operated slightly differently in their purchasing practices. The maintenance and transportation departments needed a modified system where they could get some items that were too small for individual purchase orders or the immediate nature of their needs were such that the time required to get a purchase order worked a hardship on the functioning of the department. For maintenance and transportation, I authorized blanket purchase orders for each vendor for $1,000; when the department reached the purchase order limits it was paid and a new purchase order issued.

We gained better oversight into the financial practices and reduced waste to an almost nonexistent state through this system of managing expenditures.

It was neither easy nor fun changing the lax practices from the loose or at-will buying to a systemwide process with built in controls. Making some individuals pay for their own indiscretions helped to give everyone incentive to abide by the policy. Sometimes even grownups are childlike in their behavior and learning a lesson the hard way is the only cure for their deviant activities. Over time, using sound financial practices and management, the financial condition of the school system improved. By the time I left office, the school district had constructed over $5 million in facilities, and had over $300,000 in reserve for contingencies. Throughout my remaining time as superintendent, I never had to worry about financial accountability and controls again; I think letting staff be responsible for their own actions that conflicted with a clear policy helped to bring about that accountability. As for Mrs. Baucom, she served me very well as finance officer; her expertise was so good that she continued to serve as finance officer with the school district through the tenure of several school superintendent's after I moved on. She stayed there until she chose to retire—I think that speaks highly of her ability to do the job and her willingness to work with everyone.

DIFFICULT CHOICES

There were times when I had to make politically and/or socially offensive recommendations to the school board on the delicate issue of school integration. When I did, people from both camps would line up down the hall of the courthouse waiting to tell me what a "Sorry S-O-B" I was. I never took the insults personally; I felt for both groups who were using me as the lightening rod to vent their genuine frustrations. But even though I could understand their points of view, my focus and responsibility had to be to improve the overall school system for both the near and long term.

One really sensitive and volatile case in point was when I recommended that the Douglass School, which was a colored school housing grades one through 12, become an integrated middle school for grades six through eight. I could sense, and agreed with, much of the public's concern. The Douglass School facility was constructed during 1952 and 1953. During the early 1950s a lot of colored schools were built throughout the South to avoid integration. Most of the buildings were inferior and to make matters worse they were poorly maintained; the Douglass facility was no exception.

The design of the school was a finger-type; it had a central walkway and extending out on either side were the classroom wings, a library, and the cafeteria. The buildings were porous cinderblock that would only slow down the cold winter wind. The classroom floors, in the older part of the building, were plain unsealed concrete. Each classroom had four globe lights, one wall plug, and no air-conditioning—which made the hot months of school more insufferable than the cold months.

Douglass was located in the southwest part of town on the edge of the colored community. The restrooms were the biggest single problem; they were all gang toilets with unsealed concrete floors. The restrooms were poorly made to begin with and spiraled downward from lack of repair; the unsealed concrete area around the urinals were saturated because of poor aiming, and just walking by or into any one of the restrooms was stomach-turning because of the odor. As if the sanitation, heat, and cold weren't bad enough, the school was painted John Deere green and trimmed in flamingo pink, which made it an eye sore to the community and an embarrassment to the students.

The Douglass School was a significant obstacle to overcome. I gave a lot of study as to how we could use the school as a part of our integration plan; we needed to do that for the community's sake. After a lot of soul searching, I recommended five things to make Douglass more acceptable to the general public. First, I recommended that we build a new administrative office on the south end of the building; second, I proposed to construct a new driveway for parent drop-off and pick-up on the south end of the building; third, I said we could erect a six-foot chain-link fence around the entire property to increase security for the students as well as to protect the property; fourth, I recommended that we repaint the entire school, inside and out, with pastel colors; and fifth, I said we should completely renovate the restrooms, replace all the plumbing and fixtures, install tile on the walls, and make the floors impervious. The board approved all my recommendations, and that was a big step toward making our facilities equitable and getting the most out of what we already had. A few years later, individual air-conditioning units were installed in the classrooms and central units were put in the dining and administration areas.

A lot of attention was focused on Douglass. Time was critical, and not necessarily our ally as we hurried to get it ready for the opening of the new school year. From the time school was out in May until classes started back in August, most all the upgrades we planned were completed; however, we did have to start the school year with a few of the projects still under way, but that didn't keep us from opening the school on time.

When schools opened in August we had two new schools, Suwannee High School and Branford High School, that were still undergoing some construction but parts of both schools were useable. The school board had two directors of maintenance; both made good salaries. After I observed their work for a few months, I came to the conclusion that neither did very much work; each of them talked as if he stayed busy all the time, but, in reality, neither produced anything with measurable results. During one of my frequent visits to the construction site at Suwannee High School, I met the site manager for the subcontractor for the electrical and mechanical systems, Mr. Laurie "Pop" Duval. I watched Mr. Duval work and organize things around the construction site; he was good at his craft.

I did some investigating and learned that he had family connections in Suwannee County; his wife, the former Sandra Willis, had been a year ahead of me when we were students. One day as I finished my walking inspection of the progress, I asked Mr. Duval to stop by my office some afternoon for a chat. A few days later he called and came by, just like I had asked him to do. I told Mr. Duval about my concerns for both the maintenance and preventative maintenance of all the school facilities in the county. As we talked, I learned he had been an industrial arts teacher in Bay County.

The priorities that I detailed to Mr. Wadsworth when he asked me to consider running for superintendent were still crystal clear; one of them was to get the very best staff I could hire. Mr. Duval certainly seemed to fit that mold—if I could get him. He had the technical skills, and from my observations of his work, I felt he also had the talent for leadership, organizational skills, and a good management approach to help solve many of the regular building maintenance and preventative maintenance problems that we had. I asked him if he would consider working as the Director of Maintenance for the school system. He said the construction job at the high school was coming to an end and he would consider it. I suggested that we verbally agree to his employment for one year, subject to the approval of the school board; after one year either party could sever the work relationship without stating a cause and without prejudice. He agreed.

I offered him a decent salary, which was higher than either of the two current supervisors, but far less that the combined salaries of the two. I told the board I preferred to have one well qualified maintenance supervisor that could manage people, organize the department, handle the day-to-day operations, and improve the department than to have the current two supervisors who weren't nearly as effective as they should be.

The school board initially expressed concern about Mr. Duval's salary, but after realizing that we would actually save money when the other two left at the end of June, they unanimously approved his employment and Mr. Duval started to work July 1, 1969. Pop Duval worked long and hard to improve every aspect of the maintenance operations. His efforts soon became visible, not only to the people working in the school system and to the general public, but also to the school board who suggested his salary be raised at the end of his first year.

Pop was a huge asset to me and the school system. He was a team player, and very dependable. Mr. Duval was also extremely conscientious; as employees under his supervision left for other career opportunities, he used the new vacancies to surround himself with staff that were more technically skilled, competent, and who had a positive attitude. His philosophy regarding the number of employees in his department was the same as mine, it was better to have fewer competent skilled workers than to have more who were not skilled or competent. I was committed to the long-term improvement of the quality of the maintenance department and to saving the tax payers dollars. My successors all kept Mr. Duval because of his hard work, loyalty, and commitment to the Suwannee County schools; he worked for the system about 30 years before retiring from the job for which he was hired. As with Mrs. Baucom, Mr. Duval made a life-long career out of serving Suwannee County schools; I made those two outstanding choices on behalf of the people I was elected to serve. And I am proud to have done that.

HOME LIFE

During 1969, JoAnn continued to work as a Suwannee County Home Extension Agent. We focused a lot of our time and energy on our home. We were busy coordinating the remodeling of our kitchen, installing air-conditioning, painting the whole inside and the exterior trim, and we installed carpet. Our remodeling project lasted for several months. JoAnn and I lived in and around the mess of remodeling for all that time. But that was a part of our plan for bigger and better things. By living in the midst of our changes and seeing the slow but steady progress, we were building our relationship just as much as we were building our house—that's what makes a house a home.

Like most young couples, we wanted to start a family. We hoped that JoAnn could quit work and be a stay-at-home mom. Wisdom and fiscal prudence told us that we should complete our home improvements before she resigned from her good-paying job to be a homebody.

Sometimes a small town has its drawbacks. One of our biggest nuisances was that everyone knew our business—but that's a normal and natural part of rural life and when you are a public figure everything is magnified.

JoAnn and I both had good jobs that paid us well. We weren't rich by any stretch of the imagination, but relatively speaking we were better off than most. Wherever there is jealousy, envy and resentment won't be far behind. There was a small undercurrent of bitterness that flowed through our community; it was kept alive by a group of unpleasant people who resented that both JoAnn and I had public jobs with decent salaries. There were those who felt that she should not work since I had a good job, and some of these ill-discerning citizens were brash enough to tell JoAnn their cynical thoughts. That always brought a prick to her heart because she liked people and wanted to help as a public servant.

Even though those things stung, we endured most of that kind of abrasiveness with a grain of salt. And when JoAnn chose to quit working to raise a family, those sentiments were not a part of our decision—though some probably thought it was. Both of us were involved in a lot of community and civic clubs and organizations. I was a member of the Rotary Club, which met at noon, and I was in the Lions Club, which met at night. Adding to our social calendar, we were increasingly involved in the activities of our church. Our lives were lived out in the public eye because we were high-profile people within the district; it continued to be as if we were on display for the whole community to watch our every move.

BETTER STAFF

I unrelentingly lived up to my promise of getting the best staff possible. After being in office about a year, I recommended replacing the General Supervisor with Mr. Marvin Johns; and I created the new title of Director of Instruction. Mr. Johns had been a teacher in the county for many years; he was an excellent teacher. In fact, Mr. Johns was the state's *Star Teacher* one year.

While some wouldn't believe that politics didn't play a part in my staff selections, it was nonetheless true. One of the promises I made to myself was that politics would not enter in to any decisions I made if I were elected school superintendent. My commitment to that goal never changed. While I never asked, I was certain that both Mr. Johns and Mrs. Baucom had supported one of my opponents in the election, their former high school principal. I believed then and still do, that was their choice; frankly, I didn't care.

For me, the election and politics were laid aside until the next voting season, and my goal was to find the best people available for each management-level job and then have them become an integral part of the district leadership team. I wanted staff who were not "yes" people; I wanted a staff that would assume responsibility for their actions, and exercise leadership skills.

With time, Mr. Johns became the confidant I turned to most often for brainstorming sessions; he was good at what-if scenarios and always provided helpful and constructive feedback. One of the best things about him was that he didn't always tell me what I wanted to hear, but he always told me what I needed to hear. He had my ear more than any other person did, and I can't recall ever receiving any bad advice from him.

Mr. Johns' primary responsibility was curriculum, but because he was such a good asset, he also helped Ms. Baucom in the budget building process each summer. On the downside for him, Mr. Johns was the lightning rod for many of the hard decisions that we made in the curriculum area. He and Mrs. Baucom were so unpopular at times that my successor said both of them would be dismissed if she were elected superintendent. However, Mrs. Bass, my successor, didn't follow through with her threat to fire them once she had the personal opportunity to learn their true value to the school district.

Mr. Johns was highly competent, and he worked just about all the time; he developed a plan in 1973 to achieve full accreditation of all schools in the district by 1976. It was a well-conceived and aggressive plan for accreditation. Mr. Johns was the driving force and provided organizational and leadership skills that led to the full accreditation of all schools in the district by the Southern Association of Colleges and Schools (SACS) in the summer of 1976—just as he planned and on schedule. When I took office as superintendent, there was not a single accredited school in the district; when I left office, every school was accredited. Accreditation was due in part to the loyalty of Mr. Johns and Ms. Baucom. They were valuable staff and I believed they would be loyal to any superintendent that would give them a chance; they were committed to the schools, not just an individual. Mr. Johns, like Mrs. Baucom and Pop Duval, stayed with the school system and retired from the position for which he was hired.

By the end of my second year in office I had most of the core staff in place. That gave me the opportunity to continue my quest to improve every component of the school system from transportation to food service. School desegregation was still going as well as I had expected it would, and much better than many thought.

INCOMPETENT TEACHERS

Some of the principals said they had several marginal to unsatisfactory teachers in their schools. I wasn't surprised at the news; it wasn't a revelation. Military training had taught me to have those directly responsible to attend to any problem under their control; if they couldn't, then I would. Growing up in a large family had also given me firsthand experience in confronting a problem, solving it, and then moving on. So between the military and my home life, I was prepared to handle the hard job of dealing with lack of ability.

I treated the news of poorly performing teachers just like any other problem. I assessed the options before us and then requested the principals to counsel the teachers personally. My advice was for the principals to give specific information during private conferences and then follow up with a formal letter regarding their poor performance as teachers. I suggested that the principals identify in detail the aspects of their jobs that were not up to the districts expected standards and explain what they could do to improve to a satisfactory level.

One of the principals with the two worst performing teachers gave me some backup material on the teachers, but refused to confront them because they were colored. We had some very unhappy parents who had given me a significant amount of documentation that clearly demonstrated the teachers were incompetent. The principal was unhappy and ill at ease; so were the teachers and the community. I was disappointed in the principal and fed up with the teachers. At the end of the school year, the principal resigned, but that didn't solve our teacher problem.

Both teachers were tenured so my only option was to file charges of professional incompetence against them, which I did. We had hearings before a hearing officer with the Professional Practices Council. I served as my own attorney (I know one shouldn't do that—and there's the old saying to prove it, "A man who serves as his own lawyer has a fool for a client"). But aside from the perception and the cliché, I felt comfortable representing myself because after being an elementary school teacher, I knew the educational and curriculum questions to ask that would prove the case of professional incompetence against these teachers.

I won and lost at the same time. I won the professional incompetence part of the case but wasn't allowed to terminate the two teachers at the end of school in May 1969. I was allowed to return each of them to an annual contract without loss of pay.

In an effort to salvage as much for education as I could, I hired two of the best teacher aides available and placed them in the classrooms with those teachers the following year. Since I had been required to keep those teachers, but only on an annual contract, when the next school year ended I didn't renew their annual contacts.

It didn't matter that both teachers were well beyond retirement age and that neither had any sort of classroom control. Unfortunately, the only thing that really made a difference was that both teachers were colored. When I didn't renew the teacher's contracts, the local chapter of the NAACP brought accusations of racism against me; they marched and protested. They brought in the activist Reverend Gooden from Tallahassee and set up a meeting north of town in a colored country church for about 10:00 p.m. I agreed to meet with them, and I was the only white person there.

The meeting seemed to last forever. One of the most ridiculous things on their agenda was their demand that I not take any action against any black employee without their involvement. I would not, and could not, give in to such a one-sided demand. I reminded the group that I was elected to serve all the county, whites and blacks alike, and I wouldn't limit my options just to appease their grievance and desire for control. Because of that, I had several years of strained relations with the local chapter of the NAACP, but it was still the right thing to do to remove incompetent teachers and it was also right to not give in to their arrogant demands to share the lawful exercise of elected authority. No decision should be based on race; all choices should be made on doing the right thing. And that's what I did.

After that, almost every incident at a school or on a school bus, regardless of how small or insignificant, if the event involved a white and a black child, the occasion was treated as racially motivated and used as a tool to incite further animosity—and that was wrongheaded and morally unjustified. The principals, when dealing with these incidents, and no matter what the facts were or how the incident was resolved, the solution was always unsatisfactory to one side or the other. Still, I tried to make every decision based on fairness and what was right, and not to lessen any group or individuals with the final judgment. If we don't serve what is right, we will certainly end up wrong. Rosa Parks, in the midst of her struggle against racism, said that we should do the very best we can to look upon life with optimism and hope; she was right, but not everyone in our community shared her views or willingness to strive for what is right.

Racial tension wasn't the only issue pressing against any action hostile to teacher incompetence. The teacher's union was a strong and, at times, almost malignant force to deal with. I knew actions against any teacher would bring the wrath of the teachers union down on me. Still, there was my charge to do what is right and what is best for school children and for the school system. And that included rustling some teachers' feathers and incurring the fury of the union along with it—I ran for office with fairness and justice in my heart and then swore an oath to that effect.

I wanted to improve classroom instruction. I wanted meaningful instruction on every subject at every grade level, and I made directives to principals and teachers to bring about the much needed improvements. Whenever radical change is made, you can bet it won't be supported by everyone. Sure enough, the reactions came across as a threat to those who were complacent teachers. It was difficult for me to understand how professional teachers could rally behind and support incompetent teachers, but they did. To make matters worse, the union was neck deep behind those poorly performing teachers. If anyone took an objective look, it appears that the union's main purpose was to collect dues, grow fat off their clout, and protect incompetence because it paid them to do so.

Suddenly, I was in a vice. The NAACP was on one side wanting to be involved in every decision I made regarding colored teachers, and now the union was applying their considerable pressure for me to share my decision making with them in dealing with incompetent dues payers. I gave the union the same speech I gave the NAACP, if they wanted to run the school system they should seek office and get elected. I told them emphatically that I would never share any decision making authority with them under any condition. As you might guess, I had a strained relationship with the union leadership throughout my time as superintendent. It wasn't a head-butting contest; it was a matter of doing the right thing and leaving personal feelings and political agenda's out of the way.

ANOTHER VOID

Loneliness is a killer. It's also cruel. Whenever a couple builds a life, they are a single unit—one in everything. After Mama passed, Daddy had a hole in his life that would not and could not be filled. On June 17, 1969, less than six months after I started my first term in office, Daddy made the hole in our family larger but joined the one he loved most in eternity.

Daddy was sick for a very short time and didn't suffer long; that was a blessing. I was at National Guard summer camp when Daddy got sick. My brother, Ronald, got in touch with me and said Daddy's illness was really serious. By the time I got to Shands Hospital in Gainesville, he was still alive, but unaware of my presence. Daddy lingered on through the night and passed away the next day. Our family had now lost its matriarch and patriarch, sadness seemed to overwhelm my brothers and sisters, all our families, and me. I was the youngest, so I had been with him the least amount of time, but that certainly didn't mean I hurt any less at his passing. Being the youngest, I may have had the closest relationship with our parents; and their departure certainly hurt more than I imagined it could.

I took some comfort in the way things had turned out in the course of Daddy's last years. During the 28 months he lived after Mama's passing, he saw a lot of changes in my life. I completed graduate school, and I ran for office and won with his helping me campaign. JoAnn and I met, dated, and were married. I was the only military officer in our family, and I was a company commander. I hoped that I had made him proud of his youngest son; Daddy was 76 years old when he joined Mama.

MORE TRAINING

Throughout 1969, 1970, and 1971, my Guard unit's performance continued to improve on individual soldiers' qualifications and in operational effectiveness. Because we were so efficient and organized, our Guard unit earned the Governor's Trophy as the best overall unit in the state of Florida. I was, and still am, proud of that distinction.

On February 1, 1972, the Live Oak National Guard unit was once again reorganized. This time we were made into the 269th Engineer Company (Construction Support). While the name stayed almost the same, the mission, organization, manning, and technical skills required were significantly greater. This unit was much larger, more complex to organize and manage, and the size of the unit about doubled in the number of personnel required. In addition to the headquarters functions of administration, supply, and mess, we had an asphalt paving platoon, a quarry platoon, an equipment platoon, and a maintenance platoon. Basically, it was a military horizontal construction company that had all the equipment to quarry and crush rock, a plant to make asphalt for paving roads or airport runways, and we had several pieces of heavy equipment such as D9 bulldozers, loaders, 40-ton cranes, 20-ton cranes, ditch diggers, and other heavy equipment. Besides all the equipment, we had the maintenance and supply necessary to support the whole operation.

The unit was also a natural asset to the Suwannee County Board of County Commissioners. Since I controlled far more earth moving equipment than the county commissioners had, I told them if they would provide the front-end loaders during the weekends we had Guard Drill, then I would have the unit haul sand, rock, and clay to build or stabilize many of the dirt roads in the county. I explained that this arrangement could meet three objectives: first, the Guards trucks needed to be exercised monthly; second, our truck drivers needed training with loaded trucks; and third, the county needed materials moved from one location and placed at another.

The county commissioners appreciated the help of the Guard unit; since I was also school superintendent, I was able to get the county to provide clay for the baseball field, and fill dirt to place a good thick layer on top of a former landfill site which was developed into a two-acre playground. The county commissioners provided the equipment to do the finish grading of the baseball field and landfill site. We had a good triangle between the school board, Guard unit, and county commission that proved to serve everyone in the community quite well.

For several years after JoAnn and I were married, I spent most of my evenings and weekends working on the sub-courses required for completion of the various military subjects. Training funds to pay for Reserve and National Guard officers and enlisted personnel to attend active duty schools was very limited. Not only were training funds scarce, but the time to get away from civilian jobs to attend the active duty schools and still hold down full-time jobs was almost impossible. Most National Guard officers, like me, chose to take the hundreds of hours of military required courses relating to specific subjects by correspondence. This, in my opinion, was the most difficult way to study and learn the required operational and technical subjects.

I completed the Armor Officer Basic course, five of the phases of the Engineer Advanced Officer course, and two other required phases by attending a two-week active duty course at Fort Belvoir, Virginia, for each of the phases. All these courses had time limits for completion and were prerequisites to military promotions. Often times, I would wonder whether the reward was worth the effort. An ancient Arabic proverb says, "Dwell not upon thy weariness, thy strength shall be according to the measure of thy desire." Sometimes you have to get to the end of a journey to know if the demands were worth the struggle; in retrospect, it was, and for that I am thankful.

I always enjoyed command. I made it my business to know something personal about each soldier; usually it was about his family, his children, their ages and grades in school, and where he worked. Some people do that for political gain or as a parlor trick; I did it because I cared and wanted to know everyone and I wanted them to know that I cared. That personal touch always makes people happier and encourages them to want to try harder. I always made an effort to speak to every soldier by name, usually in the chow line, and ask them something about their family, such as how is the son doing in football this year, or something like that.

It was personally rewarding to work with officers and enlisted soldiers building solidarity as a unit. I always saw myself as a servant leader. That's the way anyone should lead. In fact, our Lord showed us how to be a servant leader when he washed the feet of his Disciples. Those were people he led; those were people he looked up to. Now, I didn't wash anyone's feet, nor do I dare compare myself to the greatest

Leader of all. But I always felt it was my responsibility to enable each soldier to excel in his job and to be successful, and my job was to remove obstacles and barriers when required. That's what a servant does; that's what a leader does, and that's how I have always tried to be throughout my life.

I always took my physical training (PT) test with my soldiers; I wanted them to know I had to live by the same military standard they were required to live by. I wanted them to know my PT test scores, good or bad. I simply couldn't impose one set of standards on them and have a different benchmark for myself, whether it was a PT test, drug test, or any other task where there was an established measurement which each of us had to meet. I always emphasized that there was only one standard we all were measured against, and that was the Army standard. My command philosophy was to never ask a soldier to do something I wouldn't do, or hadn't done. I tried to always command in a fair, firm, and impartial manner. I respected each soldier, and considered each to be my superior in some way. Each of them knew more than I did in some area of their military job. We can, and should, learn from everyone whether they hold the highest office or lowest position in society. Soldiers are no different; a youthful private can know things a seasoned general doesn't know simply because of life's experiences. It is foolish of a leader to let such a wealth of knowledge go untapped because of position. We should always remember the Psalm, "Out of the mouth of babes and sucklings hast thou ordained strength," which literally means that even the least can teach the greatest.

When we were on duty, I tried to visit each soldier every day at his work site. I always felt my responsibility was to take care of the soldiers, and they would take care of me—they never let me down. As a commander, I was always responsible for every action of every soldier, good or bad. When other senior officers gave a commendation or praise to an individual soldier, a platoon, or the company as a whole, I always gave them the credit and also praised them for their performance.

The burden of command has with it a two-edged sword. Whenever someone in your command fails, as commander, you are responsible and there are consequences. On a few occasions I was reprimanded for some action of an individual, platoon, or unit; whenever that happened, I accepted full responsibility and didn't offer excuses. Afterward, I discussed the reprimand I received, and put in place the corrective action necessary to the individual, platoon, or unit. As part of command, one of my unpleasant duties was to dispense discipline.

Disciplining soldiers, regardless of rank, was always done in private, and just between the two of us, unless the seriousness of the discipline required a witness. Again, fairness was always my objective, and performing as near perfection as possible was always my goal.

BIRTHS OF OUR DAUGHTERS

JoAnn resigned her job about February 1, 1970. Later that spring we learned that she was pregnant. We really wanted a baby and now we were blessed with the news that our wishes would be granted. JoAnn spent most of her time during the remainder of that year preparing for the baby that was due sometime between Christmas and New Year's. On December the 30th shortly after lunch, JoAnn called me at the office and said I should come home right away because she was having labor pains. I bolted out the door, got JoAnn, and we went to the hospital.

JoAnn's labor wasn't too bad; it only lasted about two hours after we got to the hospital. A new star was added to my life when our daughter, Becky Ann, was born on December 30, 1970. Less than two years later, another star entered our lives as Brenda Sue blessed us with her arrival early one Sunday morning on September 17, 1972, just weeks following my second primary victory for school superintendent. Dr. Hugo F. Sotolongo was our family physician and delivered both our children. He was a good doctor, and we were friends. I guess when we make close personal friends and then share something as intimate as child birth, there is a bond that can't be broken. I still appreciate Dr. Sotolongo and his family.

One hot summer evening soon after Brenda was born we were churning ice cream on our back porch and had several neighbors over. We all started discussing swimming pools; one idea led to another, and before our neighbors left to go home, four of the families had agreed to build a community pool for the four families and their guests. Our across-the-street neighbors, Doc and Jo Kennon, had a large fenced lot just beyond their back yard and they offered it as a site for us to build our pool. The Kennon's son, who was an attorney, drew up some basic legal documents, and in less than eight weeks we had a 20 foot by 40 foot pool that was nine feet deep on one end.

Our pool had a diving board, concrete deck with cool seal, an aerial light, and it was enclosed by a six-foot chained-link fence. Each of the four families had the combination to the lock, and we all took turns cleaning the pool and checking the chemical levels of the water. That pool was a great investment for our family for two reasons; first and foremost, it wasn't in our back yard, and second, the pool was quickly accessible and always available. Becky and Brenda loved it; Becky learned to swim at about age 2½ and Brenda learned to swim before she was two. They wanted to stay in the pool, and after they learned to swim, they wanted to go more often. Since we had to cross a street to get to the pool, we always took them out of an abundance of caution. And besides, children must be watched in the water to prevent accidental disaster.

A SECOND CAMPAIGN

By the end of my first four-year term as superintendent, I was tired and burned-out. I had an almost two-year-old daughter, and was expecting a second child. Since I was feeling pulled between the responsibilities of being a public figure and having a private life, I considered the possibility of not running for a second term.

As I weighed the options, I discussed my feelings with school board member Mr. E. A. Collins; he treated me to some fatherly advice. Mr. Collins told me that I had done a great job, and he thought most of the people in Suwannee County felt the same way. Mr. Collins made a point that I hadn't really thought about; he said I had learned a lot about the school system, and the tax payers had paid for it. He added the clincher when he said I owed it to the tax payers and citizens to offer myself for another term because of their investment in me.

Mr. Collins was right and I knew it. I should run because I owed it to the community. As fate sometimes has it, I had an old familiar opponent: Mr. Henry Folsom. He was superintendent before me; I took the office from him; and now he wanted to return the favor and take the office back from me. When Mr. Folsom announced his candidacy, I was faced with a baseball scenario where it was a double elimination match to win the crown. I would have to beat the former superintendent in a second match in order to remain in office.

I didn't have the intense drive or incentive to get out and campaign for reelection, as I had done during the first campaign. Nonetheless, I gave the second campaign everything that was in me, just like I had done four years earlier.

REASSIGNED

I served nine years in command of the same hometown National Guard Company I had joined 15 years earlier. During that nine-year period, due to reorganizations, I had commanded four totally different types of units with very different military missions. Thanks to Chief Warrant Officer Lawrence Lee, my unit made nine superior ratings on our annual Inspector General (IG) inspection reports. I was proud of the soldiers, the unit, and our performance during my command. I was not a perfect commander; no one is. I always strived to improve the unit, but I know some things were worse when I left, and some I had caused to be improved.

On February 5, 1973, I was reassigned to the 50th Rear Area Operations Center (RAOC) at the Cedar Hills Armory in Jacksonville. I was the Engineer Plans and Operations Officer and served on that assignment until November 30, 1974. The very next day, December 1, 1974, I was promoted to Major, and reassigned to Headquarters and Headquarters Detachment, 53rd Signal Group in Tallahassee as the Administrative Officer. I served there until May 7, 1975, when I was reassigned as Communications Systems Engineer for the 53rd Signal Group. I was reassigned as Radio Systems Officer for the 53rd Signal Group on October 1, 1975.

That sounds like a lot of assigning and reassigning, and it was, but that's part of military life. In the grand scheme of things, getting all those different experiences helped me throughout my career in both the military and civilian walks of life. Besides that, soldiers need to master as many duties as possible in order to best serve their country if and when the need arises. I have learned through a long career, that if you are patient, opportunity will knock; if you are ready, then you can seize the moment and serve with a generous background of experience to guide you to success where others with less experience may fail.

Once I was assigned to the Signal Corp, I had to take all the courses required to be a qualified signal officer. These courses were technical, and not being an electrical or electronics engineer, the courses were very difficult for me. But I had learned a long time before that no matter how technical or difficult the content may be, the course was designed in such a way that persons of average intelligence who were willing to study, work hard, and apply themselves could pass the courses—which I did. All my military staff assignments required hours of detailed work and planning during drill, and I also spent many evenings and additional weekends on the various technical assignments. The tactical communications systems we were designing were complex and detailed.

The only way to master them was to commit the time, energy, and effort required for success.

GOOD PERSON BAD LEADER

I had a high school principal that ran a good school, but he simply would not address teacher incompetence. He had two problem teachers; unlike the episode when I had two incompetent teachers who were colored and I was called racist for confronting the problem, this time both teachers were white, one male and one female. The principal spent a lot of time telling me how terribly these two teachers performed in the classroom and that neither could maintain classroom control. He said that he or an assistant principal would have to visit each of their classrooms two to three times a day just to get the students back into the classrooms.

Drawing on experience and a good understanding of the labor laws we operated under, I advised the principal that since both poorly performing teachers had been granted tenure, he needed to be making notes of the poor classroom teaching performances and record it on their annual evaluations, which were due about the first part of April every year.

Principals always brought teacher evaluations to the superintendent's office for filing. When this principal brought his evaluations to the county office, I told him to just come on into my office and let me briefly review the teacher evaluations with him. I flipped through the stack he handed me until I found the two he had complained about; he had made it a point to grumble to me several times that year about those two teachers. I expected him to do something to correct the problem; when I looked at his evaluation of their performance, my mouth dropped because both were rated as being perfect in every area.

I got fuming mad as I read his written evaluations and compared them to all that he had said about those teachers during the school year. I told him that either what he had been telling me was a lie or the evaluations were a lie; I summed it up by saying that one way or the other, he was lying. I knew what he had been telling me about the male teacher was true because he had taught next door to me for a year and I had to regularly round up his students and put them back into his classroom and make them be quiet so my class next door could study. I told the principal I was tired of his promoting the stealing of educational opportunity from the students he was hired to serve by not having a backbone strong enough to do what was right for those kids.

In a cleansing motion, I told the principal that his services would be terminated June 30th. He got angry and red-faced and reminded me that the male teacher was a Baptist preacher, and he himself was a Deacon in the First Baptist Church. The principal added that I couldn't terminate him like that. His effort was defensive, but I made it clear to him that the teacher wasn't hired to be a classroom preacher, and he wasn't hired to be a deacon. Since the principal had chosen to insert the church into the issue, I told him that as far as I was concerned it didn't matter to me if he was the preacher of the First Baptist Church; his termination date was still at the end of the fiscal year. He grumbled some more, but he had left me no choice but to protect the students and the best interests of the school system. If the principal had performed his duties correctly, we would have either disciplined or dismissed the incompetent teachers. Instead, I hired a new principal who demanded reasonable performance from the teaching staff. With time, when those two teachers had to perform at a reasonable level, they chose to quit teaching and resigned their positions.

THE BIG LIE

Branford High School had grades kindergarten through 12th grade. About halfway through my tenure as superintendent, I began to get complaints from the faculty and staff at the Branford school. The whole staff seemed to believe they were being spied on and their conversations were secretly being monitored. The Branford principal ran a well-disciplined school operation, and he lived just across the street from the school so he was always onsite for any event or need that might arise. I spoke to the Branford principal several times over the span of about a year regarding the complaints. His response was always that he didn't know what they were talking about, and that he would never do such a thing.

During the Christmas holidays, on a Sunday afternoon, Pop Duval, the maintenance supervisor, called and said he was going to drive down to Branford to make sure the kitchen freezers and some other equipment was okay. It was just a routine follow-up to some recent equipment problems. I told Pop I wanted to ride with him to the school, and I asked him to bring along a step ladder because I needed him to help me check something out at the school.

The Branford principal was a minister and served in a church about 60 miles away, so I figured he wouldn't be home on Sunday afternoon while Pop and I were at the school. Something was gnawing inside me and I wanted to confirm or refute the Branford staff's fears of being spied on. Once we got to the school, we started looking to see if there were any bugging devices. When we examined the back panel of the school intercommunications system, we found four or five wires leading from the back of a panel that didn't match the other wires. Pop removed some panels from the drop ceiling, and we traced wires with a microphone attached in at least four locations. The material in the drop ceiling panels had been scratched away until only the thin finished panel membrane was left and a microphone had been secured to the panel touching the thin membrane. The microphones transmitted to a console in the principal's office, and were controlled by switches to listen in on any area. We found microphones embedded in the ceiling of the teacher's lounge, the two main entrances where students would wait for school to start, and the library.

Following the first staff meeting in January, I told the principal I would like to meet privately in my office. Again, I confronted him about the continued complaints regarding the school being bugged. Again, his response was that the staff didn't know what they were talking about, and that he would never do such a thing because he was a Christian and that would be against his ethics. After his pious declaration, I asked him about the microphones embedded in the ceiling and I named their locations.

The principal was baldheaded, and when he knew that he was caught, his bald head and face turned as red as a turkey wattle. When I explained what I had personally seen, he said that his son, who was a high school student, must have placed them there without his knowledge. I told the principal the microphones were placed too strategically to have been placed there by his son. Then I asked how his son could enter the building without his keys and his knowledge. He didn't have an answer. I felt betrayed because he lied to me and because he was using such underhanded techniques to spy on teachers and students; I told him that even though he ran a good school and had otherwise done a good job, his credibility with me was gone, and his employment with the Suwannee County School Board would end June 30th. To this day, I don't know why someone who has authority and good leadership abilities would jeopardize a good career over such foolish things.

REPREHENSIBLE

That which is tragic in a person's private life, is disastrous in a leader. A teacher inappropriately getting involved with a student is not a new problem. As reprehensible as it is, unfortunately, it happens; and when it does, the damage is long-lived. When I was superintendent, I had a sad, firsthand experience dealing with teacher misconduct and a student.

My encounter was with a female teacher, whose husband was also a teacher in a high school in the neighboring county; both were born and raised on farms in our area. Both still had parents living locally, and together these teachers had two elementary-age children.

Some of the high school boys were aware that the female teacher and one of her sixteen-year-old male students were having a sexual relationship. Some of the high school boys told the sheriff's department and then agreed to notify the sheriff whenever they were fairly sure of the time and location where the teacher and student would meet. A couple of weeks later, the teacher drove the student to one of the springs in our area; the sheriff's department had been advised where they were going and was waiting for them.

Law enforcement officials don't rush into action, they usually plan efficiently and effectively to make sure that their actions aren't outside the limits established by our laws. I'm sure that in this kind of case, it was harder to have restraint and wait. But they did, and after a period of time, the deputies approached her car and caught the two in the act. She was arrested, and criminal charges were filed against her. We fired her.

As soon as the illicit event became public knowledge, she divorced her husband, gave him their two children, and left town with the sixteen-year-old boy. She and the boy were married; somehow, she got another teaching job and supported him until he was old enough to join the armed forces. When the young man joined the Air Force, she followed him in his military career. Although she left, the tarnished image remained infamous in the school system and community for a long time.

BUS PROBLEMS

About two years into my tenure as superintendent, I had a school bus route in the northwest part of the county that was so bad that bus drivers wouldn't tolerate the deviant behavior; the drivers' solution to their dilemma was to simply quit their jobs. It was a bad situation. The students on that bus route were so mean and rowdy that none of the drivers we hired could maintain control; consequently, they would just quit out of frustration.

The students on the bus that caused the most problems came from one family; their mother's first name was Sarah. I had known Sarah, and her parents and brothers and sisters, for years and knew she was a very rough and tough character, afraid of nothing, would fight anyone, and yet she was kind-hearted and a hard worker. Hoping for some relief, I called and asked her to stop by my office the next time she was in town, and she did.

I was blunt and told Sarah her children were just mean as hell, and because of them we couldn't keep a bus driver on that route. Sarah offered a solution; she said, "Hire me. I can straighten them all out, and there'll be no more problems on that bus." I didn't know just how wise it was, but I told her she could have the job. After all, since most of the problems came from her family, the least I could do was let her try to solve them. Sarah regularly drove a large truck while helping her husband; so I knew that she could drive a school bus.

Sarah started her new job the next day. About the second day of her new job, on the way home from school one of her own children got loud and mouthed off to her. He was sitting about two seats back behind the driver's seat and leading a ruckus that involved several children. Sarah's report on that event was that she stopped the bus, called her kid to come up front, and in her own words she, "Slapped the hell out of him." Sarah said all the other children calmed down and she never had any more trouble from her children or from anyone else on the bus. Sarah turned out to be a blessing because she filled a vacancy we couldn't keep filled, and she got control of a bad situation and made it good. Besides driving the bus, during the school day Sarah worked part-time in the primary school cafeteria.

Sarah was territorial in what she considered her domain; she was also a dedicated employee. One morning, several months into her bus driving job, Sarah came by to see me after dropping off her students at their schools. I knew right away that something was wrong; Sarah looked awful, her blouse was torn, her face and arms were scratched, and she was sporting two swollen black eyes. I told her how bad she looked and asked her what had happened. Before she went into the event that left her so disheveled, she said I ought to see the other woman. I really didn't want to; Sarah looked bad enough for both of them.

Sarah told me that the afternoon before, one of the mothers on her route had given her some smart talk while her child was getting off the bus. She said the same mother met the bus again that morning and started giving her more verbal abuse. Sarah wasn't impressed with the woman who had returned for a second go at her. She turned off the ignition, set the emergency brake, got off the bus and invited the woman to fight and settle the issue that was causing her grief. The woman willingly obliged Sarah, and they fought outside the school bus for a few minutes. When Sarah was satisfied that she had whipped her, she got on the bus and completed her normal route.

Sarah's eyes were swollen shut and she couldn't see to drive the bus for a couple of days, so her husband drove for her. I was sure the irritated mother would file a complaint or suit against the school board, but she must have been satisfied after her brawl with Sarah because I never heard anything else about it. And that bus route continued to be a peaceful one because Sarah wouldn't tolerate rowdy behavior from students or parents. Maybe we need a few more Sarah's to help solve some of the behavior problems we face today on bus routes and in classrooms. She may have been rough around the edges, but she got the job done—which was more than any of the other drivers had been able to accomplish.

THE WORK PERMIT

A fair request should be followed by the deed in silence. Dante.

One day, probably in about 1972, I was in the office working late. Keeping long hours wasn't uncommon, but what I saw outside was unusual. There was a small colored boy who appeared to be about 11 years old and he was lingering around outside. I noticed him on several glimpses outside; I could see him through the sheer curtains and it appeared he was waiting to see me. I went and unlocked the front door, introduced myself, and welcomed him into my office. He introduced himself and told me he wanted to get a work permit.

We normally issued work permits to students who were 14 years of age and older. There were several restrictions as to when the students could work and what types work they could perform. I asked him if he had a job and he said that Mac's Fish Market, which was just a couple of blocks from my office, had offered him a job cleaning up, wrapping fish in newspaper, straightening the stack of used newspapers patrons would bring in for Mac to use to wrap the fish, and do other light errands. He said Mr. Mac wouldn't let him do anything dangerous. I knew that he wouldn't be allowed to do any potentially harmful jobs; and I also could see the aspiration for work in the young boys face.

Here was a young kid who wanted to work, and needed to work. He wasn't old enough according to some bureaucratic rule to work for money, but he was old enough to be left hungry and needy. Whenever red-tape is harmful, we sometimes have to go ahead and do the right thing. I typed out a work permit and gave it to him. The lad gave me a big, toothy grin and thanked me. He was happy to have a job, and I was thankful to be in a position to help.

I called Mr. Mac and he told me the kid was a good boy who only wanted to make a few bucks a week and that he wouldn't allow the young boy to handle any sharp knives, ice picks, scale fish, or do anything he thought would be dangerous or where he might get hurt. I thanked him for being willing to help out good kids like this one.

A couple of weeks later, the state wage and hour man came by Mac's Fish Market and took the boys' work permit that I had given him. The young boy came back to my office that afternoon and was troubled that *the man* had taken his work permit. I told him not to worry about it and I gave him a new work permit. In a few weeks *the man* took his second permit. Again, the boy came to see me and again I gave him a new work permit. Once more, I made the young kid happy, and again I was glad that I could help.

Then, in about two more weeks, *the man* came to see me. He wanted to get tough with me. I was glad that I had personally signed each of the work permits issued to the young boy; that way, no one else had to deal with the matter but me. *The man* had the work permits with him that I had signed. He told me how I was violating the law by issuing a work permit to an underage person. He curtly added that since I was an elected official I didn't have the right to knowingly violate the law. I told him I knew all of that, and if he wanted to bring charges against me, go ahead and I would ask for a jury trial—we would see what the public thought of his refusing to let someone work who wanted a job.

We argued back and forth, and I told *the man* that if the kid lived on a farm, he could work in the fields all day from daylight until after sunset doing all kinds of work that was far more dangerous than what he was doing at the fish market, and the kids working on the farm were exempt from the requirements of having to have a work permit. I told him I thought it was people like him that was encouraging young kids to be lazy, sorry, and have no incentive to work, and that I thought he was a big contributor to the society of, "Let someone give me what I need or let me steal it; I certainly can't work for it!" When he left my office, I wasn't sure what might happen next. I wouldn't have been surprised if he had filed charges; though, in the end, I think he understood that all I wanted to do was help the kid. Either way, I never heard from *the man* again, and the young boy worked as long as he wanted to and was never bothered any more. Oliver Wendell Holmes said the character of every act depends on the circumstances in which it is done—serving people who need a helping hand is always right under any circumstance.

GOOD END TO A BAD PROBLEM

During my two terms as elected superintendent, the Suwannee County School Board was the largest employer in the county. Whenever any institution employs several hundred professional and nonprofessional individuals, there's going to be personnel problems. I certainly had my share; some problems were sad, some difficult, some resulted in terminations, some turned out to be opportunities, and others turned out much better than expected.

One problem that turned out better than we anticipated happened in about 1974. Mr. Rufus Loper, a lifelong resident of Suwannee County, and a very good and competent math teacher at Suwannee High School, came by my office one afternoon. Mr. Loper told me he had been indicted on federal income tax charges. Not that he had evaded paying federal income taxes, but that he had prepared income tax forms for others in his community and had taken their word for some of the information they provided, which wasn't true or accurate in some cases. Nevertheless, he prepared and signed the forms and was held accountable for the accuracy and validity of the tax filing information. He didn't deny any of the allegations made by the IRS, and said he took full responsibility for his actions.

Mr. Loper sadly said that he had to start serving a jail sentence at the Federal Prison in about six weeks, and he asked me how I thought he should handle the situation. I told him that he was going to lose his job no matter what happened; he could voluntarily leave with the hopes that someday his resignation would reflect better than if the board terminated his teaching job. I told Mr. Loper that I thought he should appear in person before the school board and explain his situation openly and candidly, and then submit his resignation. He agreed that was probably the best approach. Mr. Loper met with the school board and explained his dilemma, submitted his resignation, and left to serve his federal prison sentence, which I believe, was for four months.

Mr. Loper returned from prison and came by my office to discuss his future once again. Since he had done an excellent job before the board explaining his previous dilemma and the events that had caused him to wind up in prison, I suggested he meet with the school board again and let them know he had paid his debt to society and would appreciate any consideration they might give him toward reemployment. Once more, he followed my advice and spoke to the board.

After a brief discussion, the board voted unanimously to reinstate Mr. Loper as a teacher, and they also restored his continuing contract. I think the boards' response surprised Mr. Loper. He was expecting them to refuse his request; most of his anxiety regarding the school boards probable course of action was based on what some in the community had told him. Mr. Loper was led to believe that since he was a black man and the board members were all white, he couldn't possibly expect fair treatment.

Interestingly enough, within a week or two, the local teachers union filed charges against the school board for reinstating Mr. Loper; to make matters worse for the union, Mr. Loper was a union member. The union also filed a complaint with the Commissioner of Education; the union claimed that we didn't properly handle the situation with Mr. Loper.

Whenever there is a complaint filed with the State Department of Education, there is always some kind of follow up. This time, someone from the Commissioner's office called me and asked what we were doing. I wasn't interested in discussing the issue because we had already done our part locally and it didn't require any outside influence. I told the caller that I thought the five school board members and I, who were all duly elected by the voters in Suwannee County, could manage the situation in a fair and reasonable manner. As he persisted in his quest for information, I said that we didn't need the help of the Department of Education in our personnel matters and then I ended the call.

Shortly after my brusque encounter with the Department of Education that had been spawned by the teachers union, a union representative from the Florida Education Association (FEA) in Tallahassee came to see me. Now, the union wanted to tell me what I should and should not do, and their representative stressed that my actions and those of the board were wrong and perhaps illegal. The union contended that we were reemploying a convicted criminal, and the union felt it was in everyone's best interests to help us do the right thing. That meeting with the union didn't last long. After the union representative stated the union's position, I told him what I thought of him and the union; then I showed him the door and suggested he go back to Tallahassee and mind someone else's business, we could manage the school system without his help, advice, or input. Before he could get through the door, I added that we had totally integrated the schools with perhaps the least problems of any of the counties in our geographical area, and the union's actions toward Mr. Loper seemed racist. At that, he left.

Mr. Loper continued to teach until he chose to retire. Soon after he retired, he ran for a position on the school board. As a teacher, Mr. Loper had excellent credibility in the classroom and in the community. If he hadn't been an outstanding teacher, the board would never have reinstated him to teach. Mr. Loper's trustworthiness found even more support when the entire county elected him to serve on the school board. Sometimes life goes beyond a second chance to make a bad situation better and then gives us roses instead of thorns.

TEACHER CERTIFICATION

Another huge problem I faced was the overly large number of uncertified teachers we had on the payroll. These were teachers with less than a four-year degree, and teachers who were teaching out of their field or area of professional training. About one-fourth of our teachers were in one category or the other; my work was cut out for me.

We had several elementary teachers that had been trained to teach a specific high school subject such as home economics, history, social studies, or physical education, but didn't want to teach in their professional field; previous administrations had allowed those teachers to transfer to elementary schools. High school teachers could transfer to a lower grade, but elementary teachers couldn't transfer and teach in a high school unless they were certified in the subject area. I guess the thought was that anyone could teach elementary school because the students don't know enough to challenge the teacher in the subject matter—and that is faulty logic. An expert teacher encourages thought and learning; a teacher's job is to open the door to a world of knowledge. Anotole France said that the whole art of teaching is to awaken young minds; I agree, and the skill is the same no matter what the grade.

Many of the teachers, at least those I observed, had poor classroom organization and worse subject matter delivery skills. I directed principals to improve the certification of every teacher who was lacking in any area where they were teaching. I knew it would take a long time for the district to achieve full certification of every teacher, but we had to start somewhere.

The most logical place to begin was with the employment of new teachers. We had a small committee to interview applicants for any teaching vacancy. The interview committee was made up of members of the district staff and the respective school principal. The school principal was the only committee member that had absolute veto power over the other committee members, and the principal always had to agree to receive any new employee. It was my policy to give veto power to the principal because if a teacher couldn't meet expectations, I wanted the principal to be responsible and to take corrective action or recommend termination. I didn't believe in making political appointments; therefore, neither I nor the board assigned an employee to a principal without the principal's consent. It just didn't make any business or common sense for me to assign a teacher to be supervised by a principal and then hold the principal responsible for my personnel appointment. I still hold that same opinion today.

We had several teachers that had less than a four-year college degree, and some of them had taught for several years. Again, I told the principals we were moving toward full certification of every teacher and principal. Those teachers that didn't have four-year degrees were given a reasonable time to earn degrees as long as they were making satisfactory progress each semester. Our teachers with four-year degrees, but teaching out of field, were also given time to become certified in the field they were teaching or else be transferred to teach in a subject area where they were certified.

Some of my policies, especially on certification, ruffled feathers, and then the discontent would expand to the entire family. I had weighed the problem against the outcome and knew that our school children's education was hanging in the balance. When ruffled feathers were matched up against a poor education, it didn't bother me to side with the children. Each year we improved in teacher certification and teaching in field; when I left office, all of our teachers had at least a four-year college degree and all but two were fully certified in the areas they were teaching. Those two teachers were both diligently pursuing certification; one was working on certification as a speech therapist, and the other certification in special education. These were critical shortage areas, not just in Suwannee County, but also throughout the state and just about every school board was accommodating some kind of schedule to help teachers gain certification for these special programs.

NEW CLASSES AND NEW OPPORTUNITES

We started offering several new educational programs during my eight years as superintendent: summer academic programs, summer recreation programs, adult education programs, adult vocational classes, exceptional student educational (ESE), kindergarten, and the NJROTC program at Suwannee High School. Our programs were expanding and so were our borders; I worked with Hamilton County (a neighboring school district) to develop a multi-county exceptional child education program and educational center at the Greenwood School in Jasper. Getting a joint effort between school districts wasn't a common thing, so I was pleased to be a part of the innovation that led to expanding educational offerings outside our own school boundaries. We were working to innovate educational service as much as we could, and in 1972, the school system had its first School Psychologist, Mr. Raymond B. Carver, and its first Occupational Specialist, Mr. Wendell Roberts. These additions were staff that would be common in later years because of a federal law requiring their services, but that federal law wouldn't surface until 1975, so we were a few years ahead of the law and already implementing programs that would someday be required—we saw the need and met it without having to have a law to demand our compliance.

In 1976, the school board voted to provide daily transportation for students to and from North Florida Junior College in Madison. We were able to negotiate for the college to reimburse the school district for gas and the use of our bus. Again, this was a service that wasn't required, but it was a community value that made higher education easier to get, and accessible to some who would otherwise have no chance to go to college. Cooperating with NFJC repaired an injustice that Suwannee County had engineered when I was a student at the college; no more students in Suwannee County had to struggle for transportation to go to college because of poor politics. I fixed that one.

Several building projects were either started or completed during my tenure as superintendent. I wanted to do everything I could to improve the schools and the programs that supported the schools. Some of the bigger projects included a child care building at the

Suwannee-Hamilton Area Vocational and Technical Center, and an exceptional education building at the Suwannee Middle School (the former Douglass School). In June 1973, plans were begun to construct a new Elementary School (which would become Elementary East) to contain two wings with space for 600 students in each wing and a central administration suite. In June 1976, we prepared architectural plans for the construction of a new school bus garage for Live Oak, and we planned for portable buildings wherever they might be needed.

I certainly can't say that we solved all the problems that were facing the school system when I took office, but I can say with pride that every area and every level of education improved during my tenure as superintendent. The school district successfully transitioned from a segregated school system to a fully integrated school system during my first year in office. None of the neighboring counties integrated as soon as we did, and none of our constituents integrated their school systems as smoothly as we did. Suwannee County was first, and the other counties integrated in some shape, form, or fashion within the next three years. If nothing else, we served as their role model.

POLICY MATTERS

Several school board members played major roles in the success of the school system for the period when I was superintendent from January 1969 through January 1977. I was fortunate, for the most part, to have school board members who knew their role was to set policy and not to administer the day-to-day functions of the schools. Most of the board members worked hard to stay out of the administrative arena.

One of the big-ticket items a school board has to purchase is school buses. There has to be a plan in place to replace old, worn out buses; so, by the very nature of wear and tear, a board has to be diligent in their timetable to make sure they buy replacement buses on a regular schedule. Since there will always be new, older, and very old buses in the fleet, there will also be political and personnel problems surrounding their acquisition and allocation.

We usually purchased five new school buses each year. The standard practice before I took office was for the superintendent to contact each board member and allow the board member to decide which driver in his district would get a new bus. The first time we received new buses after I took office, Mr. Collins, who was a great board member, stopped by my office and wanted to know when I was going to ask the board members to let me know which drivers to assign the new buses. I told to Mr. Collins that the board was only involved two times in the acquiring of new buses: first, when the board voted to buy the buses, and second, when the board approved payment for the new buses. I think I surprised Mr. Collins with my response; he asked how I was going to decide who would get the new buses. I told Mr. Collins that I wouldn't decide, it would be Mr. Sumner, the county transportation supervisor. Since I wasn't the transportation supervisor, I shouldn't make that decision. I said that I had instructed Mr. Sumner to assign the five buses to the five longest routes with the oldest buses, and not to consider political districts. Mr. Collins said that was fair and the board never again, during my tenure, got involved in assigning new buses to particular drivers.

Whenever you have a board of any type, there will always be different personalities. That's a good thing—it provides balance and diversity. The school board was no different. Some of the members were, for the most part, objective and wanted to work together; they didn't seem to have a personal agenda for serving on the board and they wanted to help move the system forward; these members were Alvin Brown, Henry Mangels, Clyde Bass, E. A. Collins, and Pete Collins. The other board members I dealt with during my tenure as superintendent were fine individuals, but either didn't serve for very long or weren't as involved as some of the other members; these were L. C. Davis, James Shields, Goldie Gaylord, and Frank Norris. Mr. Davis and Mr. Norris died in office.

A THIRD TERM

There is an old saying that the third time is a charm. There's probably more truth there than we know. When I ran for superintendent in 1976, I figured that my chances of reelection were slim. I had two reasons for believing I might not gain reelection, though I felt strangely compelled, against my beliefs, to run for the office one more time. First, I knew that the longer I stayed in office trying to do the right thing instead of what was politically expedient, I would gradually lose support because politics usually trumps in the end. Second, was the history of the office; no one in my lifetime had ever served three consecutive terms, so I had nothing to convince me that the established practice of holding public office would change with me. The nature of people simply voting for change would likely continue and ultimately prevail.

Mrs. Verna Bass, who had just retired from teaching, with the backing of the local teachers union, challenged me for the office of superintendent. Mrs. Bass was the wife of school board member, Dr. Clyde Bass. Dr. Bass was well liked as a board member, so Mrs. Bass already had a lot of support, name recognition, and political backing. She didn't have to "beat the bushes" to become known.

As with all things political, there were some things that were not correctible. Mrs. Bass didn't have a degree in Education Administration and Supervision, though many thought that she did. Usually, there are specific criteria for certain highly important jobs—school superintendent is one of them. Generally, the public expects the school superintendent to have certain credentials, much as if you would expect certain credentials from the person performing surgery on a loved one. To that effect, I received a letter from Dr. Herman Frick, the Florida Chairman of the Accreditation of the Southern Association of Colleges and Schools, stating that having a candidate without proper administrative credentials would jeopardize the accreditation of our school system.

In the wake of that revelation, educational preparation became a big issue during the campaign. Dr. Frick and the Southern Association of Colleges and Schools ruled that educational preparation was essential for holding the office of superintendent. Since the teacher's union was supporting Mrs. Bass, they challenged the ruling. Under pressure, Dr. Frick flip-flopped. That was at a time when the ERA was a hot-button topic all across America and challenging the social will of change was more or less taboo. Regardless of the political undercurrents, we both ran hard campaigns. But in the end, I lost the election by less than 125 votes.

When I left office in January 1977, the school system had an annual budget of over $7 million, and I had an annual salary of $24,000. The districts budget had more than doubled and the superintendent's salary had almost doubled while I was in office. The student body had increased to 4,869 students and we expanded our grades to include kindergarten. We had grown to a total of 255 professional staff of teachers and administrators, and the beginning salary for a new teacher with a four-year degree was $8,400—about a 40 percent increase from when I was first elected.

I took the oath of office the first time when I was 28 years old; I tackled the hard problems of bringing order out of the turbulence that had existed for several years. When I left office I was 36 years old and probably older than my natural age; I had achieved nearly all the educational and leadership goals I had set for the school system. I was proud the day took the oath of office; I was even more proud the day I left.

I never regretted seeking election for the third time; the choice had been mine alone to make. Mr. Collins advice was reasonable and solid when I sought a second term and his counsel was so good that I used the same logic to run for the third term—though, this time I had different results. The day after the election, all my supporters had long and sad faces; however, I didn't. I knew what was facing Mrs. Bass; she didn't. The day following her election, I called Mrs. Bass and invited her to come by the office and talk about the future and the interim actions I would have as superintendent. I told Mrs. Bass that I wouldn't recommend any new employees, or reassign any existing employees without her concurrence; I didn't want to make the transition any harder than it had to be and I didn't want to strap her to any of my decisions or actions.

When I was first elected, the outgoing superintendent and school board hired me as assistant superintendent to let me gain as much experience as possible before I took the helm. That had been a good thing, so I asked Mrs. Bass if she would accept appointment as assistant superintendent; she said no. I think she made an error in judgment by not getting involved, but that was her choice. Hoping to make the transition easier for her, I said that I wouldn't respond to, or file away, any correspondence until she had reviewed it. That way she would at least be able to transition into the office with some knowledge of the activities she would inherit.

Before I officially left office, the superintendent-elect and the school board gave me tenure as a teacher and as an administrator. Mrs. Bass and the board asked me what job I wanted upon leaving office. I told them my desire was to go back to the classroom as a teacher. My request was honored. I told Mrs. Bass that I would be more than willing to come by any afternoon, or talk to her on the phone, about any problem, situation, or give any advice or assistance I could offer; everything I had was hers for the asking. To her benefit, she called me several times and we had a very cordial and professional relationship after I left office.

As with just about all leadership positions, it didn't take long before her staunch supporter, the teachers union, was giving Mrs. Bass a hard time; and to add insult to injury, the school board was at odds with her because she had strong union ties. As a side note, Dr. Bass resigned his position as a school board member so there wouldn't be a conflict of interest between his serving on the school board and his wife being the elected school superintendent.

BACKWARDS GLANCE

As I look back at some happenings in our family between the summers of 1974 and 1977, I realize our past experiences prepared us for the future. JoAnn enjoyed being a stay-at-home Mom, but she wanted more from life and wished to fulfill the challenge she felt in her spirit. In the summer of 1974 she expressed her desire to teach. While I was superintendent, it was my belief that she shouldn't work in the school system where I was the chief school officer. It seemed to me that it was a conflict of interest to do that, and it certainly would have given rise to discontent and allegations of favoritism. Fortunately, the High School Home Economics teacher in Lafayette County, which is just south of Suwannee County, was going to take a year's sick leave and JoAnn was hired for that job.

We got a new experience when JoAnn went to work. We had to find good day care for our two preschool-age children. Brenda was 24 months old, still in diapers, and Becky was a little over 3½ years old. Since both were toddlers, JoAnn and I had to share our family responsibilities and enlist the help of others. We got some really great help, but it took several people to make up the group who would share in our daily lives. My sister-in-law, Lois Boatright, Carol Warren who was a stay-at-home mom, and Kathern Hines who was a part-time domestic helper and baby sitter, helped us make it through that year.

It probably sounds like we only worked. But we had our fun times too. We bought some property on the Suwannee River south of Branford in Lafayette County and built an A-frame cabin where we would spend part of our weekends from Friday afternoon to Sunday mornings. Church was always important to us. We believed that families should worship together. And we planned our weekends, even when we were on the river, to include going to our much-loved Presbyterian Church in Live Oak every Sunday morning. It wasn't always easy or convenient, but it was always our schedule. When JoAnn worked in Lafayette County, on Thursday nights she would pack what was needed for our weekend on the river. Since I always took the girls to their daily care each morning, on Friday afternoon I would pick them up and meet JoAnn at our river cabin.

JoAnn's year of working in Lafayette County helped prepare us for my career change. After I lost the election, JoAnn took a teaching position at Suwannee High School in the fall of 1976. She was hired to teach food classes in Home Economics and 9th grade general science. Since teaching science was out of her field, she took night classes for certification to teach science. I drove with her and took the same earth science course.

We learned to depend on Kathern Hines as our babysitter. Kathern was a faithful black lady, middle aged, and competent; she turned out to be the best domestic help for our girls while JoAnn worked. In fact, as a special treat to Kathern, when her granddaughter graduated from high school, I made arrangements for her to go to Disney World. Since I would be taking my family with me to a superintendents related meeting in Orlando, I planned for Kathern to travel and stay at a hotel near the convention center. After their weekend at Disney World, Kathern and her granddaughter rode back with us to Live Oak. We did that on two occasions because Kathern had two favorite granddaughters and we wanted to help her treat them to a special time.

Traveling has always been a high priority for JoAnn and me. I guess this desire has been passed on to our children as a family trait. We have always tried to make the best of our opportunities; one special trip we took was in a rented motor home. In the fall of 1975, a year after JoAnn went to work in Mayo and I was still superintendent, we felt that we deserved a family vacation, something that would be far from my job as superintendent. After a little thought, we decided to go to New England to see the leaves change color—something we didn't get much of in Florida. We used a motor home for our trip and invited JoAnn's parents to join us. Her father was recovering from a stroke-like illness that required early retirement, so her parents had the freedom to go with us. Our girls were ages three and five at the time and the motor home was a real treat for all of us to travel in. We had a 14-day trip driving from Live Oak to Washington D. C., to Jamestown, Virginia, New York City, to New England, and on into Canada with tours and a memorable collage of sights all along the way.

When Mrs. Bass assumed the office of superintendent on January 18, 1977, I felt a huge burden had been lifted from my shoulders. In a sense, it had. I left office after eight grueling, yet highly productive years as superintendent. Somehow, I knew in the long-term I would be better off, and so would my family—I just didn't know how the future would play out, but I had faith that, as the Scripture says, "The steps of a righteous man are ordered by God." I believed that, because I knew that righteousness means that we serve God and not what we can earn by what we are or what we do; so our future truly was in His hands. The steps we would take would be ordered by Him.

BLUE CROSS/BLUE SHIELD

DIAL COMMUNICATIONS DEPARTMENT OF EDUCATION COMMAND OF THE 202ND MEDICAL GROUP

The turtle only makes progress when he sticks his neck out.
James Conant.

ON THE DAY Mrs. Bass assumed the office of Superintendent of Schools, I reported to Suwannee Middle School, the former Douglass School, to begin teaching seventh and eighth grade science. Since I was certified in both junior high math and science I felt comfortable teaching either subject.

CHANGING ROLES

The principal of Suwannee Middle School was Mr. Earl Carter; he was a good man and he ran the school efficiently. It was kind of odd though. I was teaching at his school, and I had appointed him to the position he held—which was now my supervisor.

Soon after I became superintendent I recommended to the school board that Mr. Carter be one of the assistant principals at Suwannee High School. Even though he didn't have certification in education administration at the time, his performance was outstanding. Mr. Carter was well respected in both the white and colored communities; as assistant principal, he made an immediate and positive impact in managing the discipline problems that arose whether the problem was with a student who was black, white, or between the two.

Before I recommended Mr. Carter to the school board as assistant principal, I asked him if he would agree to take summer school classes during the next two summers and get a Masters Degree in Education Administration and Supervision. He agreed but said he had only one problem, the assistant principal job was a twelve-month position. I told him I knew his boss and we would work around his summer school class schedules.

Mr. Carter and I worked well together and he was always very supportive of me. He wasn't threatened or intimidated by my presence, and I offered to assist him in any way I could. I really worked to keep a low profile at the middle school and stay within the teacher ranks. I didn't want any special privileges just because I had been superintendent. I really liked teaching and enjoyed every day in the classroom.

JoAnn was continuing to teach a home economics food class, earth science, and general science at Suwannee High School. Becky was in second grade and Brenda was in kindergarten.

When spring break came that year, we loaded our 1972 white Volkswagen camper and headed toward South Florida. The first day we stopped in Ocala at *Six Gun Territory*, after that we went on down to Titusville and spent the next day touring in Cape Kennedy. From

Cape Kennedy, we traveled on toward our destination of Key West, stopping along the islands in the Keys and spending the night in our Volkswagen camper. It was a full week of travel and we packed in as much adventure as we could. With spring break behind us, we were ready to finish the remainder of the semester teaching school.

PROMOTED

Late that spring, Mrs. Bass asked if I would be assistant principal and reading and mathematics curriculum coordinator for the middle school and divide my time between Suwannee Middle School and Suwannee Elementary School West. I agreed and my appointment was approved by the school board for a ten-month contract, the same as a classroom teacher, for the following school year 1977-78. The ten-month contract was good for me because I wanted to do some traveling with my family, which I hadn't been able to do for the past eight years. We needed some quality time together and travel was a really good way to get close.

Even though I had a break from the extreme demands of school superintendent, I still had a lot of responsibilities in the National Guard. I held the rank of Major, and was the Radio Officer in the Operations Section of the 53rd Signal Group, Florida Army National Guard, with Headquarters in Tallahassee. I attended annual training that year in late July and early August at Fort Bragg, North Carolina, and served as Liaison Officer with the 142nd Signal Group from Alabama.

A NATIONAL TOUR

The 1975 motor home trip to New England had whetted our appetites for a longer trip. Soon after leaving office as superintendent, and after I knew the dates for my National Guard annual training, I went to Jacksonville and rented a 34-foot Class-A Winnebago motorhome that would sleep eight. I got it for five weeks beginning June 10, 1977. Once again, I asked JoAnn's parents to travel with us. At first, they said no; I think they declined our invitation because they didn't want to be in the way or feel like they were an additional burden, but after our insisting and a little convincing they agreed to travel with us.

I drove and Papa helped me setup camp each day; JoAnn and her mother (Memie) planned our meals. The girls were almost five and 6½. JoAnn's father purchased a senior park pass, which provided free admission to all national parks. We had no travel agenda or preplanned route; mainly, we wanted to see as much of the United States as possible within the time available.

The national park pass proved to be a valuable asset because we loosely built our itinerary around visits to national parks. Visiting the national parks gave us the opportunity to see some of the natural beauty of our country that has been preserved. We spent each night in the motor home. As soon as we parked for the night in a national park or in a KOA campground, I would set up the motor home, level it, and connect the electrical power, sewer, and water. While I did the set up, JoAnn would cook a full meal, just as if we were at home. Papa and Memie would take the girls to the playground, and about every other day we would do laundry in a campground laundromat.

Our trip took us to see the Painted Desert, Petrified Forrest, Grand Canyon, Sequoia National Park, Yosemite National Park, and the Golden Gate Bridge. We traveled the famous California Highway 1 along the Northern coast of California all the way to and through the Redwood Forest. Then we headed northeast to Crater Lake National Park in Oregon. From there, we traveled north crossing the Columbia River into Washington state to Mt. Rainer National Park. The next leg of our trip took us east toward Spokane, Washington, across the northern part of Idaho and down through Montana to Yellowstone National Park where we stayed three nights. One day while visiting Yellowstone Park we traveled down to Jackson Hole, Wyoming, and saw the Grand Teton Mountains along the way. While in Yellowstone Park, we visited Leon and Ann McDonald who were from Live Oak. Mr. McDonald had previously served in the Florida House of Representatives and had owned a grocery store in Live Oak. Their middle son, Tommy, had been my roommate during my first semester at FSU living in Kellum Hall. It was a great visit that we hadn't expected when we started out on our journey.

Leaving Yellowstone National Park, we drove to Mt. Rushmore in South Dakota, and from there we drove down to the Rocky Mountain National Park, near Denver, Colorado. We then headed east toward Kansas City; about midway through Kansas we turned south and drove to Tulsa, Oklahoma, and visited Oral Roberts University. Next, we drove east, stopping in Memphis, Tennessee, to sightsee (this was just a few days before Elvis Presley passed away at his mansion in Memphis; we didn't visit Graceland, but I kind of wish we had). After that, we drove east toward Nashville, Tennessee, and spent the night at a campsite at Loretta Lynn's Ranch before visiting Opryland the next day. Opryland was the only commercial park we visited during the entire five-week trip. We left Nashville and two days later arrived back in Live Oak.

Our trip had taken us more than 8,700 miles. Gasoline prices were about 50 cents per gallon in most places; in some of the more remote areas it was 10 to 25 cents higher. Since motor homes don't get good gas mileage, we had our national tour at a good time—I don't think it would be something most folks could do today.

BACK TO WORK

When school started back in the fall of 1977, as assistant principal, my mornings were spent at the middle school dealing with bus problems, attendance issues, and discipline. I spent three afternoons each week at Suwannee Elementary School West working with Mr. Rutledge and his staff developing and writing the first mathematics curriculum continuum for elementary grades. The other two afternoons I spent at Suwannee Middle School developing and writing a middle school mathematics curriculum continuum. For the first time, that gave the district a written mathematics curriculum continuum from kindergarten through eighth grade. Since I was certified to teach elementary school, and math and science at the middle school, along with my immersion in mathematics curriculum during my graduate school studies, I felt comfortable and confident in developing the mathematics curriculum continuum. Things went well during the fall of the year, and I was achieving success at both schools.

MILITARY CATCH UP

I was behind with my military education because of my time as superintendent. During the fall of 1977 JoAnn and I both continued to teach, and I was still assigned as Radio Systems Officer for the 53rd Signal Group. On November 1, 1977, I was reassigned to be the Communications-Electronics Systems Engineer Officer for the 53rd Signal Group. I only had about two years left to complete the Army Command and General Staff College or get out of the National Guard.

The Guard was a good thing, but it was also demanding. It took a lot of time away from my family. JoAnn and I discussed ending my military career. Staying in the Guard would increase my responsibilities and require more of a time commitment because of the additional duties I would have. JoAnn said that she knew how much I enjoyed the Guard and that staying in or getting out was a choice that I would have to make; whichever decision I made, she promised to support me. I appreciated that; some military wives are not too understanding when the demands are so severe and the commitment so great.

During Guard drill that next weekend, I discussed the situation of being so far behind in my military education with the Signal Group Commander, Colonel Edwin P. Stewart. I told him perhaps I should just go ahead and end my National Guard military career in about four months, since I would have 20 years of service at that time. He said he understood my predicament, but he wanted me to stay in the National Guard and asked if I would apply to the active duty Army Command and General Staff College; he said that if I were chosen then he would like for me to go to the school. I told him that I would; it seemed like a good thing and if the opportunity were to materialize, then I would feel satisfied that I had made the right choice. If I were to not be chosen, then I could know that destiny had intervened to change my life for another direction. Either way would be okay with me.

I filled out all the paperwork that weekend and got a current physical examination at the Army examining station of Florida in Jacksonville the following week. In less than five weeks, the Adjutant General of the Florida National Guard recommended me, and the active Army approved me, to fill one on the 32 slots offered to the National Guard and Army Reserve Officers for the active-duty Command and General Staff College starting January 3, 1978. I requested a leave of absence from the school district for the spring semester 1978; the board graciously granted my leave.

The Army Command & General Staff College was in Fort Leavenworth, Kansas. That training lasted for five months and prepared me for more advancement in the National Guard. I drove our VW Camper out to Kansas so that I could have my own transportation while I was there. I left Live Oak on January 1, 1978, and reported to Fort Leavenworth on January 3rd.

As with all military training, it was intense, demanding, and took a lot of self-discipline to keep focused. It was also challenging and rewarding. Still, I knew that my absence from our family placed an extra burden on JoAnn, but she was a strong trouper and gave me all the support and encouragement she had to offer. I appreciated that then; I appreciate it even more now. She was always strong that way.

JoAnn stayed home working at her job teaching school and kept our daughters busy with gymnastics, dance, and music lessons.

When I completed the course in Kansas, she flew out with the girls to meet me. It was great to be back together. It's unbelievable how much you miss those you love when you have to be apart. Though duty sometimes requires it, such a sacrifice is never easy, and as General Douglas Macarthur said, "Americans never quit." So as long as there were opportunities, we had to keep meeting their challenges—even though they were demanding and painful.

Army life brings many people across your path. Some become friends; some are merely acquaintances. True to army lifestyle, I developed a friendship with Ken Rhodes; he was a classmate from Idaho. Like me, his wife and two children were not with him. Again, like my family, they planned to join him at the end of the course. Ken and I made plans for our two families to travel back to Florida in my VW camper and then he and his family would take our VW camper and go on to Disney World. Our families enjoyed that time together on the road to Florida.

THE OLD AND THE NEW

I returned in the fall of 1978 to the same job as assistant principal and reading and mathematics curriculum coordinator for the middle school and Suwannee Elementary School West. I picked up the pieces, the best I could, at the point where I had left off.

The next big change came during the fall of 1978 when a friend whom I worked with in the National Guard, Major Jim Williams, who was Director of Office Services for Blue Cross and Blue Shield of Jacksonville, mentioned that he would like for me to come work for him. He asked me on two different occasions during Guard drill, but I was happy and content where I was and didn't want to move to Jacksonville. Our family was enjoying some freedom and stability where we were and we were having more time together than we ever had.

Major Williams kept encouraging me to at least come see his workplace; finally, I agreed to go for a visit on Veteran's Day, November 11, 1978. After I saw the various departments and functions he was responsible for, he and his boss, a senior vice president, took me next door to the *Green Derby* restaurant for lunch. During our lunch the senior vice president made me a job offer with a good salary and great benefits. In fact, the offer was so good that I accepted the job right then. After agreeing to the terms of my new job, I drove back to Live Oak and we began to make preparations to move to Jacksonville.

I resigned my job with the Suwannee County School Board. With this career change, as a family, we went through a culture shock. JoAnn stayed in Live Oak and continued teaching high school to let our children finish the school year; she also used the time to sell our house. JoAnn was always dependable during difficult times and she never failed to take on additional burdens to help me pursue advancement either in the job market or the military.

In Jacksonville, we bought a house that was still under construction and had a pool put in our back yard. The four-family pool we shared in Live Oak had spoiled us to the luxury of our own swimming hole. We moved into the new house in July 1979, six months after I started working in Jacksonville. During that first six months I stayed with Alfred and Annette and went home on the weekends. That was a good time with my family and helped to ease the pain of not being with JoAnn and our children.

The new start in Jacksonville was great for Becky and Brenda; they were about seven and 8½. We enrolled them in a private Baptist school close to our home, because in the public schools they would have been bused across town to a school about 20 miles away and would have had to ride the school bus for about an hour or longer each way.

With our school choice made, we went church shopping. After a few tries we found a house of worship that had some good programs for children. It was the Evangel Temple Assembly of God and since it met our needs at the time, we joined. We had some friends who were members of an Episcopalian congregation so we went to an Episcopal church as well. Since JoAnn and I chose to attend a church different from either of our denominations when we married, and then in Jacksonville we expanded into two other Christian groups, we became somewhat eclectic with our church going. I think that's a good thing because you can broaden your view and still stay true to Christianity—it's not a matter of a denomination, it's a matter of faith.

I reported to work at Blue Cross and Blue Shield on January 2, 1979. My job was Manager of Purchasing and Fleet. We were annually purchasing several million dollars worth of supplies, materials, and equipment—mostly paper products. I had four buyers and a fleet supervisor and secretarial support. I was responsible for purchasing all corporate goods and services except advertising; that made me responsible for about $55 million annually.

When I had been there about 15 months, for reasons I don't know and don't care to know, my boss, Mr. Jim Williams, who had been with the company about 25 years at the time, was demoted to my job and I was promoted into his job. I felt awful for him, and extremely awkward in the new working relationship. Jim assured me things would be fine, and they were; our working relationship remained great, and our friendship untarnished. Jim convinced me that his reassignment had nothing to do with me, but was something about him. So after about 15 months on the job, the person that hired me to work for him was now working for me. Sadly, he died suddenly with a brain aneurism one weekend about six months later.

A BIGGER JOB

My new job as Director of Facilities and Office Services was very broad. It provided all the major office support systems and services which included mail operations, micrographics, reprographics, purchasing and fleet, warehousing, shipping and receiving, facility maintenance and operations, landlord functions, parking, and safety and security. My new areas of responsibility included nine operating departments with about 200 employees and a $10 million operating budget. During my time in this job I was responsible for recommending space standards and the realignment of functional areas. I coordinated a massive facility use project that resulted in renovating, remodeling, improving the work area environment, and relocating work areas to improve production and communications within work groups; and I accomplished it all in a six months time frame without disrupting operations for the 18 of the 21 floors of the building we occupied. Just to show how broad and complex my responsibilities were, I was purchasing about $21,000 in postage every workday.

The job paid me well, but I was putting in at least 12 hours a day. The more I worked, the more the company expected. Being a perfectionist, I continued to provide more, but there was a limit to what I could do. When I reached my limit, I asked my boss, a senior vice president, to get someone to replace me who had better management and technical skills than I had; he said he didn't want anyone else. For me, I felt I was somewhat over my head with the things I was required to do and it seemed only reasonable for the company to get someone trained for the jobs they wanted done.

In late 1983, when I realized that I had spent the night in the same house as my family for the past two weeks and hadn't seen my children awake, I knew it was time for me to leave. I told my boss of my plans to leave; he still didn't make an effort to find a replacement. I believe he thought I wouldn't leave because the salary and benefits were so good. He was wrong. To me, my family was far more important than just making more money.

My job wasn't the only thing demanding attention. I continued as the Communications-Electronics Systems Engineer Officer for the 53rd Signal Group in Tallahassee. This was a nice little commute for me one weekend a month; lucky for me, JoAnn's parents were living in Tallahassee, so the family always rode over for drill with me; I drilled, while JoAnn and the girls visited her parents. At least we got to spend the time on the road together, so that was a small benefit.

TRANSFERRED AND PROMOTED

On August 1, 1981, I was assigned as Commander, 146th Signal Battalion (Corp Area), in Jacksonville at the Maxwell C. Snyder Armory on Normandy Boulevard, about 2½ miles from our house in Jacksonville. I was promoted to Lieutenant Colonel on August 3, 1981. Guard duty was now almost in my backyard.

The 146th Signal Battalion was the largest battalion in the Florida Army National Guard. I had an authorized strength of 807 personnel assigned to the Headquarters and Headquarters Company (my headquarters), along with four more identical Signal Area Companies; all five companies were housed in the Maxwell C. Snyder Armory. The Battalion had over 30 full-time soldiers to support the various battalion administrative, supply, and maintenance functions that had to be performed on a day-to-day basis. I was extremely proud and honored to get command of the battalion.

One drawback to commanding that battalion was that it had high personnel turn-over, and to maintain adequate personnel strength through retention and recruitment was constant work. The signal gear was an older Viet Nam era generation of equipment. The radios didn't work well and all the equipment was labor intensive to maintain, but that is what we had, and I intended to make the best use of it. In the summer of 1982, during my first annual training as Battalion Commander, we went to Camp Blanding. Using rented building scaffolding, we constructed four towers on which we attached our radio antennas, some as high as 130 feet into the air, to get above the pine trees and gain line-of-sight to other towers. We had to have a clear line of sight to operate our signal equipment.

My command had about 35 officers and warrant officers, and about 100 non-commissioned officers (NCOs). This large number of subordinate leaders gave me the opportunity to provide the type of servant and caring leadership I had provided at the company level, except it was five times larger. I always demanded openness and honesty. If things were good, I wanted to know; if things were bad, I wanted to know that too. I told the staff and subordinate commanders, just like I had told Mr. Airth about hiding the school districts financial problems, that bad news doesn't get better with time. I always wanted the facts about any problem or situation, I didn't want staff or subordinate commanders to evaluate the facts and give me what information they thought the facts were and what they thought I needed to hear, or wanted to hear. I would always say, "Just give me the facts, and I can draw my own conclusions, I don't need the facts filtered."

I constantly demanded a lot from individuals, and when they performed well, they were recognized, and when they fell short, as we all do at times, I accepted the blame. Junior officers and NCOs cannot function in a zero error tolerance environment. They have to be allowed to make errors and then correct them in a non-threatening command structure. Did I have to discipline officers and NCOs, of course, some very severely such as courts martial and lesser military punishment, but just like in the civilian world, most often, discipline was the result of personal behavior, usually not as a result of poor military job performance. I wanted commanders at every level to experience the great pleasure and satisfaction of a job well done, just as I had experienced years earlier. I saw my role of commander as leader, a role model (both what to do, as well as what not to do), a coach, and a mentor. This particular annual training event was highly successful and I enjoyed it very much.

The following year, things were improving for the military since Ronald Reagan had become President. The 146th Signal Battalion was affiliated with the 501st Signal Battalion at Fort Campbell, Kentucky. Our two battalions trained together as often and to the extent possible, and supported each other in many ways. The 501st Signal Battalion Commander invited my battalion to Fort Campbell in 1983 to conduct a joint training exercise with his battalion. This seemed like a good idea, but I certainly didn't look forward to a military convoy of 650 miles with 223 vehicles stretching over several miles strung up and down Interstate 75.

RIDE THIS TRAIN

Another National Guard friend, Lieutenant Colonel Donald Roberts from Panama City, was at Camp Blanding during my previous annual training, and one evening we went to eat at Pizza Hut in Starke. While eating, we discussed the possibility of my battalion training at Fort Campbell the following year and the main drawback was the distance, wear and tear on the vehicles, and the valuable training time we would lose due to the additional days required for travel. Somehow in the conversation, and I can't recall how, we came up with the idea of testing the nation's rail system. We outlined on a napkin a plan to request funding and approval to conduct a full battalion Mobilization Exercise (MOBEX) using railroad assets to transport all of my battalion's military supplies, equipment, and vehicles to Fort Campbell.

I took the scribbled notes from the napkin and made them into a formal, presentable request to conduct a military exercise using the railroad. It was a great idea, but neither of us had any real hopes that our brainstorming session would be approved as a project. Surprisingly, in about four weeks, my formal written request had been approved up through my chain-of-command, and it was sent on to the Pentagon where the proposal was approved.

A lot of coordination with the CSX Railroad was done in preparation for transporting the 223 pieces of rolling equipment which required a train consisting of three locomotives, 80 trailer railcars like those used to ship loaded semi-trailers, and four boxcars. There was also a lot of coordination required with Greyhound Bus Lines to provide the unit with 14 chartered buses for transporting the troops.

As the time for the MOBEX approached, the battalion was becoming more and more prepared. I assigned Chief Warrant Officer Patti Vickery, from the Battalion Logistic Section, to be in charge of the coordination and administration of the total movement to and from Fort Campbell. She performed her job in a superior manner, and I received several letters of commendation regarding how well the entire rail movement exercise was planned and carried out. The joint training exercise we conducted during annual training at Fort Campbell with the 501st Signal Battalion was a great success, which also complimented the rail movement exercise. I think the idea of using the nations' railways was something like the Italian proverb that says, "If the wind will not serve, take to the oars," which can be interpreted to mean be creative and use what is available, but untapped. We have great resources all around us; we need only identify them and put them to work.

GIVING NOTICE

At the end of December 1983, I submitted my letter of resignation to my boss at Blue Cross and Blue Shield of Florida. My resignation was effective as of February 1, 1984. However, I had told him of my intentions before I submitted the formal letter, which effectively gave my boss an additional 30 days notice so that he could find a replacement for me. He was happy for me to stay on the job as long as I would, but I was ready to go. The good part of my job there was that we continued to have a great working relationship for as long as I worked.

I was planning to move to Tallahassee and work for my brother-in-laws' family business. JoAnn's brother, Bill Newton, with the able assistance of his wife, Sybil, had established an underground utility contracting company in Tallahassee; their company was Dial Communications. The family-owned business had grown into a several million dollar business with 175 employees and had offices in Tallahassee, Panama City, and Brooksville. Bill had casually discussed my being a manager for him and I considered the offer. During the Christmas holidays, I told him I would accept his proposition to work for him and would start the first workday in February.

Managing construction workers is certainly different from managing professionals or soldiers. I enjoyed the work, though it involved all the labor, turnover, and personnel problems I normally had dealt with. Still, understanding management and understanding construction workers is two different things. The new job had a totally unrelated set of day-to-day crises associated with construction projects.

When I started to work in Tallahassee, JoAnn stayed in Jacksonville until the summer to sell the house and allow our children to finish the school term. She was able to sell the house and we moved in July. We purchased a lot in the Lafayette Oaks subdivision in the eastern part of Tallahassee and had a two-story house built; the subdivision had a community pool—a luxury we had learned to enjoy. During the time our house was under construction, we stayed with JoAnn's parents. Becky entered 9th grade at Lincoln High School, and Brenda started 7th grade at Fairview Middle School. Our furniture from Jacksonville stayed packed in a Dial Communications semi-trailer from July until our house was completed in October.

Shortly after moving to Tallahassee, we were back to looking for a place to worship. Our search didn't take long. We found the place that seemed to suit us perfectly and transferred our membership to the Thomasville Road Baptist Church; where we continue to be members today.

GIVING NOTICE AGAIN

In July 1985, while grocery shopping, JoAnn bumped into George James, a person I had hired back when I was superintendent in Suwannee County. He had left Suwannee County and was working for the Florida Department of Education, Office of Educational Facilities, under Mr. Alfred Bowen, Manager of the Educational Plant Survey Section. George told JoAnn there was an opening in the Survey Section, and suggested that I apply for the job. I always had a high regard for the work done by the Survey Section, and had known Mr. Bowen since my early days as superintendent when he was the General Supervisor in Hamilton County. We had been in several meetings together and we had a worthy mutual respect for each other.

I contacted Mr. Bowen, and he gave me an interview for a position in the Educational Plant Survey Section (the section that evaluates and conducts an analysis of a school district's educational facilities needs) of the Office of Educational Facilities. The Florida Department of Education hired me based on his recommendation. I started that job in mid-August 1985.

I had worked for Dial Communications for 1½ years, and enjoyed working as a manager. The company was good to me and it provided me the opportunity for our family to relocate to Tallahassee and be closer to JoAnn's parents.

Working for the state gave me an opportunity to rejoin the Florida Retirement System, where I already had a total of 14 years vested. Getting back into the Florida Retirement System was one of two key deciding points of my going to work for state government; the second key was working for Al Bowen. I started work as a Program Specialist III in the Educational Plant Survey Section. Even though I had extensive administrative experience at the school district level, there was still a steep learning curve to master all the many technical and detailed pieces required to perform the facilities job effectively. A seasoned employee was with me on every job in the school districts for the first 1½ years, helping, training, monitoring, assisting, and assuring that everything met the expected standards. I wanted to learn, and with my several years of school district experience, my knowledge grew rapidly. By the second year, I was directing Educational Plant Surveys for medium-sized school districts.

REFORGER

In 1984, the 146th Signal Battalion from Jacksonville, along with the 53rd Signal Group from Tallahassee, and some active duty signal battalions from Fort Huachuca, Arizona, combined for a joint National Guard/Active Army signal exercise at Fort Bliss, Texas. It was a four-week field exercise, and due to the extended time requirements, I split my headquarters into two command and control teams. I used the railways to ship out two signal companies' equipment and one command and control team from my headquarters. The two companies set up and operated the signal equipment for the first two weeks. When we deployed the other command and control team and two companies, we embarked a day early to provide an overlap and to hand-off duties and responsibilities with a smooth transition.

Along with signing over the equipment from the first group to the second, the second group continued the exercise without interruption. They broke down the signal sites, packed up the equipment, and shipped it home. The personnel for both periods were transported from Jacksonville to El Paso by chartered commercial aircraft. This exercise was more successful than the previous year because we had terrain at Fort Bliss that was much more favorable to signal operations; since there were no trees in this area, we had less signal interference.

In early 1985, my battalion was selected to participate in perhaps the largest Army exercise of 1986: the *Return of Forces to Germany* (REFORGER). The battalion had been through demanding and major military exercises for the past three years. I always required more from each unit of the battalion than each thought they could deliver. Somehow, the subordinate units always met or exceeded my goals and expectations. I think that is a good example of how we achieve excellence in anything—demand more than seems possible, but be willing to know and accept when the maximum is reached.

In the summer of 1985, annual training was held at Fort Gordon, Georgia, the home of the Army Signal School. We convoyed the entire battalion, all 800 soldiers, equipment, and the 223 pieces of rolling trucks, from Jacksonville to Fort Gordon. The 501st Signal Battalion from Fort Campbell, Kentucky, convoyed down and assisted, helped train, and evaluated our training and signal exercise. Attending summer camp at the home of the Signal Corp allowed the unit to get some intensive signal training by elite soldiers in some of the hard skill and more technical jobs. For the remaining soldiers, we conducted a shake-down signal exercise to prepare for the overseas deployment of equipment and personnel that was scheduled for REFORGER 86, which was during the first three weeks of January 1986. The training at Fort Gordon really proved beneficial to our preparation for REFORGER 86; it gave us a slight edge that we wouldn't have had otherwise.

Upon returning from Fort Gordon, the battalion immediately began intensive preparation for our three weeks of overseas deployment, with personnel departing on January 3, 1986, and returning on January 24th. Our REFORGER 86 mission was to provide tactical, high-capacity lines of communication throughout Belgium and extending down into Germany. In 1985, I spent all or part of 42 weekends working on regular National Guard duties or in preparation for the upcoming deployment. It was an extremely busy time with intense preparation going on around the clock.

I, along with many of the battalions' lead officers and NCOs, had made several trips to Belgium to evaluate the terrain, assess existing commercial and military communications equipment and locations, and calculate the detailed technical information needed from the Belgian Army to do the meticulous communications systems engineering required to support the mission. These additional duties required advanced coordination regarding the logistics required during deployment, which included food, shelter, and fuel for the vehicles and generators. In short you don't simply deploy 120 pieces of rolling stock and more than 400 soldiers to a foreign country without detailed planning, coordination, and cooperation and support from the host country.

One of the most extensive individual requirements was that each soldier had to pass a written drivers examination and receive an endorsement on their military driver license to operate a motor vehicle in Europe. While every soldier was not required to have a military driver's license, I required one for every deploying soldier just in case someone had to drive unexpectedly. The drivers test had 100 questions, and only four questions could be missed for a passing score; more than four incorrect answers meant the written test had to be taken again. It was a very hard test, and only about 10 people passed the first time, and I wasn't one of them.

We also had to issue cold-weather uniforms and sleeping gear because of the very cold climate where we would be operating. Our vehicles and equipment were shipped by sea. Since there was a rather large amount of secure communication equipment mounted in the signal vans, we had to send along six soldiers as super cargo to guard and check the equipment while the ship was at sea. The equipment was loaded onto a roll-on roll-off ship at the Port of Jacksonville during the second week of December. The ship arrived at the Port of Zeebrugge on the North Sea in northern Belgium just before Christmas. The vehicles were off-loaded from the ship and stored at the port to await the arrival of the main body which was scheduled to get there about January 4th. Transportation of the main body of around 400 soldiers was provided by the United States Air Force using three C-141 aircrafts, and departed from Naval Air Station, Jacksonville.

The flights, like most flights on tactical military aircraft, were very uncomfortable and an unforgettable experience within itself for most of the soldiers. For upwards of 75 percent of the soldiers, this was their first experience flying in an airplane. Command and control was very difficult during the deployment phase because the aircraft departures were staggered three to four hours apart. After each aircraft had landed in Brussels, Belgium, and the soldiers were regrouped, we departed by chartered buses to the Port of Zeebrugge to pickup our vehicles. Once the vehicles were ready we had to deploy by military convoy to several locations spread out all over Belgium.

Even though all drivers had strip-maps to their destinations, a few got separated or cut-off from their assigned convoy because of traffic or traffic lights and got lost. Just like flying, for about 95 percent of the unit this was their first time in a foreign country. They couldn't speak the language or read the names on the road signs; however, they could read the traffic signs—and that was fortunate, but it wasn't good enough to keep us all grouped together.

CHOW DOWN

All of our meals were provided by a contract vendor. The vendor provided plenty of food, but it was European, and since many of my soldiers came from rural north Florida, the European food and especially their breakfast of hard bread, jelly, poached eggs, and cold-cuts of meat, fruit, coffee, and juice didn't satisfy their appetites. The noon and evening meals seemed to be fine with most soldiers, it was just the breakfast meal that was a real problem.

After the second day the food vendor came to see me. He was concerned because the soldiers weren't eating what he considered perfectly good food and asked me what was wrong and how he could provide what the soldiers would eat. I told him I could suggest a quick and easy fix that would make everybody happy and be easier and less expensive for him. Saving money and pleasing us made him curious. I told him I would send two of my soldiers to the commissary at the Supreme Headquarters Allied Powers Europe (SHAPE), which was a short distance away in Mons, Belgium, and get 200 pounds of grits. I assured him my people would show him how to cook them, and he would have no difficulty with breakfast in the future because we would buy grits whenever they were needed. I suggested that every day's breakfast be the same menu: grits; scrambled eggs; bacon, ham or sausage; fruit juice, milk, coffee; bread and jelly. I told him that these foods would make the soldiers happy every day.

The first morning after we got him the grits our food merchant prepared all the same stuff as before and added our grits to the offering; sure enough, the grits, eggs, and meats were cleaned out and all the other stuff was left. From that day onward, we had grits, eggs, and meats for breakfast; that ended the food complaints.

The REFORGER 86 exercises went well, and except for so many soldiers coming home sick with colds or flu, the mission and training experience was outstanding. Following the exercise, we prepared the equipment and stored it at the Port for shipping back home. The main body flew home all together on one charter commercial 747 aircraft, except for the six personnel super cargo that came back on the ship with the equipment.

After 4½ years in battalion command, I was becoming tired and weary, and so was much of my staff. I had commanded one in-state and three out-of-state deployments for annual training, and one overseas deployment; that had taken a toll over time. Nonetheless, it was a great opportunity to command the battalion during those five annual training periods. I have great memories of all the things we accomplished together, many of the subordinate officers and soldiers taught me a lot, and I just hope I provided the leadership and support they needed.

On February 1, 1986, I was reassigned to the Installation Support Unit at Camp Blanding; I became the Director of Plans and Training for the military post. I served in that capacity until February 6, 1989, when I was reassigned as Deputy Commander, 53rd Signal Brigade (the signal brigade was the former signal group), with its Headquarters in Tallahassee. I was promoted to Colonel on February 7, 1989, and served as the Deputy Brigade Commander through annual training 1989. During that annual training we held a major signal exercise that extended tactical communications systems across north Florida from Tyndall Air Force Base near Panama City, to Tallahassee, to Live Oak, to Camp Blanding, and on down to the Orlando International Airport property.

COMMODORE

My work at the Department of Education marched right along; and this was about the time when the personal computer technology began to emerge on a reasonably large scale. I had a jumpstart on most people because of my Blue Cross employment; so, I purchased a *Commodore 64* computer for home use. The Office had a personal computer for us to do some advanced work and I was trying to learn as much as possible about *WordPerfect* and *Lotus 1-2-3*; these were our word processing and spreadsheet programs and were the most advanced packages of the day for personal computers. Most employees in the Department of Education had limited knowledge about personal computers because just about everything was either done manually or on mainframe computers at the Northwest Regional Data Center. Computing, for the most part, was not an individual responsibility but that of programmers who served the whole department for information storage, retrieval, and analysis.

My interest in personal computers and the various office programs kind of went hand-in-hand; I have always enjoyed learning new things and then using them in my work. The Office of Educational Facilities had a staff of about 75 professional and support employees, with a Director of the office, and two bureau chiefs, and each bureau chief had two managers. My bureau chief was over the Educational Facilities Planning and Budgeting Bureau and had a staff of about 35 employees. He had a Manager over the Educational Facilities Planning and Evaluation Section, and a Manager over the Educational Facilities Budgeting Section.

The other bureau chief, who had a staff of about 40 professional and support staff, was over the Technical Review and Training Bureau, and had two section managers. One was a manager over the Technical Review Section consisting of architects, mechanical engineers, electrical engineers, and structural engineers who reviewed and approved all public schools and community colleges architectural plans for compliance with building codes. The other manager was over the Training Section which consisted of specialists that traveled to school districts and community colleges to provide training on environmental issues and fire safety procedures; they also spent time training building custodians and building maintenance staffs on the technical and best-practice methods for those types of services.

During the spring of 1987 our bureau chief, Mr. Sterling Bryant, retired and his job was advertised as a vacancy the state wanted to fill. There were about six people that applied, including three with PhD's, and with anywhere from 10 to 15 years experience in the office. Mr. Bowen, my supervisor (a black man), also applied for the job. Mr. Bowen told me that he knew he wouldn't be selected to fill the position because the Director of the Office didn't like him, and besides he was too close to retirement to be appointed bureau chief. Mr. Bowen encouraged me to apply. I told him I had been there less than two years and all the other applicants had many more years of experience and most had doctoral degrees. He said all that was true, but none had the extensive real world and in the trenches experiences that I had. He felt that my eight years as superintendent would give credibility to my appointment if I were selected as the successful candidate.

Mr. Bowen knew I was a straight shooter; I wasn't going to play politics, and I would tell things as I saw them: good or bad. Mr. Bowen's last point was the clincher that really encouraged me to apply; he said that he knew he wouldn't get the job and he would rather work for me than for any of the others applicants.

I realized that if I applied and was selected for the job, I would jump two management levels and would suddenly become my boss's boss. I remembered that as superintendent every person in every management position was older than me, most had been in their jobs for a long time, and we all got along well. Also, when I was Company Commander of the local National Guard unit, every commissioned officer, warrant officer, and platoon sergeant in the unit was older than me. I never drew attention, or mentioned the age inversion as a factor; I just tried to deal with each person respectfully, and professionally. I took Mr. Bowen's advice.

All the applicants for the vacant Bureau Chief position were interviewed, and I was selected for the job. The Office of Educational

Facilities was in the Collins Building at the time, and we didn't move to the 10th floor in the Turlington Building until late summer, 1989. I was very busy learning all the functions and details of the job at my level and the next level down. Mr. Bowen, the manager that originally hired me, was extremely helpful and supportive of me as was all the other staff. Many had a hard time figuring out how I got the job, but there was no need to explain, all that was required for me was to just do my job.

Betty Castor was the Commissioner of Education when I was appointed Bureau Chief; many thought I knew her before I got the job and that was how I got hired. I have never in my entire career, civilian or military, attempted to use leverage from friendships, political connections, or any other means to secure a job. Again, what the other applicants didn't know was that I had never met or spoken to Betty Castor; I learned later that it was my past experience as a superintendent, and my reputation of honesty, fairness, and hard work that allowed me to edge out the other more senior, and more experienced applicants for the job.

CHILD LABOR

By the fall of 1987 my National Guard duties and work with the Department of Education had become more demanding. It was like having two full-time jobs—one civilian and one military. JoAnn was, for the most part, a stay-at-home mom doing all those tasks a mother does to keep the family running. However, when we moved from Jacksonville to Tallahassee in 1984, JoAnn continued to keep her teaching certification current in order to do some substitute teaching at Lincoln High School, where our daughters attended, and at Lively Vocational Technical School in the child care program.

The girls were in high school. Becky started having part-time jobs during her first year in high school and continued to work throughout high school. Her first job was at a yogurt store in Governor's Square Mall. She worked three hours a night and made about $3 an hour. Since she was only 14 years old, we had to drive her to work, return home, and then drive back and pick her up from work. It would have been much cheaper for me, and easier too, if I had just given the money to her, but she wouldn't have gained the valuable work experience, understood the effort required to earn money, and appreciate the value of her earnings. As Becky began her senior year at Lincoln High School, she was involved in several high school activities as secretary of the senior class and working on the yearbook. As a senior she was selected through the high school business department to work part-time for IBM. I bought a used *Honda Civic* for her to drive herself and Brenda to school each day, and she could also drive herself to her part-time job. That gave me a little relief from all the extra duties I had.

With Brenda's school activities, she began to drive after Becky left home for college at The University of Florida. She took piano lessons in high school. Brenda was a good swimmer and made the swim team for three years and served as team captain her senior year. During her senior year, swimming practice at a city pool was early in the morning from about 5:30 a.m. to 6:30 a.m. The fact that she had her drivers' license, drove herself to swim practice, returned home, and dressed for her school day helped her learn more discipline and responsibility.

Both Becky and Brenda were excellent students, self-motivated, and made good grades. At home, any time JoAnn and I discussed their future, in any way, we always referred to their lives as "after you graduate from college." We tried to discuss college as a matter of fact, as if there were no other options. We never had to nag or beg either of them to study and get their school work done.

One time Becky made a C in geometry and came home all upset about it. She wanted to discuss it with me and asked, "Are you upset?" I told her I wasn't upset over the grade, but if she was upset, then I was happy; because I knew if she was upset, she could do something about it; there was nothing I could do. Becky didn't enjoy mathematics, but she still performed quite well in her math classes despite her dislike for the subject.

Brenda, on the other hand, was more into the math and science courses. She always said she wanted to attend The University of Florida and be an engineer or dentist.

Starting in high school, Becky always planned to attend The Florida State University. One night in the fall of 1987, Becky told me she wanted to talk. I knew it must be serious; at least it was to her. Becky wanted to know what I would say if she wanted to attend The University of Florida; I told her that would be fine with me. She said some of her friends were going there and she wanted to join them. I think part of her reason for wanting to go to The University of Florida was to get farther away from home. Children need the opportunity to grow up, and that can be hard for them to do at home or even in college when they are in the same city with their family. So, during her senior year, Becky changed her mind and after graduating from high school she went to The University of Florida.

There were no college prepaid tuition programs when we were preparing for our daughters to attend college. The *Florida Bright Futures Academic Scholars* program wasn't available when Becky finished high school, but it was offered when Brenda graduated. Brenda was able to take advantage of the scholarship program and it paid most of her first four years of college. We didn't save for their college, but knew with their help and being frugal where possible, we could pay-as-you-go, and that's what we did.

When each of our daughters graduated from high school, thanks to their help, JoAnn going back to full-time work, Becky's part-time work and Brenda's scholarship, their college was paid for. Both took college classes at FSU in the summer following their high school sophomore year, and got college credit in humanities for a 21-day European travel/study trip following their junior year. Each of the girls also took as many dual-enrollment classes as possible at Lincoln High School, and each finished high school with about 28 semester hours of college credit.

We told both our daughters that they had to attend a state college or university because we simply couldn't afford to pay private college or out-of-state tuition. I also told them they had no choice but to live in a college dorm room at least during their freshman year at the university. We made that decision for two main reasons; one was the cost, and the other was that each of our daughters had always enjoyed their own private bedrooms and I felt that they needed to learn what it was like to share a small room with one or two other people. I believed that living on campus gave them a greater opportunity to be a part of the university and to participate in all the various activities that were going on in the university environment. We wanted them to start college immediately after graduating from high school, because by enrolling in summer school, taking a couple of classes, gave each a chance to learn their way around campus before the mass of students arrived in August. Both stayed in the college dorm their freshman years, both pledged to the Delta Gamma Sorority during their freshman years, and each lived in the Sorority house during their sophomore and junior years, and then lived in a rented house with two or three other girls during their senior years. Actually, both followed the same track through college, Brenda was just always two years behind Becky.

Becky began classes at The University of Florida in the summer session of 1988, and Brenda started in the summer session of 1990; each started immediately after graduating from Lincoln High School. This was about the time JoAnn launched into full-time employment with the Florida Department of Education. Becky earned a degree in Speech Communications and Brenda's degree was in Industrial Engineering. Both girls later completed graduate work. Becky, shortly after getting married, earned a Masters Degree in Adult Education from the University of South Florida in Tampa. Brenda, after working several years, earned a Masters Degree in Business Administration from Emory University in Atlanta. They are proud of their accomplishments, and so are we.

SURGEON

With our children in college, JoAnn and I took advantage of some traveling opportunities associated with my positions at the Florida Department of Education and the Florida National Guard. In 1989 I was asked to go, as a delegate, to the national meeting of the National Guard Association of the United States in Nashville, Tennessee. Other National Guard Association related trips included: September 1990 to Reno, Nevada; September 1991 to Alaska and Hawaii; and in September 1992 to Salt Lake City, Utah. These were almost like vacations even though I had to spend a lot of my time on official duties. Just having the freedom to go places, even though it was work, was a new experience that JoAnn and I enjoyed.

On May 1, 1989, I was reassigned as the Deputy Commander at Troop Command, in Jacksonville; the Headquarters was commanded by Brigadier General Thomas Sprenger. In civilian life, General Sprenger was an orthopedic surgeon in Bradenton, Florida. General Sprenger was militarily very technically and tactically competent and demonstrated outstanding leadership skills; he was also great to work for.

In January 1990 I received a telephone call from General Sprenger; he asked if I would like to become a surgeon for the military. I told him, "If that's required, I'm ready." Of course, he was kidding me about being a surgeon. But he did say he wanted to place me in command of the 202nd Medical Group, and wanted to know my thoughts on the idea. I told him that would be fine and I looked forward to the challenge; after all, command is command and what is most important for a commander is leadership. Still, inside I was wondering who had I teed-off that would cause me to get this kind of assignment. Nevertheless, it was a Colonel Command, and even though I had never dreamed of commanding a medical unit, I also realized there were very limited Colonel Command positions in the Florida Army National Guard, and General Sprenger had given me a great opportunity.

DESERT STORM
SMART SCHOOLS
CLEARINGHOUSE
RETIREMENT

It's a fine thing to rise above pride, but you must have pride in order to do so. Georges Bernanos.

I REALLY LOOKED FORWARD, though with mixed emotions, to command of the 202nd Medical Group located at the Cedar Hills Armory in Jacksonville. Foremost in my mind was the fact that I had always found it difficult to deal with the military medical community; they seemed to march to a different drum.

Brigadier General Sprenger and Major General Ensslin told me they had complete trust in my ability to straighten out the problems that plagued the 202nd Medical Group. I knew I had their full backing and support to take what action I felt necessary to fix the problems and to bring the unit to a higher level of operational readiness—military style.

General Ensslin was The Adjutant General (TAG) of Florida. He and General Sprenger began the seemingly impossible task of getting the Army Medical Department at the Pentagon to allow me to take command of the 202nd Medical Group. Even though I was willing to attend the Medical Service School at Fort Sam Houston in San Antonio, Texas, the Surgeon General of the Army wouldn't allow me to go there because I was a Colonel, which according to guidelines made me too senior in rank for that particular school.

The 202nd Medical Group staffing called for a medical doctor to be in command; therefore, I couldn't qualify to command the unit. Nonetheless, I started doing the job functions as if I were the commander. The current commander, a Colonel and also a Medical Doctor (Psychiatrist), became a shadow commander with me doing the actual leadership. Even though the Doctor was technically in command, I was essentially performing all the duties and functions of commander.

From a structural perspective, I had strong reservations about taking the command because it was, after all, a medical unit; from a tactical position, I was still elated to have a command at the full Colonel level because, organizationally, to me, it was just another leadership assignment. I assessed the management of the organization and realigned several staff members, terminated a few, and ridded the unit of some poor or non-performers which included one doctor.

Once the organizing began, we made great progress. What the unit needed was leadership, direction, and organizational effectiveness. I immediately began making plans for two weeks of tactical medical training during annual training at Camp Blanding; and to provide a few selected required short medical courses for the Medical Professional Staff during the annual training period. With the new structure, our annual training went well for our headquarters, and for the subordinate medical units under my command, which included two separate medical companies: a MASH hospital, and several medical detachments of various types. The actual Medical Group commander was present during annual training and I saw him about once a day, but in reality, I was totally in charge of the exercise. He didn't interfere with anything I did or question any changes I made; one thing that worked in my favor was that he didn't like commanding because of all the operational and personnel problems that went along with leadership. I rather enjoyed the challenge so we made a good team.

The mission of the 202nd Medical Group was to provide command and control of three to seven hospitals or battalion-size units; upwards of about 3,000 soldiers. The unit didn't offer any definitive health care but did provide professional coordination, guidance, and consultative services.

COMMAND

After several months of negotiating by the senior leadership of the Florida National Guard and the National Guard Bureau in the Pentagon, the Army Surgeon General finally agreed to a 24-month technical waiver for me to command the 202nd Medical Group. I officially assumed command on July 21, 1990. The 202nd Medical Group had subordinate units in Jacksonville, Camp Blanding, Tallahassee, Tampa, Saint Augustine, and Miami.

After getting rid of some of the deadwood in the group, the unit began to turnaround and function more like a military operation. As soon as I was given unofficial command, I started making serious changes in the crucial positions. During the first six months, I relieved the Executive Officer, a Lieutenant Colonel; a Medical Doctor, who was a Colonel (my rank); an active army Captain; reassigned some Majors; reassigned some senior NCOs; and began to develop a working professional military staff.

The medical doctor simply didn't want to work and do what he was instructed to do, so I zeroed in on his lack of performance and gave him two options: work or resign. Since he was so lazy and sorry, he chose to resign. The military was better off without him.

It quickly became obvious that there was a new sheriff in town after I fired or relieved a few staff of their responsibilities. Everyone in the unit had a very simple choice, get on board with the improvements or get out of the way. Since my job was to create a well-oiled military machine, I really didn't care which option they chose because we were going to achieve our goals with or without any particular individual. We had several disgruntled people who wanted to transfer and I was happy for them to leave because their replacements all had better attitudes and work ethics; for the most part, the replacements we received had a higher quality of technical and tactical skills as well. Those who wanted to stay already had the values and ethics we needed for success. So, it wasn't a matter of getting rid of everyone; it was only a matter of fine-tuning what we had and replacing what didn't work.

For the first several months our staff meetings were tense because of the change from a long-entrenched low level of expectations, sloppy paper work, and poor organization to a unit with rigid structure and fine-tuned operations. It took me about six months to bring about a total transformation, which wasn't too bad for the task I was given.

Throughout my military career both my superiors and subordinates noted that my strength was the ability to bring order out of chaos. By the time official approval was authorized for me to take command, the operational readiness of the unit had improved with every guard drill. I gained more confidence in the unit and was pleased when I considered its potential in the wake of our new direction. The primary staff I placed in the vital positions began to click as a team and they told me they were comfortable with me and their job requirements. As usual, I continuously emphasized professionalism, meeting the Army standard, raising the percentage of Military Occupational Skills (MOS) qualifications, and total unit readiness.

WAR

One month after I was approved for command, Iraq invaded Kuwait; the invasion was in August 1990. By October, National Guard and Army Reserve units were being mobilized to support the Persian Gulf War. Even though the pace of mobilization for the Persian Gulf War continued to increase for certain units in the Florida National Guard, the 202nd Medical Group was not on the initial planning list. On a Sunday afternoon, November 18, 1990, I received a call from Troop Command Headquarters informing me that General Sprenger, the Troop Command Commander, was on his way to the 202nd Medical

Group Headquarters to see me. I suspected the 202nd had been placed on the planning list and General Sprenger was coming to give official notification and discuss our mobilization readiness. He arrived some 30 minutes later and told me that earlier that morning the 202nd Medical Group had been placed high on the list. We began intense discussions about post-mobilization planning and command and control of my other subordinate units in the event we were mobilized.

After General Sprenger left I called in the staff and notified them of the unit's status and advised them to focus on preparation for mobilization. I told the staff that we had been placed on the planning list for possible mobilization and deployment to the Middle East and that I would inform the entire unit at the final formation just before dismissal for the weekend.

As I addressed the entire unit on that Sunday afternoon, I shared openly the very real possibility of our mobilization and deployment to war. I instructed our soldiers to get their personal finances, business dealings, and family affairs in order because our mobilization could occur at any time. I shared with the unit what I had shared with the staff earlier regarding what I thought would be required by the unit and each section to prepare for mobilization. The discussion was very frank, open, thought provoking, and a sobering experience. The purpose of the discussion was to build confidence and not to make our troops fearful of war. I didn't say it, but the words of General George S. Patton would've fit in quite well to build confidence among our troops; he said, "The object of war is not to die for your country but to make the other bastard die for his." General Patton was rough spoken, but he had great insight into how we should view warfare.

I shared my thoughts regarding the individual and unit preparation required to meet the challenge of leaving home and going to war, if it should come our lot to go. No one was negative and an air of positive commitment prevailed. For parents with young children, especially mothers, certainly there was additional anxiety for their families, and at the same time, they had the commitment of being professional soldiers. I told everyone that my personal thoughts were mixed with professional responsibility of command, leadership, and maintaining a positive can-do, will-do attitude. I added that I also had to think of my own personal circumstances, my employment, and getting my personal affairs in order. That discussion with the unit proved to be beneficial because we entered active duty a short 11 days later.

MOBILIZING

On Friday, November 23rd at approximately 1:15 p.m., I was called by Colonel Bridges; he was director of the Plans, Operations, Training, and Mobilization for the Florida Army National Guard. Colonel Bridges issued the pre-alert message. I immediately notified Major Hartley who was my full-time Administrative Officer; Major Athanaseas my Operations Officer; Major Greene my Logistics Officer; Command Sergeant Major Finnerty; and Lieutenant Colonel Mason my Executive Officer.

I instructed Major Hartley, Major Athanaseas, and Major Greene to immediately mobilize the five individuals we had identified for placement on active duty; they were ordered to report on Saturday, November 24, 1990. By that evening, which was Thanksgiving weekend, Major Hartley reported back to me that everyone had been alerted.

I visited the headquarters in Jacksonville on Saturday, November 24th, to review preliminary plans, and visit the members already ordered to active duty along with the other full-time support staff. During that meeting we discussed any potentially non-deployable personnel and their possible replacements. The intensity of preparation continued with stepped-up emphasis on everything by everyone.

I notified my civilian boss, Dr. Jim Schroeer, Director of the Office of Educational Facilities, and Betty Castor, the Commissioner of Education, of my pending deployment. Commissioner Castor suggested that I submit an annual leave request for the next 12 months, using annual leave for the first day of each month, and taking leave without pay for the remainder of each month. That was helpful since I never officially left the state payroll and kept my benefits, such as medical insurance and my parking space, in force throughout my deployment. Commissioner Castor also wrote me a nice personal letter while I was deployed. It's good when our leaders recognize the sacrifice we make and then they act to personally acknowledge what we are doing. Soldiers appreciate that; I was no exception.

The official activation notice came on Tuesday, November 27th at approximately 2:30 p.m. We had less than a day and a half to transition from civilian jobs, work out our problems with employers, and finalize any individual preparation of packing in order to report for active duty at 8:00 a.m. on November 29th at the armory in Jacksonville. Everyone reported to the armory on Thursday morning with no AWOLs. At the first formation, the detailed plans for preparing for deployment were shared with the unit.

POWER STRUGGLE

I had been on active duty less than four hours when I started getting telephone calls from a Colonel in the medical service office at the Pentagon. He suggested that I resign and he assured me that he and his constituents would make absolutely certain that I wouldn't deploy with the unit as its commander; his sole objection was that I was a Signal Officer and not a Medical Officer. The Colonel said that he couldn't command a signal group and didn't feel I could command a medical group. I didn't agree, and the medical service officer was making a mistake. There's an old Kurdish proverb that says a man shouldn't throw the arrow which will return against him—that's what the Colonel was doing. But his ego was so involved that he couldn't objectively see what he was doing.

After he persisted in making demanding calls for me to excuse myself from deploying with the unit, I bluntly and clearly expressed myself to him. I told him I agreed he probably couldn't command a signal group, but I was sure I was a far more experienced and capable commander than he, and I had every confidence that I would do a perfect military job in my command. That made him furious; I believe he wanted to command the unit, and he saw me as an obstacle to his personal desires. I think the Colonel wanted to get his ticket punched as having combat command experience which would look good on his military record and résumé. Since the Colonel was having a difficult time pressuring me into compliance with his whims, I wanted to make it perfectly clear what my intentions were. I told him it would be a cold day in hell when I requested to be relieved of the command because of his influence; I also told him that I didn't ask for the command and I would never ask to be relieved of it unless I thought my being in command would bring harm to the unit—which I didn't believe was the case. An old Japanese proverb says something like when the character of a man is not clear to you look at his friends; I would like to have seen this Colonel's friends—if he had any. He just seemed too power hungry to me.

I wasn't concerned about getting a ticket punched, or a promotion; all I wanted was to continue to provide good leadership to the staff I had just molded together. To me, at the group-level command, all anyone can do is primarily manage people, time, and resources. While I agree that it is helpful to be technically and tactically proficient in the special area one is commanding, I believe it is less essential in the medical corps since I had medical doctors on my staff that could provide me with technical advice whenever I needed it. I soon found that most, not all, but most doctors make poor leaders and commanders; they are too technically and skill driven to have to deal with managing things on a large scale. Doctors, by and large, function independently, make independent decisions that are unique to medically related conditions, and most have their offices and practices managed for them. That's a good thing because when patients need medical help, they don't need an administrator to organize surgery or prescribe medications—they need the precision skills of someone who works on a specific problem.

MORE PREPARATION

Each operational section of the unit began its in-processing, inventorying, packing, labeling, blocking, and bracing of our equipment for movement to our mobilization station in Fort Stewart, Georgia, on Saturday, December 1, 1990.

Much of our required peace-time immunizations had been completed during the guard drill weekend held October 21st & 22nd at Camp Blanding by the 131st Mobile Army Surgical Hospital (MASH). Nevertheless, there were some pantographic X-rays, Powers of Attorney, Defense Enrollment Eligibility Reporting System (DEERS) forms, Dependent ID cards, ID card photographs, and several other small tasks to be completed on Thursday and Friday. Chief Warrant Officer Tom Martin, a United States Property and Fiscal Officer (USP&FO) representative, was there to help with the transfer of property from state control to federal use. Family support personnel were available to help families. The news media made at least two visits. All of our meals were provided from local restaurants under a food service contract. The most laborious task was the inventory, packing, and bracing of property. Sleeping accommodations were contracted at the Ramada Inn for everyone who lived more than 50 miles from the armory.

The work required for deployment of the advance party was completed late Thursday night and they left for Fort Stewart at 5:00 a.m. on Friday, November 30, 1990. While coordination with Fort Stewart was being conducted by the advance party, final plans for deploying the main body were completed by 8:00 p.m. The unit formed at 7:00 a.m. on Saturday, December 1st to complete the last minute loading of sensitive equipment and soldiers' personal baggage. While in the final formation prior to boarding the buses, brief comments were made by Florida's Adjutant General, Assistant Adjutant General, Troop Command Commander, and numerous City of Jacksonville and local Legislative officials. Besides all the troops and officials, there were many family members and friends who had come to watch their loved ones leave for war. I guess their anxiety was higher than that of our soldiers—at least soldiers are prepared for the possibility of war. Family members know that soldiers go to war, but they don't have the training or psychological benefit of drilling and preparing for it.

The Adjutant General personally walked the formation with his wife, Faye, along with others and wished each soldier well. This was an emotional and difficult time not only for families but also for the many military and civilian friends that came to see the unit off.

At approximately 9:15 a.m., the charter bus and the remaining military vehicles left in convoy with a supportive community wishing us well. The main body arrived at Fort Stewart at noon and began its pre-deployment phase. We were met by the advance party and escorted to billeting facilities in the reserve component area. After the unit settled in during the afternoon, the balance of the day, which took until after midnight, was used preparing and painting our vehicles a desert-brown color. Military efficiency should be lauded, in less than 12 hours on post, all our vehicles were re-painted. The unit spent Sunday completing the in-processing requirements: dental screening, finance, ID cards, and immunizations. Monday was spent at required pre-deployment briefings. Tuesday was consumed on the firing range zeroing weapons, shooting for familiarization, and qualification with weapons.

We used all day Wednesday for NBC (Nuclear Biological Chemical) training. The nine NBC stations were carefully planned, staffed, and operated. Anything to do with nuclear, biological, or chemical issues was extremely important to each soldier because of the high level of threat we expected once we reached the theater of operations. The instruction we got was both superior and well received by our troops. Thomas Huxley understood the value of excellent instruction; one thing he said was that the most valuable result of all education is the ability to make yourself do the thing you have to do, when it ought to be done, whether you like it or not. To me, that pretty much sums up preparation for war. We had the training offered to us, and we endeared ourselves to it.

The Adjutant General, General Ensslin, the Assistant Adjutant General, General Capps, and the Troop Command Commander, General Sprenger, visited the unit at MOB station and gave us their support. We spent the rest of our time in CTT (Common Task Training) requesting supplies and packing equipment that was to be deployed with the unit. Some of our time was devoted to staff planning, revising and updating the units operating procedures, and clarifying operational responsibilities and procedures.

Our unit contacted the ARCENT Surgeon's Office at Fort McPherson, in Atlanta, several times trying to get clarification on our mission and subordinate units. Clarification can sometimes be a tedious and time-consuming task simply due to the mass and scope of the venture and the number of people that make and then relate official orders. Our Operations Officer contacted the subordinate units on the TPFDL (Time Phased Force Deployment List). We shared what limited information we had, which wasn't much, but it was the best we could do and it kept everyone informed—at least to some degree.

The validation of the 202nd Medical Group for deployment was completed on the 12th of December by the Second Army Commander, Lieutenant General Crysel, and a departure date was scheduled for December 18, 1990. Family members were permitted to visit only at a specifically designated time. I gave the unit members a 24-hour pass to be with their family who made the trip to Fort Stewart. Most soldiers spent the day on Saturday doing some shopping and enjoying a few civilian meals, and then on Sunday morning attending church services with their loved ones.

JoAnn and I agreed that she wouldn't see the unit off from Jacksonville; she brought our daughters, Becky and Brenda, from The University of Florida to visit me on the last weekend. I made arrangements for us to stay as a family at a nearby motel. This gave me an opportunity to gain strength, support, and insight from my family that also helped me to understand how the deployment of troops into war affects every family. I learned, firsthand, just how heart-wrenching and painful it is to leave those you love the most and head into a situation that can kill you. It is something soldiers do by choice through patriotism, but few, if any, ever enjoy it. While duty is an honor, it has a definite measure of fear and uncertainty that goes along with it.

While at Fort Stewart, Lieutenant General Crysel (three stars), the Commanding General, Second United States Army, Headquartered at Fort Gillem, Georgia, came to visit and evaluate the training and readiness of the units deploying to the Persian Gulf area. During General Crysel's visit, he sent word for me to come see him at Post Headquarters. Since there had been a move launched to keep me from commanding a medical unit, I considered that since General Crysel had to validate my unit as combat ready, perhaps he had some reservations about me commanding the Medical Group. I knew that he was fully informed about my signal/medical situation. And since the Colonel who was so interested in the command had not succeeded in bullying me out of command, I was certain that he had called higher ranking officials to try his hand at outmaneuvering me.

General Crysel was quite personable, and he assured me that I would deploy into the Theater of Operations in the Persian Gulf area as Commander of the 202nd Medical Group. He also said that his authority and control ended once we landed in the Theater of Operations; General Crysel added that he didn't know what would happen to me once I arrived in the theater; in fact, he said that I might be sent home, not because of my ability or performance, but simply because I wasn't qualified in the Medical Branch.

Also while we were at Fort Stewart, General Vouno (four stars), the Chief of Staff, United States Army, Headquartered at the Pentagon, came to visit and evaluate the training and readiness of units deploying to the Persian Gulf area. Like all the others, he was pleased with our readiness. He, too, had probably received an earful trying to get me relieved, but he never mentioned it.

A military deployment frequently generates personal actions and decisions that have long term effects. Speeding up plans for marriage is a classic example. One of my male soldiers asked me for permission to marry before our deployment. Since there was still time, and it seemed important to the soldier, I gave him my permission and blessing. I gave the bride away, and the entire unit attended the wedding ceremony; we were all dressed in BDU (Battle Dress Uniforms), and the only civilian present was the bride's mother. I made an exception to the standard mobilization policy and we collected enough donations to give the newly married couple a one-night honeymoon.

While getting married one day and leaving for war the next is not necessarily the most logical or brilliant personal choice someone can make, it is still a persons individual choice. If I had denied the request, I would have been seen as insensitive and not caring about the soldiers in my command. I did care; that was why I authorized it, participated by giving the bride away, allowed the soldiers to collect money from their ranks as a gift, and then approved a one night leave for the newlyweds—while all other married soldiers stayed with the unit. That is the kind of thing that makes loyal soldiers; preventing them from exercising a personal choice only creates bitterness and resentment— and these can be real morale killers, and worse in a war zone.

ON THE WAY

We deployed using two aircrafts, one C-141, and one C-5. The unit deployed with eight male officers, 27 male enlisted, two female officers, and seven female enlisted for a total of 44 individuals. As the last of our equipment was loaded into the C-5 aircraft, the unit looked around one final time at the USA and realized that our departure was for real; it wasn't an exercise or a training maneuver. We were going to Saudi Arabia. This was the first truly emotional feeling we had felt about going to war. We departed at 3:15 p.m., Friday, December 21, 1990, and made a refueling stop at Torrejon Air Force Base, Spain. A hanger had been set up for all military personnel traveling to Saudi Arabia, which included a cold shower, hot meal, video movies, coffee, and cookies. There were ice crystals on the ground because it was so cold outside; that was our first nature encounter that was different from our 70 degree winter-weather in Florida. But nature was waiting on us everywhere we went; and Mother Nature never was at a loss for surprises.

We arrived in Dhahran, Saudi Arabia, at 8:30 p.m., Saturday, December 22, 1990. It was an awesome, overwhelming feeling unloading on the tarmac in the dark with jets flying overhead and numerous military C-5As, C-141s, and commercial 747s parked and unloading passengers, bags, and supplies. It looked as if we were going to be there a while with a lot of soldiers from all over the United States. As we looked around, we experienced our second emotional experience that this was for real. The baggage and equipment were off-loaded and buses (school bus type, with foreign nationals as drivers) were there to transport the unit to its temporary holding facility at a place called *Cement City*. We had arrived at the world's largest sand box.

Cement City was a temporarily closed cement factory with enough general purpose (GP) large tents to house approximately 6,000 troops. We had 32 people living in one tent along with all their personal belongings. Living conditions were miserable. Our females told us when they awoke the first morning they were greeted by other female soldiers, who had been there for quite a while, with the greeting, "Welcome to hell." When it was daylight and we looked around, we agreed that Satan probably was the mayor of Cement City and maybe even governor of the Province.

DESERT ACCOMMODATIONS

We had to wash our clothes with bottled water and hang them on the tent ropes to dry. Because of the wind and sand, we usually had to shake out a lot of sand before we could wear any garment that had been hung out to dry; and most especially underwear because the grit was as abrasive as sandpaper and would remove a substantial amount of skin if given the opportunity.

Shower facilities were crude with forever long lines and an overbearing Sergeant outside yelling, "Your seven minutes are up, move it!" There was no such thing as a long leisurely soak in a tub or a refreshing shower that lasted long enough to relieve the never-ending stress that was made worse by our hostile surroundings.

Latrine facilities were port-a-let style wooden boxes with screening around the top; these things smelled terrible. They were pumped out daily by civilian contract personnel, but because of the heat they still smelled awful. The latrine architecture was similar throughout the theater, and we soon forgot what porcelain felt like; but not so much that we didn't wish for it. Our latrines were located about 100 yards from the sleeping tents, and the cold nights made latrine runs a real challenge. It was amazing how fast we could do the 100 yard dash.

The dining facilities also left much to be desired; food was cooked in a tent but all eating was done on the outside on benches, tables, or sitting on the ground. T-rations were served for breakfast and meals-ready-to-eat (MREs) for lunch. The King of Saudi Arabia paid for us to have a hot meal at night, which was actually very good although the food was cold by the time we got it to the table. Nonetheless, we all appreciated his gesture of kindness.

The living tents had wooden floors, but with the dust storms (talcum powder-like dust), sand was in everything we owned within 48 hours. While tents do provide some measure of protection from the elements, they are a far cry from the luxuries, or even basics, of home.

The unit was planning to deploy, almost immediately, to Oman along with its subordinate units, but like all military operations, the time wasn't right—it had to be staged correctly and in order. In the military, timing is everything, so there is a lot of what most soldiers call, "Hurry up and wait." The waiting seemed endless, but trips to the Post Exchange (PX), mail call, Physical Training (PT) each morning, and trips to a hotel downtown to make phone calls made each day pass a little more quickly. Our only communication with loved ones at home was through telephone lines; since a lot of troops were trying to make phone calls, standing in a very long line was our only option, but that was something that was worth the wait.

CHRISTMAS IN CEMENT CITY

Along with thousands of other soldiers, we had a memorable Christmas in Cement City. While we were still at Fort Stewart, we had drawn names to exchange gifts; then, everyone received at least one present on Christmas Day. We brought a Christmas tree with us, which we set up with gifts under it for everyone. There was a Christmas box for each soldier with about $10 worth of goodies for *"ANY SERVICEMAN."* Individual US civilians sent these, and we thoroughly enjoyed the treats and knowing that someone really had remembered us. I read the Christmas story from the Gospel of Luke and Major (Medical Doctor) Fouts led the unit in prayer after which gifts were exchanged.

We had a delicious Christmas dinner with all the trimmings provided by the Saudi King (including ham—which was forbidden by their customs, but he honored ours, and we appreciated that). We certainly missed our families and celebrating Christmas at home but we had our new military family, and we consoled each other during that emotional time.

CHANGING THINGS

I, along with Major Fouts, Major Athanaseas, and Command Sergeant Major Finnerty met with Colonel Tsoulos at 1500 hours on December 26th at the ARCENT/Medical Group (Provisional) Forward at Dhahran, where we were told the ARCENT Commander, Lieutenant General (three stars) Yeosock, had decided to make the Medical Group (Provisional) a part of MEDCOM (Provisional) a Major General (two stars) command effective immediately.

Colonel Tsoulos also informed us the 202nd Medical Group would become the support staff for his principal staff, in addition to maintaining command and control of the three medical hospitals the

202nd Medical Group was already scheduled to deploy to the countries of Oman and the United Arab Emirates. Colonel Tsoulos said that he had been selected by the ARCENT Commander, Lieutenant General Yeosock, to command the MEDCOM. Colonel Tsoulos laid out the overall plan for the theater in a wide-ranging, all-purpose fashion. He told me that he had a MEDCOM staff of about eight people, not counting his consultant staff which was Medical Doctors representing the different medical specialties.

Colonel Tsoulos, who was the Army's Chief Medical Officer in the Theater of Operations, was my commander and I reported directly to him. Immediately following my first meeting with Colonel Tsoulos, we had about five minutes of private time. During this brief time, he told me he knew all about me. I'm sure he had been thoroughly briefed and informed about me long before my arrival. He said he knew I was a signal officer but that didn't matter to him. He told me to take the Signal Corp insignia off all my uniforms and to replace it with the Medical Service Corp insignia. He told me he needed commanders with leadership skills far more than he needed doctors. He said we would get along great and he would be supportive of me, and for me to do my job and not to worry about being Signal Branch, just focus on the mission at hand. My new insignia left many people guessing who I really was, especially those three Colonels who were medical doctors and who commanded the hospitals under my command and reported directly to me.

Colonel Tsoulos, as the ARCENT Surgeon, was responsible for medical policy and medical supplies for the entire theater, and as MEDCOM Commander, he was responsible for all medical units at the EAC (echelons above corps) level. He let me know that the MEDCOM had no equipment; by making us part of his headquarters that gave him an instant headquarters that was staffed, equipped, and operationally ready. Tactically, it was a good maneuver on his part.

On Thursday, December 27, 1990, Command Sergeant Major Finnerty, Major Hartley, Major Athanaseas, Major Pifer, and I drove to Riyadh, Saudi Arabia—about 260 miles away. We went to make preliminary plans to move the advance party and main body to our permanent work location. We returned late Friday, December 28th, discussed our findings with the unit and made plans for the advance party to leave at noon, December 29th, to Riyadh. The main body departed at 9:00 a.m. Sunday, and arrived at approximately 2:45 p.m.

NEW DIGS

Our short stay, which was only eight days but seemed more like eight weeks, at Cement City made our move to any other location a desirable event. We spent the first day cleaning the assigned living quarters, unloading the mil-vans, setting up cots, fixing water heaters, unpacking personal belongings, and all the other organizational tasks it took to make our new location livable.

The living quarters were seven-story high-rise buildings with parking garages underneath. Each building had marble entrances, halls, foyers, and staircases. According to the information we received, the buildings were constructed in 1982 to house the Bedouins (nomads) who lived in the desert. They refused to occupy the buildings, so the structures had been vacant since their completion.

The name of the community was Eskan Village and it was a beautifully designed complex slated to house approximately 125,000 people. The buildings were German designed with bricks on the exterior poured-concrete construction. Each floor had four three-bedroom suites, two on each side of the main elevator entrance. Each suite contained a master bedroom with a private bath, two individual bedrooms with a bath between, a separate family room, kitchen, dining room, living room, and a foyer with a bath. Outside were children playgrounds and a schoolhouse, which the ARCENT Operations Center used.

I would rather kill a pig than write a letter—Alfred Lord Tennyson.

For security reasons, we couldn't tell our families exactly where we were located, and direct communications with family and loved ones back home was very limited. I was able to make a couple of telephone calls to JoAnn and she would reassure the rest of the family that I was okay. All of this was before the internet proliferation, widespread email capabilities, and the unlimited use of cell phones with international roaming and calling. Postage for us to send letters home was free, and I tried writing to my family, including my brothers and sisters, as often as I possibly could. I couldn't use words as masterfully as Tennyson, but I shared his opinion on writing; still, I put forth the effort so that my family wouldn't worry.

Most of my family thought I was living in the sand in a tent; but we had it better than that in Eskan Village simply because we were a medical unit and we needed something a little more enhanced than a tent to provide sanitized health care for wounded soldiers. Many in my family shipped boxes of goodies and other treats for me to enjoy. I guess sending me something to snack on helped them to feel like they were, in some small way, being a part of my everyday life—they were. The small care-packages were great; most all of the soldiers got them. No matter who in the unit got goodies from home, they always shared with everyone else. We had a good measure of camaraderie. At one time, I must have had at least 20 pounds of M&M peanuts in the $1-size bags. I kept anywhere from two to four bags of M&Ms in my pants side pockets all the time, and frequently they were the only lunch I had.

Monday was spent further developing the living area and making preliminary plans to establish a work area for MEDCOM headquarters. On Tuesday morning, the decision was made for us to work in a building of the same type architecture as the high-rise buildings, except it was only four-stories high and each floor contained two three-bedroom suites. The MEDCOM occupied the bottom two floors and the signal command occupied the top two floors.

When we set up the facilities for our occupation, we taped the windows to prevent shatter and covered them on the inside with heavy black visqueen for blackout operations. Our own military switchboard was set up and military tactical phones were placed in all major work areas. The inside offices were wired for lights using the tactical light sets and our two 5-KW generators were carefully placed and sandbagged to provide emergency power, if needed. By Tuesday, the building was scrubbed, cleaned, and operations were established. Again, just as expected, we had a precision move and set up; our soldiers were almost flawless in the performance of their duties.

Communications was the biggest single challenge for us to become operational, and tactical phone circuits were extremely limited. My signal background and experience proved to be valuable almost immediately. I made friends on the first day with officers of Company C, 167th Signal Battalion, from Fort Gordon, Georgia, and with their help, we were able to get limited phone service in about 48 hours. Thanks to Sergeant First Class Jon Allen, my Communications Chief, we were able to get access to the commercial phone service. All of these individual factors, some seemingly small, were extremely important overall because the ARCENT Surgeon/MEDCOM Commander was still in downtown Riyadh at the MODA (Minister of Defense and Aviation) building, which was about 40 minutes travel time away. By January 9, 1991, communications in the MEDCOM headquarters building was sufficient and stable enough for the MEDCOM Commander to move the command group from downtown out to our location at Eskan Village.

The command section of the MEDCOM consisted of the Commander and ARCENT Surgeon, Colonel D. O. Tsoulos; Chief of Staff, Colonel Frank B. Holland; me, as the Commander of the 202nd Medical Group, and Acting Deputy MEDCOM Commander; Colonel William Brock Watson, MEDCOM Chaplain (he was State Chaplain for the Missouri National Guard); Major Stanford Sur, Adjutant; and MEDCOM Command Sergeant Major Finnerty (my CSM).

Colonel Tsoulos' medical specialty was as a general surgeon. He was a chain smoker, screamed and yelled at and about everything and everybody, and used curse words in just about every sentence. Most of the 12 doctors on his staff seemed to fear him, but for some reason he was never anything but professional, polite, and helpful to Colonel Holland and me. I think it was because he knew we both worked every waking minute of the day to make his command successful. I believe he realized it and appreciated it. But for everyone else, it was hell.

The 202nd Medical Operations unit had obtained seven Zenith laptop computers with seven printers and ample software and fax machines at Fort Stewart in preparation for deployment. The USP&FO for Florida had provided the unit a new copy machine; a piece of equipment that proved to be invaluable since the MEDCOM didn't have a copy machine nor did any of the other units located in our vicinity. We were definitely the best-prepared unit to go to work and accomplish our assigned tasks either in a tactical or built-up environment. Our field equipment was easily adaptable to the built-up area and served the MEDCOM well during the entire operation.

The 202nd Medical Group had opened an account for local purchases while we were still in Cement City near Dhahran and we were able to pick up a lot of the supplies we needed to get the operation going. We got electrical parts, civilian telephones, copy machine repair services, printer ribbons, and other office supplies.

We were also able to obtain certain creature comforts for our living area, which included electrical adapters, a TV for each suite, a small refrigerator for each suite, a small foam mattress for each cot, and cleaning materials for each suite. The unit had brought a microwave oven, coffee pots, and other things from our home station in Jacksonville—these were some of the most useful items we had. The laundry facilities in Eskan Village provided excellent, three-day service, pressed BDUs, and folded fluff at no charge. As time went by, our living conditions got better: we had beds instead of cots, then thicker foam-rubber mattresses, and finally we got metal wall lockers with hangings on one side and shelving on the other side. Each of these conveniences made for slightly improved living conditions, but then every little bit helps and each little amenity becomes a blessing. For our comfort, heating and air conditioning units were installed in each room, courtesy of the Saudi King. For the first part of our stay, we had access to three mess halls that were run by the Air Force; they did an excellent job serving us.

RENEWED ACQUAINTANCES

One day, a group of non-medical soldiers showed up at my headquarters and wanted to see me. When I saw who it was, I couldn't believe it; it was the company commander and some of his people from the 269th Engineer Company, from Live Oak. I had commanded that company some 18 years earlier, and Captain James Black, whom I had taught in sixth and seventh grades 24 years earlier, was now the commander. I felt really proud that I was on their minds, and especially proud to know that a kid I had taught in public schools was now a company commander just like I had been. I felt moved to know that both my military and educational backgrounds had touched another life and maybe somehow made a difference.

The engineer unit and Captain Black were doing some site work for a Patriot Missile Battery that was located just about a mile away. From halfway around the globe and a peaceful little community with everything anyone could ever want, we had found common ground in a war-torn desert that needed a hometown model.

SPREAD THIN

Throughout MEDCOM operations, I, along with the 202nd primary staff, maintained command and control and provided support for its three Evac Hospitals. The units were the 129th Evac Hospital (USAR) from San Diego, California, located in the province of Dubai, in the city of Dubai in the United Arab Emirates; the 311th Evac Hospital (USAR) from Bismarck, North Dakota, located in Abu Dhabi province in the United Arab Emirates; and the 365th Evac Hospital (USAR) from Niagara Falls, New York, located at Seeb Air Force Base in Muscat, Oman. These units were all commanded and controlled by the 202nd Medical Group concurrently while it provided the support staff for the MEDCOM. The nearest unit to us was approximately 600 miles away and the farthest unit was about 750 miles away. Because we were so spread out, my command and the control of subordinate units was primarily done by telephone. Command visits took a minimum of three days, so making a command visit was no easy task and certainly wasn't something done quickly. Travel time on the Star run (C-130 aircraft) with stops in Dhahran, Al Dafra, Alain, Shaijah, and finally at Seeb Air Force Base, took 12 hours and 45 minutes one way.

The MEDCOM was the higher headquarters for the four medical groups (the 202nd Medical Group being one of the four) functioning at the EAC (echelons above corps) level and 11 other direct-reporting units.

There were two occasions when Colonel Tsoulos went to one of the other Medical Group Headquarters with the intent to relieve the commander of his command. The first time occurred after I had been working with Colonel Tsoulos for about eight weeks. On both occasions, he had me to pack my bags and accompany him because he intended to leave me in command if he actually relieved the Medical Group Commander. Colonel Tsoulos planned to bring the relieved commander back to work in a staff job in his MEDCOM headquarters. Colonel Tsoulos told me that he had more confidence in me than he had in many of the other active duty commanders. He said Colonel Holland, the Chief of Staff, could act as the Deputy Commander, if I was reassigned to another unit. Fortunately, for me, the differences were always worked out and I never had to assume one of the other commands.

ADAPT AND DELIVER

Initially, the war to liberate Kuwait was a come-as-you-are logistical war. Medical logistics were the most complex and challenging aspect of the war effort. Providing health care services in a war zone isn't an apple-a-day-keeps-the-doctor-away business. War creates injuries that are unimaginable except to medical staffs in major trauma units. The medical care and services learned and provided in war are the benchmarks and training grounds for improving medical services on the home front. Most people don't realize it, but the burn units in our modern hospitals owe their skills and services to the practices developed to help treat injured soldiers in wartime.

Besides having the medical services available for our troops, we had to be able to transport the wounded to where our doctors were. We suffered under a shortage of ground transportation to bring casualties from the airfield to the hospital. But two soldiers in my unit solved the problem. Fifty intra-city buses were purchased, and under the leadership of Sergeant First Class Dillhyon and Lieutenant Bartlett, my Detachment Commander, 26 of the buses were converted to carry from eight to 12 litters. So our American ingenuity and willpower helped to make our mission accomplishable.

Most of the medical supplies we needed were sole-source items, civilian and/or unique in nature (such as CT cat scans), things that have short shelf-lives, are controlled substance (drugs like narcotics), require special handling and/or storage (things like oxygen and blood), or are critical professional request items. The MEDCOM contained about 50 operating rooms with a total of about 100 operating tables, and had over 160 medical doctors and more than 1,000 nurses.

A DIFFERENT MINDSET

My three evacuation hospitals were told to not deploy to the theater with any military equipment except weapons, protective masks, and military identifications. They were placed in Host Nation Support (HNS) hospitals, both military and civilian, and were to integrate with the HNS staff. The 365 Evac Hospital in Oman integrated with the Air Force's Contingency Hospital. This arrangement benefited both services, proved to be a viable working solution, and provided 1,000 additional beds for the theater.

Host nation facility negotiation was an interesting mission for the 202nd Medical Group team in United Arab Emirates at two separate hospitals. Meetings were held with the Minister of Health in that country who requested full integration of US staff and the civilian staff at his hospitals. They gave us full cooperation and ultimately we all benefited from the seemingly awkward arrangement. This new concept of HNS integration precipitated its own specific problems such as the required wearing of white uniforms, caps, no weapons or protective masks, and nurses not performing certain nursing skills (starting IV's, drawing blood etc.). In two countries (Oman and United Arab Emirates) civilian clothes had to be worn at all times. All this was quite a change for hospital nurses who were prepared for the front line casualties, only to learn that their evacuation hospital mission had changed to that of a convalescent hospital. The trauma physicians expressed frustration as well. This new mindset affected the integration of nursing and physician staff with the local civilian staff of the HNS hospital.

While I can't elaborate on the day-to-day military operations and activities of the MEDCOM and the 202nd Medical Group, I can say that throughout our entire deployment the 202nd Medical Group was the backbone of support to the MEDCOM through the initial buildup, through the air bombing campaign, through the ground war, and during the recovery and restoration effort in the liberation of Kuwait. We provided the bulk of the daily manpower required to support the MEDCOM for Administration and Personnel functions, Operational and Intelligence functions, and Logistical support for regular military items as well as the special and unique medical equipment, supplies, and pharmaceuticals. The 202nd Medical Group also provided these same services and functions to our direct reporting hospitals; proverbially speaking, we were always wearing at least two hats.

There was a definite culture clash for all of us. We were in a country that held a different set of values from ours; our host country treated people according to their race, religion, and sex. We observed their social customs and followed their cultural rules of conduct. Women, including our female soldiers, could only sit and eat with males if they all ate in the designated family area of a public dining facility. If a restaurant didn't have a family area, women weren't allowed to enter; which also meant they couldn't eat. Given the long and sometimes torturous route to equality in America, our female soldiers had a real adjustment to make—it was like returning to a time where they were held to have little or no value to the community. Our women sometimes felt intimidated by the Saudi Moral Police, whose job was to enforce a dress code of not allowing the lower portion of the neck or arms to be exposed. We tried to keep the cultural law and respect the views of our host country, but that required all of us to suppress, if not temporarily abandon, our true convictions. We tried our very best to represent the dignity of our country and our own people; while some of our female soldiers could have probably given in to the natural urge to rebel against repression, they applied the concept of the ancient proverb that says, "Good behavior results from resisting temptation." Our behavior was to serve, not restructure the people and their customs. As Americans, that's what we did.

The Chief Nurse for the 202nd Medical Group was Lieutenant Colonel Mathewson-Chapman. Her performance was truly outstanding. She had a wide range of duties from monitoring subordinate units' nursing staffs to promoting the integration of nursing staffs with the civilian staffs in Host Nation Support (HNS) hospitals. She retired in about 2005 with the rank of Major General (two stars). General Mathewson-Chapman was one of our female soldiers who represented the United States with valor, honor, and integrity.

The International Marine Satellite (IMARSAT) phone was a very useful piece of equipment, especially in remote areas. This phone allowed instant access to worldwide phone communications and provided a non-secure commercial telephone service instantly, anywhere in the world. At that time, it cost $41,000 dollars per phone and $10 per minute to use—it wasn't a common piece of equipment for anyone because of the cost. Still, it was like having a 2008 simple satellite cell phone, except that those phones required a shipping crate the size of a footlocker.

Once the ground war ended and prior to our departure for home, we had some free time to go shopping at the malls in downtown Riyadh. Just about all of us used that freedom to eat at a Pizza Hut or a Popeye's Fried Chicken. We all wanted a taste of home.

GOING HOME

The 202nd Medical Group received notification of the planning dates for re-deployment on March 28, 1991. The unit carefully broke down and prepared the organic equipment for shipment home; at the same time, everyone continued to pull shifts where needed to assure that the MEDCOM stayed operational.

The building floors and walls were scrubbed to ease the clearing of the building by the MEDCOM rear detachment. The last of the military vans was packed, inspected by the military police/customs and sealed on April 7th in preparation for transport to Dhahran the next day to await shipment back to the United States within the next six months, hopefully. Our military vehicles were washed and moved to Dhahran on April 9th. April 10th was spent doing final individual packing and cleaning of the living quarters. We wanted to leave things in a better condition than how we found them; besides, it was a good relations practice as well as a social courtesy.

Colonel Tsoulos addressed the unit at 11:30 a.m. and expressed his personal appreciation and thanks to the entire unit for performing in such an outstanding and professional manner. He acknowledged that he had assigned the most difficult job to us. The Colonel took his time to emphasize in detail how well we had performed our duties. He said with pride that the active duty and National Guard personnel blended and worked together so well that he couldn't tell who was an active duty soldier and who was a National Guard soldier.

Colonel Tsoulos presented Staff Sergeant Vanderventer the Bronze Star Medal; she was probably the first female in the Florida Guard to ever receive the award. Later that day, I was awarded the Bronze Star Medal by Lieutenant General Yeosock for outstanding leadership and performance during Operation Desert Shield/Storm. I learned a lot about leadership during that time; I learned a lot about learning as well. President Kennedy was prepared to give a speech on the day of his assassination, and I think that the words he would have spoken would have echoed about as much as his now famous, "Ask not what your country can do for you; ask what you can do for your country;" those muted words would have been, "Leadership and learning are indispensable to each other." I believe that to be true in the military, in education, in business, and in the home. Tragically, President Kennedy never spoke those words; fortunately, we have them to live by.

That evening, the unit was picked up at 11:00 p.m. and taken to the customs and transportation holding area. The customs processing was completed by about 1:00 a.m. and then we were transported via bus to the Riyadh Air Base for the flight home. Our chartered L-1011 aircraft left at 4:00 a.m. loaded to gross weight. The first refueling stop was at Sigonella Naval Air Station in Sicily, Italy, about 4½ hours into the 20-hour flight. The next refueling stop five hours later was at Shannon, Ireland; well-wishers greeted us expressing their thanks and support of the Desert Storm troops. The next refueling stop six hours later was at Bangor, Maine. Approximately 200 enthusiastic supporters met us along with a high school band and refreshments. It was on American soil that we knew for certain that we had returned to a grateful and thankful nation of patriotic people. We arrived at our final destination for that flight in Philadelphia, Pennsylvania, at 6:30 p.m.; we gained seven hours of clock time, but that didn't shorten our trip any.

The military had arranged for our bags to be checked directly to the commercial airlines that would take us to Savannah, Georgia, the next morning. The Air Force got each of us individual rooms at a nearby motel; for the first time in months we could have some privacy, and that was almost as shocking as the loss of privacy when we left on our tour of duty.

We were traveling on commercial airlines to our final destinations. That wasn't a problem for us, but it was a little sensitive for security reasons because we were traveling in full combat gear with weapons, protective masks, and Kevlar helmets. It probably looked like we were invading America—in a sense, we were; we were coming home.

HOME AT LAST

Fort Stewart had planned on us being there out-processing for a total of nine days from the 13th to the 21st of April. There were only 42 of us because two had left earlier, so that amount of time was unrealistically long—besides, we wanted to get home. Some intense negotiations took place with the Mobilization Operations Center, and the time was reduced to four days, including the travel day home and having Sunday the 14th off. Following the final demobilization process, the unit departed Fort Stewart on schedule at 9:00 a.m. on Tuesday, April 16th on two charter buses and arrived at the Cedar Hills Armory at 11:30 a.m. to a happy, warm, and grateful reception. The Adjutant General, Major General Ensslin, and his wife Faye; the Assistant Adjutant General, Brigadier General Capps; the Troop Command Commander, Brigadier General Sprenger and his wife, Justine; and a host of happy spouses, children, family, and friends greeted the unit. The unit was dismissed at 1:00 p.m.

The 202nd Medical Group had been involved in numerous training exercises over the past years, particularly in Turkey; however; the *Super Bowl* of all army exercises is deploying to go to war. Operation Desert Shield/Storm presented the *Mother-of-All* challenges for each of us. Because of our unit readiness, there was a swift transition from peacetime to wartime preparedness. During Operation Desert Shield/Storm, all the individual and collective training we had undergone came together; we were prepared in weapons, technology, and leadership and then to cap that off, we had highly qualified personnel. The cooperation between branches within the Army, the other military services, support from the coalition forces, and the magnificent backing of the American people all contributed significantly to the success of Operation Desert Shield/Storm. Last but not least, throughout our deployment the soldiers in my command had a positive attitude and their motto was "whatever it takes" to get the job done always brought success even in the toughest assignments. We always remembered that we proudly represented the Florida Army National Guard, the State of Florida, and the United States of America. We were patriots—proud patriots, and we knew that America is the land of the free because we were part of the team that worked to make and keep us that way. Our faith had been tried, and so had our military training; General George Marshall said that military power wins battles, but spiritual power wins wars—we all learned that on a personal level.

BACK TO WORK

I returned home to Tallahassee the afternoon after I released the unit at 1:00 p.m. on April 16, 1991. I reported to work the following morning and there was a note on my desk along with a couple of Legislative Bills relating to Educational Facilities. The note was for me to study the bills first thing and to attend a House Committee meeting at 9:00 a.m. in Morris Hall and be prepared to answer questions about each bill, if required. I thought I was getting back to business as usual, but I really wasn't. A surprise awaited me.

The chairman of the committee learned of my return from the war, and used the opportunity to recognize me; when he did, the crowd applauded. It was humbling, and I appreciated their show of gratitude. When the applause stopped, the chairman asked if I would like to make any comments; I thanked him and the audience, and said, "Over there I knew who the enemy was, here in this room I can't tell friend from foe." Everyone laughed and then we moved on with legislative business.

After about a month back on the job, JoAnn and I went to Bradenton to visit Brigadier General (Dr.) Sprenger and his wife, Justine. On our way driving down, JoAnn and I looked up the little old lady that had packed the box that I got for Christmas which had been labeled "*ANY SERVICEMAN.*" Like many Americans who sent things to soldiers, she had put her name and address in the box. I wanted to let her know that I got her gift and that it was special to me. We often get gifts from those who know and love us; we don't often get something from strangers. Since I had the chance, I wanted to thank her personally for the kindness to me, and her loyal support of all the troops. After a brief introduction and a thank you, we moved on. It was heartwarming to meet someone who is truly the backbone of our nation; she was that backbone, just like all the others who sacrificed their time and money to send treats to unknown soldiers.

It didn't take long to readjust to life at work. I rapidly fell back into the work routine at the Department of Education.

FAMILY CHANGES

JoAnn's father (Papa) was sick for quite some time and passed away in December 1991. My brother, Carra, suffered from a severe heart condition for several years; shortly after JoAnn's Dad stepped into eternity, Carra left us in January 1992. Those were painful losses, but there is no easy or painless loss. Our hope is in our faith that we are only separated shortly and will soon be together in a family reunion that won't end. C. S. Lewis said that the pain we suffer from the death of a loved one is part of the happiness we have had; he said that just before his wife, Joy, died of cancer. I guess there is a lot of truth in that statement, but knowing that our pain is because we had happiness doesn't relieve the hurt during our grieving.

Becky started dating Scott Robert Heath while I was away in the Gulf War. Scott was in graduate school studying for an MBA while Becky was finishing her undergraduate degree.

JoAnn's mother (Meime) lived by herself for the first year following Papa's death. In the fall of 1992, Meime asked about adding some space to our house and moving in with us, which was fine with JoAnn and me. We started an addition to our house right after Christmas and finished it by the end of February. Meime moved in with us in early March 1993.

When the spring semester ended, both Becky and Scott finished college. They had achieved major milestones in their lives; now they were ready for a new life together—it seemed a good thing. With our blessings, they were married on July 17, 1993, in the Summerall Chapel on the Citadel Campus in Charleston, South Carolina. An Irish proverb says that if we praise our children they will prosper; we practiced doing that as well as following advice from the Book of Proverbs, 22:6, which says, "Train up a child in the way he should go: and when he is old, he will not depart from it." We were proud of Becky and Scott; they fulfilled our dreams and theirs.

PROMOTED AGAIN

My National Guard unit was still recovering from the Gulf War deployment. Along with the unit's slow return to its normal situation, I was getting into my second year of a 24-months technical waiver to command the unit. In early January 1992, The Adjutant General,

Major General Ensslin, who was retiring in the following month, and his named successor, Brigadier General Ronald O. Harrison, called to inform me they had discussed and recommended that I become the next Brigadier General in the Florida Army National Guard.

Once again, I was surprised by recognition. As with all my previous promotions, I had not asked for this one either. Nonetheless, it came to me. One of our truly great American Generals, Omar Bradley, said, "We are given one life and the decision is ours whether to wait for circumstances to make up our mind, or whether to act." When General Ensslin and General Harrison suggested that I start filling out my paper work immediately, I did. There wasn't going to be time to wait or consider options; they said that I would assume command of the 53rd Signal Brigade on June 1st. So time was short for me to get everything in order.

The confirmation process for any military general officer is a very long and drawn out process. It has to go through many different approval steps and leadership levels—all the way to the President of the United States and to the United States Senate for confirmation. It sometimes takes months and even years before the confirmation is final. My confirmation took place on March 11, 1993, and I was promoted to Brigadier General on that date.

As the Signal Brigade Commander, I had command responsibilities for about 1,500 soldiers in military units throughout north Florida from Jacksonville to Pensacola. I was also responsible for Military Support to Civil Authorities (MSCA) for all the 21 Florida counties west of the Suwannee River; typically, we were available for any natural disaster or other state emergency under the command of the Governor, who is the Commander-in-Chief of the National Guard, except when serving on active duty. This support to civil authorities can be for any reason the Governor may designate, but primarily the Guard is only used in that capacity for protecting life and property in situations such as hurricanes, wild fires, civil unrest, search and rescue, and delivering emergency services or support.

Two MSCA Operations occurred while I was in command of the Signal Brigade. The first one was in support of and recovery from Tropical Storm Alberto. In July 1994, Tropical Storm Alberto made landfall in the Florida panhandle and triggered over $500 million in federal disaster assistance. Most of the destruction occurred because of river flooding from rainfall in excess of 20 inches. The Choctawhatchee

River rose 15 feet above flood stage in the towns of Westville and Caryville in Holmes and Washington Counties. Flooding along the Apalachicola River caused extensive damage to the towns of Blountstown and Wewahitchka. In all, over 500 homes were flooded in the aftermath of Alberto.

The second operation was to assist in the recovery following Hurricane Opal. Hurricane Opal passed over the Florida panhandle between the cities of Pensacola and Fort Walton Beach on the night of October 4, 1995. Opal weakened to a small Category Three hurricane before landfall. Nonetheless, Opal caused major beach erosion and storm surge flooding along a stretch of shoreline extending from Pensacola to Mexico Beach, a distance of over 150 miles. During each of these operations, we had several hundred Army and Air Force Guardsman on active state duty for several days. We also had many types of military vehicles, equipment, and aviation helicopters supporting the civil authorities. My responsibility during these emergency operations was to command and coordinate the activation, assignment, and management of all military assets engaged in the area of operation to protect life and property.

ANOTHER LOSS

During the second MSCA operation in October 1995, my oldest living brother, Thomas Lee, passed away in the Veterans Hospital in Lake City following a lengthy illness. I took a one-day leave from state active duty to attend his funeral in Suwannee County; then I had to return to the difficult job of managing the troops during the natural disaster and my own pain in the wake of Tom's death. Tom had served his country proudly in World War II; his capture by the Germans and subsequent confinement as a prisoner of war left a lifelong scar on all our lives. Tom's passing left a vacancy we couldn't fill, but heaven was richer with his arrival in God's kingdom.

We had several successful annual training exercises during the years I served as Commander of the 53rd Signal Brigade. The last major exercise was in Central America, along the Panama Canal, and working with an active Army Signal Brigade. In addition, I attended many military related functions ranging from National Guard Association of the United States annual meetings to Florida National Guard Officers annual meetings. Some of the national meetings I attended were in Boston, Massachusetts; Biloxi, Mississippi; Detroit, Michigan; Salt Lake City, Utah; Hawaii; and Alaska. JoAnn accompanied me to most of the state and national meetings; she enjoyed the social environment, as did most of the military wives, and I was proud to be able to let her be a part of the experience. These weren't vacations paid for by the public; we paid for all our military related conference trips. What we did was that whenever it was possible we took advantage of these trips and turned them into mini-vacations. By making a burdensome task into something good, we used our opportunities to see places of interest that we might not have visited otherwise. For example, in the fall of 1992, as a result of my being promoted to Brigadier General, JoAnn and I attended two required one-week orientation courses, one in Fort Leavenworth, Kansas, and one in Washington, D. C.

FADING AWAY

General Douglas MacArthur said, "Old soldiers never die; they just fade away." We each have our time and our destiny. I retired from active participation in the Florida National Guard on October 2, 1997. I had about 19 years command time; throughout my career I served at levels of leadership from a Private helping other privates learn the essentials of Army tanks to Brigadier General commanding more than 2,000 soldiers.

The military was very good to me, and my family. It served me well and I made every effort to serve the military with equal fervor and enthusiasm. I received a total of 22 awards and decorations during the 39½ years I proudly wore the uniform of the United States Army. All of my military awards and decorations are listed in the appendices in the back of the book.

After Samuel Colt introduced his pistol, a gunman was quoted as saying, "God created all men equal, Sam Colt keeps them that way." To a great degree, the military is the same. Everyone has the same opportunity, the same chance, and the same benefits. Only, not everyone is willing to give everything to have what is offered. The military and marriage are a lot alike; they both require an absolute commitment to reap the full rewards and enjoy their blessings. From the day I enlisted and went to boot camp as a Buck Private, until the day I retired a Brigadier General, I gave the military everything I had—and I was giving it first and foremost to America. Just like all my brothers before me, I am honored to have worn our country's uniform.

DOWNSIZING

Political winds favor many directions. Buzzwords like "downsizing" "outsourcing" "privatization" and a whole host of others can have an attractive ring when spoken with just the right inflection. Sometimes they are good, sometimes they are not. Time usually tells the whole story.

When the state leadership switched from Democrats to Republicans, the Department of Education was downsized. As a part of the paring down, on July 1, 1995, the Office of Educational Facilities was changed from a staff of 97 to a staff of 35. The office lost many good people and the Educational Plant Survey responsibilities were transferred to the local school boards, community colleges, and to the State University System to be completed by in-house staff or by contracted services instead of the state. This was supposed to have been a move to save state money, which it did; but it certainly did not save the local taxpayer more money, because the educational agencies were now paying far more collectively for the services than it had previously cost. And instead of having a central unit with no political agenda doing the needs assessments, local school boards, in many cases, paid firms to tell them what they wanted to hear—that was one of the tragic trade-offs of downsizing and I feel this has been very costly to the state's taxpayers.

During our reorganization, I was transferred to be the Administrator of the Educational Facilities Budget Office. I served in that capacity until the fall 1997 Special Session of the Legislature. The Special Session dealt with the sole issue of relocatable classrooms. During that Session, the Legislature created a small state agency and named it SMART Schools Clearinghouse. The SMART stood for *S*oundly *M*ade *A*ccountable *R*easonable and *T*hrifty. The SMART Schools Clearinghouse was established to help school districts get special funding from the state. The Special Session also created the School Infrastructure Thrift (SIT) Program awards and effort index grants.

The Legislature appropriated about $400 million to be awarded as grants to school districts that constructed new schools that cost less than the established threshold and met the construction requirements established by the newly mandated Clearinghouse board. The Clearinghouse board had five members who had substantial business experience in the private sector. The Board was given broad rule-making power and authority by the Legislature. As a part of their moving programs from the Department of Education, the Clearinghouse was assigned to the Department of Management Services for administrative and fiscal accountability purposes, but otherwise it functioned independently.

As always, when legislation affected education, I would become familiar with the language and intent of the law. When the Special Session passed their laws, I read the functions, duties, and responsibilities of the Clearinghouse, as well as the expectations of the Legislature. I didn't want any part of it—it looked like a monster.

A senior legislative staff member contacted me and all but insisted that I apply for the job as Director of the SMART Schools Clearinghouse—he wanted me to tackle the monster. Sometimes we do what we want to do; sometimes we do what we're expected to do. Reluctantly, I applied, and within one day I was interviewed and selected by the Chairman of the SMART Schools Clearinghouse Board to be the Director. Of course, I had to be approved by the entire Clearinghouse Board, which happened in December 1997, and I started to work as the Director of the SMART Schools Clearinghouse on January 2, 1998.

The Clearinghouse Board gave me their full support, and while the job was very demanding, it was rewarding. I served in that job along with the other two full-time Clearinghouse employees until the Director of the Office of Educational Facilities resigned on March 31, 2001. Wayne Pierson, Deputy Commissioner for Finance and Operations in the Department of Education, was one of the Clearinghouse board members. He asked if I would come back to the Department of Education and be the Director of the Office of Educational Facilities as well as Director of the Clearinghouse. I agreed to assume the additional responsibilities through June 30, 2002, which was my planned retirement date. I was looking forward to having some free time for the first time in my life, and I wasn't interested in extending my working career.

Before I retired, I told Wayne Pierson and Jeanine Blomberg, my immediate superior with DOE at the time, to call me if I could ever help them in any way. Jerry Martin, the person designated to be my successor, took over the duties and functions of the Director of the Office of Educational Facilities upon my retirement.

JoAnn and I both retired on June 30, 2002. I had 32 years in the Florida Retirement System, and JoAnn had 16 years in the system. We were to that wonderful place in life where we could get to know ourselves in a different light; no regular schedule, no daily routines. We launched into our retirement with a whole set of dreams of things we could do. C. S. Lewis said that we should never forget the magic; we were looking for it anew beginning on July 1, 2002.

FREE TO TRAVEL

Even before we retired, JoAnn and I practiced what we hoped would be a way of life—travel. JoAnn and I took several trips from 1994 until our retirement in 2002. In 1994, we flew with Meime to visit Rebecca and Scott in Denver. We flew with Meime to Philadelphia to visit Gettysburg, Valley Forge, Lancaster, and Amish Country in 1995. JoAnn and I enjoyed a 22-day European trip to 10 countries in 1996. We took a nine-day family trip with our daughters and son-in-law in 1999 to the Netherlands, Belgium, and Germany. Also in 1999, we visited Brenda in Costa Rica for a week. As if 1999 hadn't given us enough travel, in November we spent a long weekend (5 days) in England. In 2000, Brenda was an exchange student from Emory University Graduate School in Barcelona, Spain, so we visited her in Spain. We also found the time to do a couple of cruises to the Caribbean somewhere along in our journeys.

BUNDLE OF JOY

The year 2001 brought several events of great importance to our family. The first was the arrival of our grandson, Cooper Boatright Heath. Cooper was born on January 31st at the Northside Hospital in Atlanta; he was our first grandchild. JoAnn's job with the Department of Health as an Area Child Care Food Program Consultant allowed her to take off two weeks to be with Rebecca during this exciting and important event in our family.

The second major event of 2001 was significant worldwide, the attacks on the World Trade Center in New York City on September 11th. That singular event changed the way we live and how we travel. The third big event in 2001 was our first trip to the Armed Forces Recreation Center (AFRC) in Germany for a Military Retiree vacation in December. The weather was cold, but the wintry countryside was very beautiful. We visited the Bavarian area of Germany and Austria on the eight-day trip and absorbed the flavor of local customs so much that we planned to return someday for another visit.

EMPTY SPACE

JoAnn's Mother (Meime) had lived with us for the nine years before we retired; she knew that we wanted to travel. Meime suggested that she rotate her visits between her three children for four to six months at a time; she figured that kind of schedule wouldn't bother the day-to-day activities of any one family for very long. Meime started by staying with JoAnn's younger brother, Bobby, and his wife, Joyce, in Eustis, Florida. After making the complete round and spending a block of time with each child, she told JoAnn's older brother, Bill, that she would like to move into a private facility. Meime had even found a place she recommended—the Broadview Assisted Living facility. Bill and Sybil took her to see it, and she decided to move there. Once her decision was made, she was ready to go and within a week, she moved. Meime stayed there for 3½ years until she passed away in December 2007, at age 89. She had lived a full and rich life, but her passing, like all the others, left another empty space in our lives. When Meime made the decision to spend time in each child's home, she was likely planning ahead to make just the one single round as a final family visit and then go to where she could have private, around-the-clock care. That was probably wisdom on her part, and caring as well.

RETIREMENT
RETURN TO DOE

The experience of this sweet life. Dante.

J OANN AND I had planned our future so that when we retired, we would be debt free; we didn't want a house or car payment to burden us down. With the benefit of my military retirement and along with our other retirement income, we were receiving more annual income than when we went into retirement. We had more discretionary disposable income the first year of retirement than we had in any year before leaving our working careers.

Our plan was to travel as much as possible. By the time we actually retired, we had already traveled a good bit and in many different ways. Our favorite type of travel was cruises, primarily because we had to only unpack once and then stay in the same room for the duration of the trip. We also realized the cost of a cruise vacation is known in advance with few or no surprises at the end.

TRAINS, BOATS, AND PLANES

Our first trip following retirement was a 15-day *Europe's Magical Waterways* riverboat cruise with Vantage Travel. The cruise began in Passau, Germany, and ended in Amsterdam, Netherlands. We flew into Prague, Czech Republic, in August 2002, for a two-day pre-cruise excursion; Prague was a beautiful city and our lifelong dreams were being satisfied with every place we saw. The local flavors and customs thrilled our senses and satisfied that eagerness we always had for exotic travel, and each new country and town only added to our excitement.

We left Prague on Friday and the rivers flooded the city three days later. I guess we were lucky on that one. The cruise included over 60 locks on the Rhine-Main-Danube Canal that connects the Danube River to the Rhine River; the river and locks system is an engineering marvel and well worth the trip if that had been all we saw. But that was just a side benefit because we saw several small towns and we made walking tours in many of them. In the larger cities, we had walking and bus tours. All our excursions were both interesting and educational. The food on the riverboat was excellent, the service outstanding, and the accommodations were great. The trip was satisfying and rewarding, and further whetted our appetites for more cruise-type travel.

In September, JoAnn and I flew to Long Beach, California, to attend the National Conference of the National Guard Association of the United States. Major General Ronald O. Harrison, the Adjutant General for Florida, was the President of the Association that year, and we wanted to support him as well as stay for an additional week or two and visit sites locally and in the surrounding areas. We planned to drive up the California Coastal Highway 1, along the way we wanted to visit the Hearst Mansion and the famous Pebble Beach Golf Club. In San Francisco, we spent a week staying in the city and taking tours of the nearby areas. We went to the famed wine country, Napa Valley, for a tour of the countryside. While we were in the area, we had the chance to visit JoAnn's second cousin, Mark Newton, and his wife Genny. Retirement travel was letting us have fun, freedom, and visit family that we didn't get to see very often.

During the fall of 2002 we visited New Orleans, Louisiana; Branson, Missouri; and Savannah, Georgia. Wherever we went, we stayed anywhere from four to eight days, which made our trip fulfilling without making it tiring. Before the year ended, we also took a western Caribbean cruise to Grand Cayman, Belize, and Cozumel. During the week of Christmas, our entire family went to Lake Tahoe, Nevada, and spent time skiing, snowmobiling, and enjoying a real white Christmas as a family. That year sure saw us rack up the miles doing just what we wanted to do.

One of our favorite cruises was in July 2003. We made a 12-night Norwegian Cruise to the Scandinavian Countries of Denmark, Estonia, Norway, Sweden, Finland, Russia, and England. While we were in Saint Petersburg, Russia, we took a day trip (flight) to Moscow to visit the Kremlin, Red Square, and other historic sites. While the one-day side trip was busy, it was also educational and enjoyable. Despite the fact that we had a structured trip, we also had the luxury of being flexible and doing some other things that we wanted to do—that's what retirees do.

A NEW ADDITION TO OUR FAMILY

When we got back from our Scandinavian cruise, it wasn't long before our family grew again. On July 25, 2003, Chandler Bowman Heath was born in Atlanta at the same hospital as his older brother Cooper; he was a healthy, beautiful baby boy with a head covered in black, velvety hair. Chandler and Cooper continue to bring an unbelievable amount of happiness into our lives. Rebecca and Scott are making wonderful parents and we appreciate them allowing us to be involved in their lives. Grandparents have a special place; they can spoil their grandchildren, let them do things they didn't let their own children do, and endear themselves to the memories of children. And then, when the grandchildren become the grandparents, they can do the same thing. Being a grandparent lets us make up in our grandchildren for what we missed in our children. I think this is probably a gift from above, and we should all enjoy it.

During the first 10 days of September 2003, we made our second trip to Germany. This time, JoAnn and I took my two oldest living brothers and their wives, Alfred and Annette, and Pete and Alice. We had a great time doing the daily tours, visiting some of the old castles in Germany, and then visiting Austria and Italy. Perhaps the highlight of the trip for all of us was the visit to Hitler's *Eagles Nest*. That kind of history is good to see and learn about; surprisingly, we were able to remember that our brother, Tom, had suffered tremendously under Hitler's reign, but we, as a family, grew closer from that trip to the heart of where the Nazi's planned and plotted their schemes for world domination. When I was a boy on the farm, I could never have imagined making such a trip; I guess Alfred and Pete shared that same sentiment—I only wish all our brothers could have made the trip.

JoAnn and I signed up for a 15-day trip to China in the fall of 2003. But when the SARS scare came in the spring of that year, I called the tour company to cancel our trip. I was told we would lose our initial deposit. I said that was fine; I didn't want to expose us to something potentially deadly just to save or use our money. I asked if the travel company had another trip leaving about the same time that we could just swap into. Fortunately, there was a trip leaving the same day for 17-days going to Australia and New Zealand. I told them to sign us up. So, from October 6th through the 23rd we spent about half our time in Australia, and we spent the other half in New Zealand. We went snorkeling at the Great Barrier Reef, which is several miles off the coast of Australia. We also got to attend a performance in the famed Sidney Opera House. While we were in New Zealand we visited Christ Church, Queenstown, and took a cruise on Milford Sound. Milford Sound is the most famous fiord in New Zealand; it's also where the movie *Lord of the Rings* was filmed.

In March 2004, we took Scott and Rebecca's family with us on a three-night Disney cruise. Cooper really liked the activity; however, Chandler was too young to realize what was going on. But for the rest of us, it was a great trip and a really good time for the entire family.

In April 2004, JoAnn and I took a driving trip to Fort Knox, Kentucky, and stayed overnight in the officers guesthouse. I had been stationed at Fort Knox with the Army about 46 years earlier while I attended the Armor School, Advanced Individual Training, to learn about the M-48 Army Tank. It was an opportunity for me to revisit a place from my earlier life. Places grow in fondness as we get older and their memories seem to sweeten with age. For Knox was that way for me.

We traveled on to Niagara Falls, a place neither of us had visited before. We took a helicopter tour over the falls. That was the first helicopter ride for JoAnn. To me, that helicopter ride was a luxury flight after the many military helicopters I had been on. We also went to Toronto, Canada, then headed west to Michigan, and then went north across the scenic Mackinaw Bridge into upper Michigan. We drove back through Wisconsin, down into Iowa, and then headed home. This trip completed our visit to all the states except for North Dakota. We needed something left to look forward to, so North Dakota was it.

In June of 2004, we visited Brenda in California, and then flew on to Calgary, Alberta, in Canada. We got a rental car and drove to Edmonton, Alberta, and visited the huge indoor mall and amusement park, and then drove to Jasper, Alberta. Some of the most beautiful country in the world is in the Canadian Rockies National Park. We drove through them and spent two nights at a gorgeous and scenic hotel, *The Fairmont Chateau Lake Louise*, located on Lake Louise. The Canadian Rockies were made more special for us and *The Fairmont Chateau Lake Louise* became the highlight of our trip as we celebrated our 36th wedding anniversary with picture-postcard scenery in the backdrop. From there, we drove down to Banff and through the Banff National Park and returned to Calgary. We were enthralled with that trip and almost hated for it to end. But all things must end, so we returned our rental car and flew back to Atlanta; from there, we drove home to Tallahassee.

In July 2004, JoAnn and I took our longest riverboat cruise. It was a 26-day cruise starting at the Black Sea, traveling the Danube River, the Rhine-Main-Danube Canal, and the Rhine River, ending in Amsterdam, Netherlands. This was a great and relaxing trip. During the voyage, we had a chance to visit Bucharest, Romania; Ruse, Bulgaria; Belgrade, Serbia; Budapest, Hungary; Vienna, Austria; Passau, Heidelberg, and Cologne, Germany; and Amsterdam, Netherlands. Even though we had been on a portion of the trip before, it was well worth seeing again. During that trip, we became friends with a couple, Coy and Lou Butler, from Chattanooga, Tennessee, who were celebrating their 50th wedding anniversary. Some friendships are just meant to be; we have traveled together two times since, and have visited in each other's homes. The Butler's friendship was a gift to us through our retirement travel and a side benefit to our newfound freedom.

ANOTHER GAP

While we were in Bucharest, Romania, I got a call from our daughter Rebecca. It seems like tragic news can find us anywhere. My sister, Winifred Padgett, had passed away. It was impossible for us to make it home in time for the funeral. We could have tried, but the odds were against us even if everything went perfectly. It was a hard choice, and painful. But I made the decision that we wouldn't put ourselves through all the disturbance, heartache, and stress and then still not make it. As painful as it was, I made the right decision; still, another flower was plucked from our family bouquet, and though heaven was richer, we were poorer.

OFFERS

Malcolm Forbes said that retirement kills more people than hard work ever did. Retirement doing nothing might kill you, but JoAnn and I were busy seeing as much of the world as we could. I had already worked a lifetime from childhood all the way to retirement age. Not only had I worked, I had the dual career of public works and a full military life. Retirement seemed good, but I got a lot of offers to work. I didn't want a job.

I got several calls during my retirement from banks, legal firms, consulting firms, and construction companies offering me employment; some wanted to hire me full time and some asked if I would work for them part time. With every offer, I thanked the caller but declined their invitation. I simply didn't want to go back to work. I was enjoying the first real free time I had ever known; besides, I was doing the things that I had always wanted to do such as visit my family, be with our children and grandchildren, and traveling. I also wanted to put together some DVD photo albums of my family and JoAnn's family. I had even taken two courses at Tallahassee Community College in *Photoshop* and *Restoring Old Photos* just so I could have the skills to put together our family histories in pictures. About the last thing I needed was a job because my days were always full of activity and there was plenty to keep me busy.

In the fall of 2004, I agreed to serve, for a short time, on the transition team for a newly elected superintendent in central Florida.

In preparation for my team assignment, I went by the Office of Educational Facilities on Friday, November 12th, to get current information regarding the school district's capital outlay funds, capital projects in process, and any other information that might help with indoctrination. During my visit, I learned that John Winn had been appointed by the State Board of Education to be the Commissioner of Education, and that Jeanine Blomberg was the new Chief of Staff for the Department of Education. Since I had known them for many years and held both in high regard, I decided to stop by Jeanine's office and just say hello and congratulate her on her appointment as the new Chief of Staff. I only intended to stick my head in the door to say hello, give congratulations, and leave. When I appeared at her door, Jeanine motioned for me to come in and told me that she had wanted to talk to me and would have called me in a day or so.

Jeanine reminded me that when I retired I told her that if I could ever be of assistance, she should just let me know. Jeanine said she needed my help and asked if I would come back to work and offered a one to three day a week option, two to six months preference, a year or more, or whatever I was willing to do. About the last thing I was expecting was an offer to return to the Department of Education; her request caught me off guard and by surprise. I said that I would help, but I had a couple of cruises booked that would cause some personal hardships if I were working. She said that was okay, I could do my planned travel and still have the job.

As I thought it over, I really didn't want to go back to work; but then I had also made a commitment 2½ years earlier to help, if I were needed. I asked what level of work obligation she really wanted from me. Jeanine said she would prefer me coming back and working full time. I told her to let me think about it, talk it over with JoAnn, and I would let her know my decision on Monday, November 15th. I talked things over with JoAnn and my girls and each said to do what I wanted.

I gave the offer considerable thought. After pondering all the possibilities, I called Jeanine on Monday, and said that I would return to work full time and would come in on Tuesday to discuss the requirements, her expectations, and finalize our deal. As with most jobs, one of the major points is money; the Department offered me the same salary I was making when I retired 2½ years earlier; at this point in my life, money wasn't that much of an issue so I agreed on the financial terms.

Once we settled the salary issue, we discussed her deep concern and frustration over the operations and staff in the Office of Educational Facilities. Her biggest concern was the accuracy of the amount of capital outlay dollars that would be required to implement the Class Size Reduction requirements mandated by the 2002 Constitutional amendment. She had doubts about the exactness of the Florida Inventory of School Houses (FISH), and the other Educational Facilities Information Systems (EFIS) programs that were developed for, operated, and managed by the Office of Educational Facilities.

I told her we could fix these problems; not easily, but with her support and the commissioner's backing, we could get it done. She told me I had their full cooperation, and knowing Jeanine, that was enough for me. I told her she should feel free to terminate me any day that she so desired and there would be no ill feelings on my part; however, I said that I wouldn't leave without giving her at least 60-days notice. I wanted to restrict myself to a long termination notice so that I couldn't, or wouldn't, quit out of frustration. We agreed on those terms. She asked if I could start to work the next day, Wednesday, November 17th; I told her that she needed to meet with the Office of Educational Facilities staff and let them know what was going on, and that I would be willing to start to work on Thursday. Again, we agreed.

On my first day, I saw that the Office was in a mess; the morale was at an all-time low. After a few hours on the job, and three or four brief conversations with people I trusted and had worked with over the past several years, I quickly realized most of the problem was not with the staff but instead had been at the management level above the Office.

I had conversations with Jerry Martin, who succeeded me when I retired. We had talked a couple of times before he resigned, which was about 18 months earlier, and I knew from my conversations with him that the working environment was terrible. The person to whom Jerry had reported made ridiculous demands; adding to his incompetence, his leadership style shifted with his moods. He was inconsistent, offered no direction except for criticism, and made constant demands that he changed as soon as he made them. To add to the problems, he assigned a person as Assistant Director of Educational Facilities who was a totally incompetent manager and was abusive to the whole staff; this person didn't produce much work, and to make matters worse, he created a lot of confusion and frustration in the office trying to be like the person who promoted him. There is an old Yugoslavic axiom that says if you want to know what a man is, place him in authority; the Department had two bad eggs in leadership positions and they did a lot of harm.

The working conditions were unbearable and Jerry Martin resigned. Jerry was very competent and knowledgeable on all issues related to the job; he just couldn't take the constant abuse that was wrongly heaped upon him. After Jerry left, the person to whom the office reported appointed Dr. Charles Wooten as the Director of the Office of Educational Facilities. Dr. Wooten is an excellent employee with outstanding technical and analytical skills. The problem, as I saw it, was that he had no direction or support from his boss or even his bosses' boss. I never met the direct boss, but I know I could have never worked in that political atmosphere with such a flagrant disregard for what the Florida Statues requires. I would probably have told the former Deputy Commissioner over Educational Facilities to go to hell. Dr. Wooten was in a no win situation, and was going to have to do all the dirty work, and be the fall-guy for anything that went wrong, all without the benefit of management's support. Unfortunately, and unlike Jerry Martin, he was in no position to retire. Had I been in Dr. Wooten's situation, I would have had no choice but do as he did, which was the best he could on a day-by-day basis.

About a week after being on the job, my friend, the newly appointed Florida Education Commissioner, John Winn, was on the elevator with me and asked that I ride on up to his office. I spent about five minutes in his office, and he expressed his appreciation for my returning. He said I would be facing some major decisions, some very unpopular, but for me not to worry about what the Governor's Office or the Legislature might say, just do what I knew was right and he would stand behind me. He also said he had the final copy of the *Educational Facilities Task Force Report* prepared by the previous Commissioner and his regime and wanted to know if I cared to review it and give him my input. I told him I had seen enough of the pieces of the report and observed the methodology for assimilating the information; as far as I was concerned, I didn't want to read it. I recommended that he trash the whole document. I never heard another word about the report. The Commissioner's comments just reinforced those Jeanine had made to me when I agreed to come back to work—the previous administration had created a monstrous mess that needed a lot of work.

THE HARD WORK

Two areas required my immediate attention. First, we had to develop a mathematical model to determine the real dollars necessary to fund the additional classrooms needed to meet the Class Size Reduction requirements in accordance with the 2002 Constitutional Amendment. Prior to the change of commissioners, Jeanine was the Deputy Commissioner of Assessment, Research, and Measurements. In that role she frequently needed capital outlay data and would contact Dr. Wooten, and his boss wouldn't allow him to share the information with Jeanine. Dr. Wooten was caught in the line-of-fire, in the conflict between Deputy Commissioners, again a no win situation. Dr. Wooten couldn't tell Jeanine he was told not to share the information with her; he had to simply not provide the information she requested. The situation understandably shook Jeanine's confidence in Dr. Wooten.

To make matters worse, Dr. Wooten was the person responsible for calculating the dollars necessary to fund the new classrooms needed to meet the Class Size Reduction requirements. The previous Deputy Commissioner to whom Dr. Wooten reported wanted the funding amount to be very low; he obviously thought that was the politically correct approach to meeting the Constitutional mandate. He also insisted that students be assigned to all school spaces whether the area was appropriate or not; and that created a false threshold of need. So, by manipulating ways to calculate the need, the numbers were unrealistic and the total need reported to the Governor and Legislature was $785 million—which was barely 16% of the real need. Jeanine questioned the amount and asked that I do a thorough analysis and determine the actual cost necessary to meet the Class Size Reduction requirements.

At this point Jeanine was ready to dismiss Dr. Wooten because of the grossly inaccurate data that he had provided under the direction of her predecessor. I insisted that she not do that, I needed his help. Dr. Wooten was the only other person in the Office with the knowledge, skills, and the background to be of any real help in this mammoth assignment. If she had fired Dr. Wooten, I would have given the 60-day notice I had agreed to give, and I would have left. Even though I replaced Dr. Wooten as Director of the Office, there was not even a hint of resentment. He has only been professional in every way and has contributed more than any one person in the office to our progress of moving the office forward.

I sat down with Dr. Wooten and together we began to determine what data we needed to assess the real need; it was a methodical and meticulous task. We determined the format of the data, and how we could systematically build a set of complex spreadsheet formulas, that when compiled and assembled would provide the most accurate results along with a defensible methodology and realistic assumptions. We worked almost continuously including late every night, Saturdays, Sundays, and all the Christmas holidays except for Christmas and New Years day. Dr. Wooten worked on the assignment constantly every moment at work, and I worked with him at every opportunity. We worked as a check and balance, but Dr. Wooten did almost all the tedious gathering and assembling of the data.

After about eight weeks of intense study and analyses we arrived at our answer, but before going any further, we provided the raw data to two other individuals and had them to replicate our work. Where our answers were different, we debugged our formulas and methodologies until we all came to the same results, yet using different formulas and methodologies.

By late January or early February, Jeanine selected Linda Champion to be her Assistant Deputy Commissioner. Linda and Jeanine would be responsible for defending the amount of money we would request for class size reduction.

After everyone had arrived at the same result for our need, we were ready to share the information with Linda, Jeanine, and Commissioner Winn. The real need was a whopping $4.9 billion, and it was verifiable through independent work. Once we explained in detail and they were satisfied with our assumptions, methodology, and logic, we moved forward with the revised estimate of capital outlay dollars necessary to meet the Class Size Reduction requirements. Jeanine, Linda, Commissioner Winn, and I met with Governor Bush and his strategic staff and again went over our assumptions, methodology, and logic. I had already reviewed it with the Governor's main education staff person, Patricia Levesque, and she agreed with and supported our findings. Jeanine, Linda, Patricia, and I got together with a joint meeting of the Florida House of Representatives and Florida Senate Appropriations Staff and again reviewed in detail our assumptions, methodology, and logic. They supported our findings. It had been a difficult task, but we had learned what the real need was and we could certify and verify our facts and figures.

THE BIG SELL

The tough part was still to come; Jeanine had to meet with the Senate Appropriations Committee and explain why the dollars needed to construct additional classrooms to meet the Class Size Reduction requirements had changed from $785 million to $4.9 billion. Raising taxes is never pleasant; telling the government that your original estimate of need was off by more than $4 billion was excruciating. The Legislature had to find a way to pay for that mistake. Telling anybody that someone else caused the problem never earns you any credit. In fact, even when the problem really was someone else's, the best approach is to face the music and tell them what the needs are—pointing a blaming finger, even a justified one, usually costs you in credibility; Major General William Napier asserted as much when he said that assuming the blame for someone else's blunder requires more disciple and a greater degree of valor than most people possess. Jeanine took somewhat of a political beating for the faulty analysis presented as fact, but in the end, with validated data, she won them over.

PLANNING AHEAD

The second major task I had was to find my successor; I called a few School District Facilities Directors and a few other possibilities. Everyone I called was making a far better salary than the state could pay. By this time, Jeanine was working full-time as the Chief of Staff, and Linda was the Deputy Commissioner for Finance and Operations, so Linda became my immediate boss. She demonstrated the same level of support to me and to the Office that I had received since returning to work.

In March, I called my friend, Major Daniel Matthew Johnson, who was on active duty in the Army assigned to the Florida Army National Guard in Saint Augustine; he had been a teacher and an assistant principal in the Leon County School System and he was my aide-de-camp when he was a Lieutenant and I first made Brigadier General. I believed he might be able to recommend someone in the Leon County School system. Major Johnson said to let him think about it for a day or so and he would get back to me.

When Major Johnson called me, he gave me the name and telephone number of someone whom he thought would be a good candidate: Alex Carswell. I called Alex at home that evening, introduced myself, and related that I had gotten his name from a mutual friend. Alex was the Assistant Principal at Columbia High School in Lake City; he had also run for the office of Superintendent of Schools the year before and lost by just over a hundred votes. Alex said he was interested, and we agreed on a time for him to come by for a visit/interview. From our meeting, I recommended him to the Deputy Commissioner. Alex came back for a follow-up meeting with Linda and we agreed to hire him.

Alex started to work the last week in May 2005. Alex was a natural; he worked well with the Office staff, school district staff, and others he met. I was proud to have him as part of my team, and looked forward to my leaving after one to two more years. I didn't want to just stay on and on. I told Alex to let me know whenever he felt comfortable with all the pieces and complexities of the Office, and I would bow out of the picture. I didn't want to stay and hold him back, and I wanted to get on with my own life. Unfortunately, Alex was offered a principal's position with the Leon County School District two years after joining us; the school district paid him considerably more than the state could. I didn't feel any ill will toward him for taking the job. Our loss was the school district's gain. Before leaving, Alex recruited Thomas Inserra, a principal in the Leon County School system, who was in the salary range for the state. We employed him in July 2007, and he is doing an excellent job preparing to relieve me of my state duties.

My third most daunting task was to fix some of the personnel problems. I started by getting rid of non-performers; that's usually the best place to begin. Next, I required all office staff to work together in harmony. It only took me one day to evaluate the poor performance of the Deputy Director of the Office, and after expounding my expectations of work hours, work quality, and work quantity, he resigned the following day.

Four other individuals had to be dealt with in a similar way. Whenever I required a demonstration of performance, each resigned or got another job somewhere else—either way, they left and the Office ran smoother and better when they were gone. The selective pruning of nonperforming and low performing individuals helped to improve the morale of the office. We began to increase productivity, run smoother, and the spirit of teamwork within and between sections started to re-emerge. These distressing individuals had caused a lot of friction within the Office and between the Office and other agencies; all of them had a divisive effect and were part of a cancerous rumor mill. I had no time or patience for such employees; these kinds of people do not belong in a public service position. I feel sure my predecessor, as the Director of the Office, would have done the same if he had had the same level of backing I had.

My fourth task was to fix the Educational Facilities Information System (EFIS). EFIS is the data source for all public school educational facilities and the Office is responsible for maintaining it. The fixing of the EFIS systems had several false starts in the past; the most recent was during 2001 and 2002, just before I retired. During that time, we were struggling with a contract that didn't include a stipulation for a finished product. The system, when completed, was conceptually to have brought together in a relational database (Oracle) the six major components of the Office of Educational Facilities information system. These were supposed to have been developed with edit checks so that data could be input on-line at the local school district or community college level. That was the idea; it wasn't what we got.

The contract hours ran out long before the work was completed. A correctly done job would have given us a fully functioning, verified, and validated system. The contract ended with each of the six components at various stages of completion—most of them just started or merely ideas. In all fairness, the Departments' Education Data Center made genuine efforts to try to complete each component to some degree of usability and functionality. But it just couldn't be done with the product we received.

We struggled and worked with what we had because of a poorly executed contract. As a result, there is still considerable work left to do; some components required more work to become functional. The six components were: Florida Inventory of School Houses (FISH); Public Education Capital Outlay (PECO) fund management; Capital Outlay and Debt Service (CO&DS) fund management; Educational Plant Survey (on-line) for school districts and community colleges; the required annual School District Five-Year Work Plan (on-line); and Project Tracking (New Construction, Additions, Remodeling, Renovations, Site Work, etc.), which is the system our office uses to track the various construction projects throughout the state.

I explained the many shortcomings of the EFIS system to the Deputy Commissioner for Finance and Operations, the Chief of Staff, and the Data Center management. I also detailed the critical need to get the system fully functioning in a reliable and integrated form. All the different data that existed in any one of the subsystems should automatically populate its data to any other subsystem. In other words, districts shouldn't have to enter any data into any report if the information resides in any of the databases maintained by the Department of Education.

All the senior leadership supported a rewriting of all our subsystems into one integrated and comprehensive system. There was only one stipulation on my part, and that was I had to agree to stay and see the rewrites of all the subsystems through to completion. Because I knew how critical this was to the overall effectiveness and efficiency of the Office, I chose to stay and see the process finalized. Because I agreed to see the project through to the end, I have been on the job about three times longer than I intended to stay. I alone couldn't have done this whole major effort. It is only through the experience, hard work, and dedication of Dr. Charles Wooten that the total rewrite of the EFIS system has been made possible. He has been the tip of the spear on every issue. I have been constantly involved, but not near to the depth and breadth he has.

My fifth task was to improve the functionality and efficiency of the Office itself. The physical office layout actually split the staff in some sections and didn't foster a logical workflow for global office coordination and management. I explained the situation, and was able to get our half of the 10th floor completely remodeled into a more functional work area. At the same time, the other half of the floor housing the Office of Food and Nutrition Management was remodeled. Even though we were temporarily housed on several different floors during the six months the floor was being remodeled, the inconvenience and extra effort to operate during the interim was well worth it. In my opinion, the newly remodeled area of the Turlington Building is the most functional and best designed office in the Department of Education.

My sixth and final task is the result of the 2007 Legislature. I was given five additional employees to provide support to the 35 school districts that are members of the three Educational Consortiums. Our office assists those small districts with their Educational Plant Surveys, Educational Facilities Five-year Work Plans, Growth Management issues, and the Florida Inventory of School Houses (FISH). We hired the five new staff members in July 2007; all of our new hires have experience in educational leadership and management. Nevertheless, even though our new staff has understanding, it still takes at least two to three years to train someone in all the aspects of conducting a comprehensive needs assessment of all educational facilities in a school district. After that training, they must learn to do a complete analysis of what is needed for each building in terms of renovation, remodeling, new construction, or reuse for another function. We are well underway with training our new staff. I think we have been fortunate and successful in this area.

Through the transition of Commissioner John Winn resigning and Jeanine Blomberg being appointed Commissioner in February 2007, and through the appointment of Dr. Eric Smith as Commissioner in November 2007, each Commissioner has supported us. We have had the freedom and support to function in a non-political environment. That is probably the single most important issue we have to face. All school board members are elected officials; superintendents are a mixed bag of elected and appointed chief school officers. All of them have some level of vested interests in using our office for political gain. Given that level of power, it is easy to see how an office that is responsible for overseeing to some degree the building of new schools and authorizing money for them can become a political football or a hot potato. It's also easy to see that because of the potential for abuse, politics should never be allowed to strong-arm the decision making process. Our last three commissioners have made it possible for us to function independently of political decisions; that's a good thing.

NOT GROUNDED

Even with a heavy workload, JoAnn and I have still found time to travel. We were able to take two Western Caribbean cruises for seven days each. Our first Western Caribbean cruise was in December 2004. We took an Asian land and sea cruise in the fall of 2005 where we visited the cities and sites in Beijing, Shanghai, Hong Kong, and Xian (the site of the terracotta soldiers), China; Nagasaki and Okinawa, Japan; Nha Trang and Saigon, Viet Nam; Singapore; and Bangkok, Thailand.

In December 2006, on our second Western Caribbean cruise, two of my brothers and their wives, Alfred and Annette, Pete and Alice, and their son, Leslie, and daughter-in-law, Amy, joined us. In the spring of 2007, we took advantage of a trip advertised through our house of worship, Thomasville Road Baptist Church. Our friend Chet Barclay coordinated this trip; he took the same tour a year earlier. We spent a week touring the Holy Land and a week in Egypt. It was great to see firsthand the lands discussed so intimately in the Bible and to stand in the places where our faithful teachers walked. When you walk in the lands of the Bible, it is overwhelming to know that you have been touched by the dust of the bones of the prophets who spoke God's word—everyone should experience that.

ANOTHER LOSS

On the most distant and remote part of our trip in Egypt, we received the sad news that JoAnn's brother, Bill Newton, had passed away. We knew he wasn't well, but we had no idea that his illness would take him from us. Bill's death was untimely and premature. Like with my sister's death when we were in Romania, there was no way we could make it home in time for the funeral. We had to suffer through the sadness from the far side of the globe and then suffer the pain of loss again when we returned home. We know that as our family leaves us, heaven gets richer and we try to rejoice and take comfort in that. But losses of loved ones hurt because we are separated for the rest of our lives on this side of eternity.

In the summer of 2008, we made two trips. The first was in July on a seven-day Eastern Caribbean cruise with our two grandsons, Cooper age seven and Chandler age five. On our second trip in August, we traveled to Garmish, Germany, which is one of our favorite destinations. Our travel friends from Tennessee joined us and we stayed at the Armed Forces Recreation Center (AFRC) as military retirees; from there we took day trips to the surrounding areas of interest. Our travel continues to charm and entertain us, and we hope for a lot more of it.

CLOSING

As all good things have a start and a finish, this part of my story is now at an end. It has been a really taxing exercise for my memory. I hope that in years to come, I will be able to read my own story with complete reflective satisfaction. As I look forward to retirement again, I don't consider this the end. Living daily with the unknown just around the corner while anticipating the future brings appreciation for the past. Yesterday's shadow is always there for us to see in our memories; tomorrow holds the promise of a new light and a new adventure, but that will slip silently into the shadows as well.

I hope you have enjoyed this short stroll with me through a few of the places and times in my life's journey. On the following pages, I want to leave you with a few things—some ideas, some acknowledgements, some pictures with a little explanation of who or what is in them. These are my salute to my family and to you. God bless America, and may He keep us safe until we join Him and leave the shadows behind.

MY MANAGEMENT PHILOSOPHY
CIVILIAN AND MILITARY

One's work may someday be finished, one's education never.
Alexandre Dumas.

THROUGHOUT my dual career, frequently I was asked about my management philosophy, both in the civilian work-place and in the military. My answer was always the same; there really was no difference; I was the same person in each role.

To be successful as a manager or leader, I believe there are some basic management principles for how a person should manage others. Know your boss's priorities, meaning the best way to get along with any boss is to find out what is important to him or her and fall in step with their priorities. Always know not only your boss's priorities, but also know what your boss's, boss's priorities are. I have two additional objectives that I expect from every person in supervisory or management positions. The first is caring for your subordinates. I am a people person. I firmly believe that, as managers, our primary job is to take care of our subordinates. If we don't take care of our subordinates, I assure you, they will not take care of us, or our work unit—and ultimately our overall success as an operational unit will fall short. The second is leadership. Anyone working for me at any level of supervising others is in a position to lead others. The combining of caring with leadership provides the vehicle to take care of our subordinates.

We have to be willing to accept the tough challenges. Being an employee or a soldier may not be the easiest task in the world, but either, if done well, requires personal dedication and sacrifices. You may be tasked for work that you feel you cannot accomplish in the short run, or even in the long term. When this occurs, it requires open and honest communication with your supervisor; I believe you have the right to explain to your supervisor why you feel you cannot accomplish an assigned task. But be very careful and be absolutely sure that you can prove that you can't do the job if you say you cannot do the task. Remember, you are being evaluated against your peers who just might accept and accomplish the task that you say you cannot do.

One needs to be innovative and take the initiative. This means being able to act on your own in the absence of guidance from your supervisor or manager. If a situation arises, and you are not sure what to do, simply take all the information that you have available regarding the situation, and make what you believe is the right decision—and usually it will be the right one. If you discover a project that you want to do, do it, and do it well. If you learn that a project can be accomplished easier or better, do it. Remember, every effort counts.

For me, getting along with others is essential, and especially my direct reports. My direct reports are the people who have my ear on a daily basis and they influence my decisions more than anyone else. My direct reports have more contact with me simply because they are closest to me. This is not to say that they are always right, but they are always in the thick of my directions to begin a project or to improve one. Arguing with them is about the same thing as arguing with me. They have had my guidance and are trying to accomplish my directives. As a manager, I have always made conscious efforts to put the right person in the right position. I expect direct report managers to support all initiatives unless they are physically impossible to accomplish. Again, always have open and honest communication vertically and horizontally within the organization.

Always be willing to learn from your contemporaries. Each type of civilian business or military unit operation is unique and requires special management skills. It is from many of our less senior employees or junior enlisted soldiers that are motivated, well educated, and technically competent from whom we the senior managers and leaders have a lot to learn. We should accept the hard lessons learned from our own mistakes and also lessons that worked well for our generation. This learning shouldn't only be limited to individual subjects but should also extend to what worked for others in situations similar to ours. Collectively, there is a wealth of information among us, we should try to get it out in the open and share the knowledge.

Don't ever forget to put your job and your responsibilities in proper perspective. Step back and take a look at the big picture. Try to analyze where you fit into that picture and how you can become a better fit. When you begin to feel comfortable in your current role in the big picture, begin to improve yourself. By this, I mean to improve yourself in the position assigned, this is especially true for any person who plans to progress up the supervision and management ladder. For me, the best way to move up in the organization is to perform your current job exceptionally well. Know your job and be both technically and operationally proficient. Always be qualified educationally for your current job and for the next higher two levels of management responsibility. Keep your current job up front but closely followed by your long-term career aspirations and responsibilities. In short, always keep yourself prepared for any future opportunity.

Never cease being a student of the profession. No matter whether civilian or soldier, you must know your job, and continue to grow in it. This is how growth and maturity can be evaluated when compared to your peers. Don't be a marginal performer—keep up, and ahead of your peers. There are many jobs any person can do; it is the positive attitude that makes the big difference in performance. Always maintain a positive attitude, and be proud to be a professional. Always be honest in all your dealings, don't show partiality between subordinates, and deal with everyone in a firm but fair manner. Show pride in your work, professionalism in your dealings with others, and demonstrate a high performance level.

Never, never, never, sacrifice values, morals, or ethics. Any supervisor or manager that suggests, or insists, that you compromise any one of the three principals: values, morals, or ethics, you must refuse, and remove yourself from that work environment as soon as possible. It may not be easy, but it is necessary.

In summary, I believe there is no dissimilarity in the way civilians are managed and the way soldiers are managed; the only difference is one wears a military uniform, and the other does not. You don't step on subordinates or other people trying to get to the top. No person is an island, and no successful leader moves up the leadership ladder without the support and efforts of many subordinates and superiors along the way. I have said many times, "If you find a gopher (turtle) sitting on the top of a fence post, you can be certain it didn't get there by itself." There is no substitute for good, honest, fair but firm, sound, and caring leadership.

Pay heed to Socrates' most important question and ask yourself to answer it regularly—"What is virtue?" Answer that question and walk daily under its umbrella, and you will master life. Always remember, there can be no compromising of integrity in a life that is well lived.

The Unknown Journey

APPENDICES

BRIGADIER GENERAL SPESSARD BOATRIGHT
Military History

Geneneral Boatright began his military career by enlisting in the Florida Army National Guard with Company A, 1st Battalion, 187th Armor, Live Oak, Florida, on March 3, 1958. His basic training was at Fort Jackson, South Carolina, and Advanced Individual Training at the Armor School, Fort Knox, Kentucky, where he was the Honor Graduate of his class. After three years of enlisted service, General Boatright graduated from Infantry Officer Candidate School at Fort Benning, Georgia, on May 2, 1961, and was commissioned a Second Lieutenant on June 2, 1961. He was assigned as tank platoon leader in Company A, 1st Battalion, 187th Armor, 48th Armored Division, and completed the Armor Office Basic Course in 1963. In 1963, he was assigned as Armored Cavalry Platoon Leader in Headquarters and Headquarters Company, 1st Battalion, 187th Armor, 48th Armored Division, and promoted to First Lieutenant. In 1964, he was assigned as Company Executive Officer, Company A, 1st Battalion, 187th Armor. He was assigned as Company Commander, Company A, 187th Armor, and promoted to Captain in June 1966. While commander, his unit was reorganized in January 1968 to Company C, 3rd Battalion, 124th Infantry, 53rd Separate Infantry Brigade. Again in December 1969, while commander, his unit was reorganized to 269th Engineer Company (Dump Truck). In 1972, he completed the Engineer Officer Advanced Course, Fort Belvoir, Virginia.

While still serving as commander, General Boatright's unit was reorganized in February 1972 to the 269th Engineer Company (Construction Support). In 1973, he was assigned as Engineer Plans and Operations Officer, 50th Support Center, Rear Area Operations. In December 1974, he was assigned as Administrative Officer, Headquarters and Headquarters Detachment, 53rd Signal Group and promoted to Major. In 1975, he was assigned as Communications Systems Engineer, 53rd Signal Group and in October of the same year, he was assigned as Radio Systems Officer, 53rd Signal Group. In November 1977 he was assigned as Communications Traffic Engineer, 53rd Signal Group. General Boatright attended the Reserve Officer Resident Course of Command and General Staff College at Fort Leavenworth, Kansas, from January to May 1978. In October 1980, he was assigned Communications-Electronics Systems Engineer, 53rd Signal Group.

In 1981 General Boatright was assigned as Battalion Commander, 146th Signal Battalion, 53rd Signal Brigade, and was promoted to Lieutenant Colonel and served as battalion commander until February 1986. While Commander, he deployed his Battalion to REFORGER 86. General Boatright was assigned as Director of Plans & Training, Installation Support Unit, Camp Blanding, Florida, in February 1986. In July 1986, he returned to the 53rd Signal Brigade as Operations Officer. He was assigned as Deputy Commander, 53rd Signal Brigade and promoted to Colonel in February 1989. He was assigned as Director, (Post MOB) in STARC in May 1989.

In July 1990, General Boatright was assigned as Commander, 202nd Medical Group in Jacksonville, Florida. While commander of the 202nd Medical Group, the unit was activated into federal service in November 1990 and deployed to the Middle East in support of Operation Desert Shield/Storm. During Operation Desert Storm, as Commander of 202nd Medical Group, 3rd Medical Command, Army Central Command (ARCENT), he was stationed in Riyadh, Saudi Arabia, with subordinate units in the countries of United Arab Emirates and Oman. His unit was released from active duty in May 1991 and he continued to command the 202nd Medical Group until assuming command of the 53rd Signal Brigade on June 1, 1992. He was promoted to Brigadier General on March 11, 1993, and retired on October 2, 1997, after the 53rd Signal Brigade was deactivated on October 1, 1997.

General Boatright received the following awards and decorations in order of precedence:

Federal Awards and Decorations:

1   Legion of Merit

2   Bronze Star Medal

3   Meritorious Service Medal

4   Army Commendation Medal

5   Army Achievement Medal

6   Army Reserve Components Achievement Medal

7   National Defense Service Medal

8 Southwest Asia Service Medal

9 Humanitarian Service Medal

10 Armed Forces Reserve Medal

11 Army Service Ribbon

12 Army Reserve Components Overseas Training Ribbon

13 Saudi Arabia Medal

14 Liberation of Kuwait Medal

State of Florida Awards and Decorations:

15 Florida Cross

16 Florida Distinguished Service Medal

17 Florida Service Medal

18 Florida Commendation Ribbon

19 Florida Meritorious Service Ribbon

20 Florida Service Ribbon

21 Florida Active State Duty Ribbon

22 Florida Recruiting Ribbon

Joseph Arch (Joe) Boatright.
Susan Elizabeth (Starling) Boatright.
This is a photo of my parents that I have blended together from two photos before they got married. The pictures were taken in 1917. Daddy was 25, Mama was 20.

This is a family photo taken December 13, 1941.

Front row (L to R) Pete, Alfred, Daddy holding Ronald, Mama holding Spessard, Billy, Sherwood.

Back row (L to R) Carra, Thomas Lee, Honorine, Winifred, Margaret.

This was prior to Thomas Lee being mobilized into active duty from the National Guard for World War II.

The home place.

This photo was taken about 1954.

The house Daddy and Mama built with their own hands using only hand tools. They moved into the house about 1920. Then it had a wood shingled roof. This is the only house they ever owned. It is also the house where all their children were born.

The smoke house.

This is where Daddy and Mama lived while they were building their house.

This house was used to smoke the pork sausage, hams, shoulders, and sides. The shelters on either side were used to store the horse drawn wagon on one side and horse harnesses, plows, and other farm implements and tools on the other side.

The corn crib.

This is where we stored corn for feeding the animals during the winter, and we also used the corn for grinding and making corn meal and grits. Syrup was stored in the crib loft. The shelter on the left side was part of the cow lot. This is where we milked the cows. The shelter on the right side is where we stored the tractor and other farm implements and farm tools.

The Tobacco Barn.
This is the barn where we cured the tobacco once it was strung up on tobacco sticks and hung in the barn on the various tiers which were about 2 feet apart. It took about 5 or 6 days of continuous heat getting up to about 180 degrees for the green leaves to dry up and turn a beautiful gold color. The two burners were fired with kerosene.

The chicken house.

The chicken house had horizontal roosting poles inside for the chickens to sit and sleep on at night. The boxes on the outside were used for the laying hens to lay their eggs. Each section had hay in the bottom to protect the eggs from breaking. We always had plenty of fresh eggs.

The syrup cooking shed.

We always ground sugar cane around Thanksgiving. We made about 450 gallons a year. The cane grinding mill (not shown) was about 20 feet in front of the chimney. The sugar kettle held 60 gallons of cane juice and yielded about 9 gallons of sugar cane syrup. The kettle was fired with a hotshot kerosene burner.

The six youngest boys.

This picture was taken about 1945.

If 1945 is correct, from left to right: Alfred 14, Pete 12, Billy 11, Sherwood 9, Ronald 7, and Spessard 5.

Mama and Daddy.
This picture was taken Christmas Day 1954.

We usually spent Christmas at home. Some of the married children and their families were usually present. Our family's big celebration was always Thanksgiving Day. Most all the family made every effort to be present on that day. This left Christmas Day available for married children to visit with in-laws, if they wanted to.

SCHOOL DAYS 1949-50
LIVE OAK

Spessard.

This picture was my school picture for the 1949-50 school year.

I was in Mrs. Agnes Folsom's fourth grade class. She was the wife of Mr. Henry Folsom. She was an excellent teacher. We were housed in one of the old World War II wooden buildings moved from Camp Blanding after the war.

Spessard Boatright.

This picture was taken in 1957.

I was a junior in High School.

The Joe & Lizzie Boatright Children.

This picture was taken in March 1958. This was one of the few photos of all the eleven children present at the same time. I was a senior in high school, just two months prior to graduation.

Front row L to R: Thomas and Spessard.

Middle row L to R: Carra, Honorine, Margaret, Winifred, and Sherwood.

Back row L to R: Ronald, Billy, Pete, Alfred.

Spessard Boatright.

This was me in my graduation cap and gown. I graduated in late May 1958.

Private Spessard Boatright.

Dressed in Class "A" uniform at Fort Knox, Kentucky. This photo was taken on Thanksgiving Day 1958. I was just about to finish the Armor AIT (Advanced Individual Training). I graduated from the Armor School just before the Christmas Holidays.

Second Lieutenant Spessard Boatright.

I was dressed in Army Officer Class "A" uniform. This photo was taken in the fall of 1961. I completed Infantry OCS School at Fort Benning, Georgia, May 2, 1961. I was commissioned in the Armor Branch. I had to wait until I turned 21 years old to be commissioned. I was commissioned on June 3, 1961.

254

Joe and Lizzie's 45ᵗʰ Wedding Anniversary.
This is December 1962. The anniversary was held at the Philadelphia Community Center, next to Thomas Lee's house.

L to R: Carra, Thomas, Sherwood, Alfred, Spessard, Margaret, Ronald, Daddy, Billy, Mama, Pete, and Winifred.

One of Spessard's Campaign Photos, 1968.

The photo was taken in the spring of 1968.

Spessard and JoAnn's Wedding June 1, 1968.

The small wedding ceremony was held in the First Presbyterian Church of Live Oak. A wedding reception was held in the church social hall by the ladies of the church. The ceremony was conducted by The Reverend James (Jim) Walkup.

Spessard Boatright, 1971.

This picture was taken in the fall 1971. By this time I had served three full years as Superintendent of Schools.

HELP RE-ELECT

Spessard Boatright

Your

SUPERINTENDENT OF SCHOOLS
SUWANNEE COUNTY

Your Vote and Support Will be Deeply Appreciated

• EXPERIENCED • QUALIFIED • DEDICATED

Spessard Boatright, 1972.

This is a copy of my campaign card I passed out while seeking a second term as School Superintendent. You can tell by the "Help Re-Elect" at the top of the card. I won a second term by a sizable margin.

Captain Spessard Boatright, 1972.

This photo was taken at Camp Blanding, Florida. I was commanding the 269th Engineer Company (Dump Truck) at the time. I was a Captain, and my driver was (Specialist Fourth Class) SP4 Woody Greene.

Spessard, JoAnn and Family, 1980.

From L to R: Becky, Spessard, JoAnn, and Brenda. This is by the pool in our backyard on Grampell Drive in Jacksonville. We lived in Jacksonville from July 1979 to July 1984. I worked for Blue Cross/Blue Shield as Director of Office Services. Becky 10, and Brenda 8, attended Trinity Christian School.

Lieutenant Colonel Spessard Boatright, December 1982.

From L to R: Brenda, JoAnn, Spessard, and Becky. I was the Battalion Commander of the 146th Signal Battalion (Corp Area), located at the Maxwell C. Snyder Armory on Normandy Boulevard in Jacksonville. This was taken at the Battalion Christmas Party held at the armory. The Battalion had five company-size units and over 800 soldiers.

The Spessard Boatright Family, Summer 1985.

This is a family photo that was included in the Thomasville Road Baptist Church Directory. We moved to Tallahassee in the summer of 1984.

From L to R: JoAnn, Brenda, Becky, and Spessard in the rear.

Eskan Village in Riyadh, Saudi Arabia, 1991.

This is where the 202nd Medical Group lived and worked during the time it was deployed for Desert Storm/Desert Shield. Each of these buildings contained 28 three-bedroom homes. At the time I commanded the 202nd Medical Group, I was also acting Deputy Commander for the 3rd Medical Command, ARCENT. My rank was Colonel.

Colonels' Boatright and Tsoulos, April 1991.

The 202nd Medical Group is preparing to redeploy back to Fort Stewart, Georgia, from Saudi Arabia at the close of the Persian Gulf War. Colonel Tsoulos is thanking my unit for the very difficult job we performed so well. Colonel Tsoulos was the Army's Senior Medical Officer in the Theater of Operations. I was his Acting Deputy Commander for the 3rd Medical Command, ARCENT.

202nd Medical Group Headquarters, April 1991.

The 202nd Medical Group is preparing to load the charter buses at Fort Stewart, Georgia for the much anticipated trip home to Jacksonville, Florida, Cedar Hills Armory. A reception was held at the armory upon our arrival home, and after a brief opportunity to visit our families. We were dismissed to return to our homes later that same afternoon.

Brigadier General Spessard Boatright, March 1993.
I was confirmed by the United States Senate for promotion to the rank of Brigadier General on March 11, 1993. This is my official photo. I am dressed in the Army Dress Green uniform. This is the photo that was posted at each of the armories where I commanded units as part of the Chain-of-Command. I commanded the 53rd Signal Group from June 1, 1992, until October 2, 1997. The Brigade was deactivated and I retired with 39½ years of National Guard and Active Duty Service.

Brigadier General and Mrs. Boatright, March 1994.

JoAnn and I were attending a Formal Military Banquet and Ball in September 1994. We attended many functions of this type both at the State and National levels through our years with the military.

Brigadier General Spessard Boatright, March 1993.
In this photo I am wearing the Army BDU uniform. The Brigadier General rank is barely visible on the collar. The Battle Dress Uniform (BDU) is the typical work or duty uniform worn for weekend National Guard training. It is also the uniform worn in the field or other general work areas. This is the uniform I chose to wear for my official retirement ceremony at the Armory in Tallahassee, Florida.

Scott and Rebecca Boatright Heath Wedding, July 17, 1993.

The wedding took place at the Summerall Chapel on the campus of The Citadel in Charleston, South Carolina.

Pictured L to R are: Spessard, Brenda, JoAnn, Rebecca, and Scott Heath.

Rebecca and Scott are the parents of Cooper and Chandler Heath in a photo by themselves.

My Brothers and Sisters, November 1994.

Front row L to R: Alfred, Margaret, Thomas, and Winifred.

Back row L to R: Spessard, Billy, Pete, Ronald, and Sherwood.

Here you can see how we all have aged.

My immediate Family, Fall 2007.

L to R: Spessard, Rebecca Heath, JoAnn, and Brenda. I retired from the Florida Department of Education as the Director of the Office of Educational Facilities on July 1, 2002, after working 32 years. I returned to the same position with the Department of Education in November 2004, and I plan to retire again in the spring of 2010.

Our Grandchildren, Fall 2007.

Cooper Boatright Heath hanging by his arms was almost 7 years old.

Chandler Bowman Heath sitting in the tree was about 4½ years old.

Their parents are Scott and Rebecca Heath.

CPSIA information can be obtained
at www.ICGtesting.com
Printed in the USA
LVHW042042221218
601287LV00001B/26/P